A Tale of Ten Cities

THE TRIPLE GHETTO IN
AMERICAN RELIGIOUS LIFE

A Tale
of Ten Cities

THE TRIPLE GHETTO IN
AMERICAN RELIGIOUS LIFE

Edited by
EUGENE J. LIPMAN
and **ALBERT VORSPAN**

*Union of American
Hebrew Congregations
New York*

c1962

PREFACE

WE ARE INDEBTED TO MANY PEOPLE FOR THEIR GRACIOUS cooperation and help in the preparation of this volume. To the subcommittee of the Commission, who served as readers—Rabbi Maurice N. Eisendrath, president of the Union of American Hebrew Congregations; Dr. Ernest Solomon; Rabbi Morris Kertzer of Larchmont Temple—go our warmest appreciation. We are profoundly grateful also to the many experts whose guidance and comments were invaluable. Among these, special gratitude is expressed to Sidney Vincent, Philip Jacobson, Dr. Everett W. Ferrill, Maurice Fagan, Jules Cohen, Robert E. Segal, Samuel Scheiner, Harrison Fry, Mr. and Mrs. Martin Schwartz, Rabbi William Silverman, Rabbi W. Gunther Plaut, Albert Chernin, Belden Menkus, Leo Pfeffer, Sam Hatow, and Rev. Will O. Campbell. While we freely and hungrily picked their brains, we—and we alone—are responsible for what finally appears in these pages.

Our indebtedness is also expressed to Mrs. Vivian Mendeles and Miss Ruth Harrison, who were tireless and gracious in their preparation of the various typescripts; to Mr. Ralph Davis, production manager of the UAHC, for his usual skilful job of designing this book; and to the late Miss Sylvia Schiff, of blessed memory, for her conscientious reading of the manuscript and proofs.

We have made a conscientious effort to describe the

realities of interreligious relations—the tension as well as the teamwork—with fairness and balance. Since we, the editors, are both Jewish and are engaged professionally in Jewish religious life, we acknowledge that some unconscious bias, however rigidly guarded against, may have crept into these pages. It is likely that this bias asserts itself in favor of a liberal approach to society and to religion.

It is our fervent hope that this book will provide some insight into what is happening in cities and suburbs across the United States. It is an effort to investigate the dynamics of interfaith relations, to examine (without preconceptions), and to seek to refine out of the resulting data some ore of truth which may help us all to understand one another and, therefore, ourselves a bit better.

Ten different cities were selected for this study. They represent a fair cross-section of America—urban, suburban, East, South, West, and Midwest. In each of them, an expert observer was asked to report the picture as he saw it, frankly and honestly. For purposes of convenience, Minneapolis and St. Paul, Minnesota, are dealt with together as "Twin Cities." Most of the reporters are not trained sociologists. Their reports are not scientific studies; they are straightforward accounts of what knowledgeable and active individuals know and see. The reporters are of several faiths and many professions. One is the religious editor of a daily newspaper; one a college professor; another a clergyman; several are intergroup relations workers. It is significant, perhaps, that several of the reporters insisted upon anonymity as a condition of complete candor in their accounts. More than one felt that his professional position would be jeopardized if his name were to appear over an article frankly describing the interreligious situation in his own city. As a result, the names of the individual authors do not appear. We assume responsibility for the entire volume.

America is undergoing many transformations. So are all faith groups in America. Is religious tension rising? If so, is that all to the bad? What are the issues which divide the faiths? On which issues are they united? Is self-isolation growing among religious groups? Are religious bodies joining together to advance social justice in the civil order? Are there constructive results from the thirty years of work and the investment of millions of dollars in the interfaith brotherhood movement? Are secularists the new persecuted minority in American life? Is anti-Semitism still powerful in American life? Anti-Catholicism? Is America a "post-Protestant" nation? Will America become predominantly Catholicized in the foreseeable future? Is there a big gap between the level of interreligious relationships among national denominational bodies and that of their local groups? Similarly, is there a serious gap between relationships among local religious institutions and their members as individuals and as families?

We do not pretend that this slim volume has definitive and authoritative answers to these knotty questions. But we offer it to readers of all faiths as a conscientious effort to face questions and to look for answers in a living source: the day-to-day realities of a number of American cities.

EUGENE J. LIPMAN
ALBERT VORSPAN

CONTENTS

A Tale of Ten Cities

THE TRIPLE GHETTO IN
AMERICAN RELIGIOUS LIFE

INTRODUCTION

Of all the differences between the Old World and the New, this is perhaps the most salient: Half the wars of Europe, half the internal troubles that have vexed European States, from the Monophysite controversies in the Roman Empire of the fifth century down to the Kulturkampf in the German Empire of the nineteenth, have arisen from theological differences or from the rival claims of church and state. This whole vast chapter of debate and strife has remained virtually unopened in the United States.—JAMES BRYCE, 1893

AS AMERICA ENTERED THE 1960's, THE CHAPTER WAS NO longer unopened. The pages are clearly spread before us. The time has come to read them.

History will record 1960 as the year a young war veteran from Boston knocked the "For Protestants Only" sign off the door of the White House. Incredibly narrow as was the victory, the election of a Roman Catholic to the presidency was an historic move in the direction of that open society which is envisioned in the American dream.

The political campaign of 1960 was also a vast educational process for the American people. The campaign illuminated many aspects of our national life. Among them were the changing relationships among the great religious faiths of America. One of the things revealed in stark clarity was that, far as we have come since 1928, we still have a long, long road to follow. Religious bigotry is sill wide-spread and deeply embedded. The faith groups still see one another across barriers of mutual isolation and distrust. Moreover, the ignorance of Americans about the religious faiths of our neighbors is boundless—and potentially dangerous.

Just as the racial crisis in America and in the world compelled us as a nation to examine our changing racial relations, so the religious issue in the campaign of 1960 compels us to focus our attention on the changing relations among American faith groups. For these relationships have been changing. The emergence of Kennedy did not create the "religious issue." It merely lighted up, with spectacular flares, trends which had been forming for a long time.

What were the lessons to be drawn from the "educational process" of 1960? These are some:

The decline in anti-Catholic prejudice since the Al Smith campaign of 1928 is encouraging—but it ought not to be exaggerated. Bruce Felknor, Director of the Fair Campaign Practices Commission, reported on the basis of careful analysis that there was a greater volume of hate material in circulation in 1960 than there was in 1928 . . . and most of it was more subtle and cleverly written. Anti-Catholic sentiment quite clearly accounted for Senator Kennedy's loss of Tennessee and Virginia and may also have been crucial in California, Florida, and Ohio. The Democratic presidential candidate ran 7 per cent behind the Democratic vote for Congressional nominees across the country, according to a study by Louis Harris, expert analyst. He was 23 per cent behind in the heavily Protestant South. What saved Kennedy was his ability to restore the big-city coalition of Negro, Jewish, Catholic, and labor voters. This—and especially his success in reversing the huge Catholic migration of 1952 and 1956 from the Democratic to the Republican columns—had more to do with the election of the first Roman Catholic President than did the softening of religious bigotry.

Actually, religious and ethnic factors have always played important roles in American political life, despite pious disclaimers about the absence of bloc voting. In a conscientious study published in 1960 by the Center for the Study of Democratic Institutions, Moses Rischin declared: "American electioneering has always given special attention to the ethnic and religious interests of the voters. History demonstrates that Americans bring to the polls their special backgrounds and pull down the levers congenial to their national origins and religious ties." Rischin concluded: "The proposition that the ethnic factor is second only to the economic factor in influencing an American's vote is unlikely to be overthrown in the near future."

Beyond the question of anti-Catholicism, of anti-Semitism, or anti-Protestantism, is the stark fact that we Americans know precious little about the realities of religious relationships in America. There are scores of studies of *race relations* in American cities—and there need to be even more. But there are few comparable studies of religious relationships on the American scene. Yet the relationships among adherents to major faiths—Protestant, Catholic, and Jew—are changing with rapidity in America. These changes are relevant to more than a political campaign; they have large implications for the future of American life.

The election campaign confirmed the idea that religion has become the primary expression of self-identification in modern America. To be an American is to belong to one of the "three great faiths." One can see this in former President Eisenhower's repeated assertion that it doesn't matter what faith one adheres to as long as one has faith . . . or in Mr. Nixon's statement during the campaign that religion would be an issue only if either one of the candidates did *not* possess any religious faith. But if religion has become a major force in American life, there is little evidence that it is successfully shaping the national conscience or that it is contributing effectively to a sense of national purpose or high moral standards in American life. Indeed, the bland faith in faith, the isolationism of individual denominations and faith groups, the absence of genuine interfaith cooperation on realistic terms, the aloofness of too many religious institutions from the great social and political challenges of our time, the superficiality and even irrelevance of much of America's religious expression—all these suggest that America's religious groups have not yet redeemed the promise of their numbers and new-found strength on the American scene.

The challenge has been ringingly described by Dr. Abraham Heschel:

"This is a time to cry out. One is ashamed to be human. One is embarrassed to be called religious in the face of our failure to keep alive the image of God in man. We see the writing on the wall, but we are too illiterate to understand what it says.

"The trouble is that religion has become 'religion'—institution, dogma, security. It offers neither drama nor exaltation; it engenders neither judgment nor repentance. Its acceptance involves neither risk nor strain. Religion is regarded as one of the amenities of Western civilization."

THE SHIFTING SCENE

Needless to say, America's religious groups do not float in an ambiotic, empty sea. Religious life and thought in America have been profoundly affected by the revolutionary social, economic, psychological, and cultural changes which have transformed our country during the past generation.

Among many changes, the following have had profound effects upon religion in America:

Most Americans now live in cities. At the time of the Revolutionary War, 95 per cent of our people were farmers. No city had a population as high as 50,000. By 1900, the urban population had grown to 40 per cent; in 1950, 64 per cent; and predictions are that it will reach 85 per cent by 1975. The farm population continues to shrink. In one year alone—April, 1956 to April, 1957—the farm population decreased by 1,861,000. In 1960, less than 12 per cent of the population actually lived on farms. Indeed, one-third of the American people were concentrated within fourteen huge metropolitan areas. The old center cities have decayed and many cities are striving manfully to arrest the processes of deterioration. Suburbia marches stridently on to greater and greater numbers and power. In the decade between 1950 and 1960, the suburbs grew at a rate six times faster than the central cities. There is abundant evidence that these trends will not be reversed in the foreseeable future.

All our means of mass communication have tended to dilute the regionalism and localisms which, in earlier generations, gave to America its many-accented, multicolored flavor. To be sure, the people on Maryland's Eastern Shore and those who cling to the cliffsides in Beverly Hills, California, live worlds apart. But the distance between them is being annihilated by magazines and movies, radio and television, paperbacks and jet airplanes. To a greater extent than ever before, American culture is a mass culture, thoroughly homogenized.

The power structure and relationships within the American economy have changed drastically. With the exception of a few pockets of depressed new immigrants, tenant and migrant farm laborers, and the chronically unemployable, there is, to all intents and purposes, no proletariat left in the United States today. There are still vast distances between top and bottom income groups, but they are, in a real sense, the differences between lowest middle class and highest middle class. The leisured, luxuried, aristocratic upper class is vanishing, with rare playboy exceptions. The lowest income groups live on a middle-class level, with middle-class aspirations and problems. The long-dreamed-of home in the country, with a bit of land around it and a car in the garage, has become mortgaged reality for more Americans than ever before.

Traditional ethnic ties have lost much of their strength in American life. As immigration to our shores has been reduced to a small trickle, Americans no longer identify themselves primarily as Italians, Germans, Greeks, Irishmen, but increasingly in terms of religion: Protestant, Catholic, and Jew. This emergent tripartite religious culture has become a major factor in American life, and religion has become a crucial form of identification for Americans. Indeed, religion has become almost an aspect of Americanism, a virtual attribute of patriotism.

The cataclysmic developments already mentioned have had both positive and negative effects on American life and thought. Combine them with two world wars, fifteen years of cold warring, the spectre of atomic destruction, and the catapult into space by both the U.S.A. and the U.S.S.R. Add the weakening of family ties, unsatisfying jobs for most, sterile leisure-time activities, and a sense of helpless futility in the face of the great issues of the day. Out of this melange comes deepseated anxiety sufficiently wide-spread to be justifiably called a crisis. It has many names: the age of anxiety, the search for identity, the crisis of fulfilment, the era of automated men. Regardless of the label, this is a time when Americans' largest questions are: Who am I? Why am I?

This volume does not deal with broad sociological, demographic, psychological, or economic theories as such. We are confident, however, that the discerning reader will see these background factors very much in evidence as we describe one arena of reality on the stage of American life: the changing relations among Protestants, Catholics, and Jews in a plural American society.

BOSTON
Conflict Along the Charles

TOURS OF BOSTON FOLLOW THE ROUTE FROM "OLD Ironsides" to Paul Revere's house, to the Old North Church, to the headquarters of the Christian Science Church, to Harvard University, then to Lexington and Concord, with a brief detour to Thoreau's Walden Pond.

These hallowed places conjure up ghosts of the Pilgrim Fathers, of Puritanism, of the flowering of Congregationalism and Unitarianism, of elegant Beacon Street, and of still ever-so-proper Brahmins.

When President-elect Kennedy addressed the Massachusetts legislature a few days before his inauguration, he recalled that the fabric of his life had been shaped by "the common threads woven by the Pilgrim and the Puritan, the fisherman and the farmer, the Yankee and the immigrant." This was a generous and nostalgic reminiscence, and it is a tribute to Yankee Protestantism that its symbols and memories have such enduring strength and pungency. But reality is otherwise in Boston today.

In a perceptive report on "Boston: The Lost Ideal," in *Harper's* magazine (December, 1959), Elizabeth Hardwick captured the image of a city once legendary with culture and gentility, now old and feeding on its own smugness and snobbishness: ". . . The Boston image is more complex. The city is felt to have, in the end, a pure and special nature, absurd no doubt but somehow valuable. . . . The image lends itself to exaggerations, to dreams of social and ethnic purity, to notions of grand old families still existing as grand old families are supposed to exist. *Actual* Boston, the living city, is governed largely by people of Irish descent and more and more recently, by men of Italian descent. Not long ago, the old Yankee, Senator Saltonstall, remarked wistfully that there were still a good many Anglo-Saxons in Massachusetts, his own family among them. Extinction is foreshadowed in the defense."

Such time-honored Protestant fortresses as the *Atlantic Monthly* and Old South Church still add to the glory of Boston. But the day of the revered Yankee is over. The Watch and Ward Society, inspired by Anthony Comstock, has been marinated into a Citizens Crime Committee. The Massachusetts Council of Churches (Protestant) at 14 Beacon Street seems a modest spiritual workshop indeed compared with the awe and glamor attending all that originates on "Lake Street," the tag line for the headquarters of Richard Cardinal Cushing. For, with the possible exception only of John Fitzgerald Kennedy, the Cardinal is the single most powerful individual in the city of Boston—and in the State of Massachusetts.

Cardinal Cushing ministers to approximately 1,550,-000 Catholics. Protestants are estimated to number 700,000 and Jews 150,000, in the area encompassed by the Archdiocese. Even allowing for the thousands of unchurched or religiously undesignated, few will dispute the claim that the city of Boston proper—the central city—is three-fourths Roman Catholic. As of 1960, no Protestant or Jew sat on the nine-man City Council; no Protestant or Jew sat on the five-man School Committee. All mayors of Boston between 1930 and 1961 were Roman Catholic.

A few steps down the street from the Bullfinch dome atop Massachusetts' State House is the ultra-modern Catholic Information Center, maintained by Paulist Fathers. Next door is Boston's staid Union Club. From the newly-constructed Catholic Information Center at 5 Park Street to 150-year-old Park Street Congregational Church at Zero Park Street is a short walk, but the symbolic distance from the Paulist Fathers' Center to Park Street Church at "Brimstone Corner," where brimstone for powder was stored in 1812, can be measured only in light years.

In October, 1944, when Richard J. Cushing was designated Archbishop of Boston, he declared:

"We shall encourage everything we believe to be for the glory of God . . . and we shall be 'anti' to every 'anti' movement that reflects against the Fatherhood of God and the brotherhood of man. . . . For this reason, we are anti-anti-Semitic, anti-anti-Catholic, anti-anti-Protestant, and anti-anti-Negro. . . . If all men knew God and loved Him there would be no anti-movements and everybody would be treated kindly, justly, and fraternally."

Ever since, Richard Cardinal Cushing has been the man best-placed for effecting a reduction of religious and racial tensions in the historic Boston area. And for those who accept an absence of fisticuffs and hot words as proof of peace and amity, Cardinal Cushing has made a gigantic contribution to the cause of Boston inter-group amity.

Behind him lie the days of persecution of Boston's immigrant Irish by the sons and daughters of Pilgrim, Puritan, and Yankee. Behind him is the sordid memory of an Ursuline convent burning in 1834. Behind him is that ignoble era of factory signs and newspaper adver-tisements warning: "No Irish Need Apply." Behind him is the period of transition when Irish precinct work-ers had to fight their way upward for dominance of the Democratic Party.

Behind Cardinal Cushing are also the days, a quarter of a century ago, when Father Charles Coughlin boasted that he drew most of his funds from Boston backers, when his *Social Justice* sold 12,000 copies a week in the city. Bostonians recall with dismay the strength of the Christian Front during World War II in the land of the bean and the cod.

Francis P. Moran, who insisted that Franklin D. Roosevelt's true name was Rosenfelt and the man a traitor, found it not difficult to promote Christian Front activities in Hibernian Hall, not far from the heart of one of Boston's major Jewish sections. In 1941 only a few voices were raised in protest when Moran's pro-Nazi followers took over the South Boston Evacuation Day-St. Patrick's Day celebration by importing the alleg-edly anti-Semitic Father Edward Lodge Curran from Brooklyn. Behind Cardinal Cushing is the dark day, March 11, 1944, when Father Curran was in Boston to bring to 700 devotees the greetings of "the greatest priest in America, Father Coughlin."

Louis Lyons, curator of the Nieman Fellows at Harvard and one of Boston's most capable *Boston Globe* alumni, has declared bluntly in his chapter on "Boston" in the Robert S. Allen compilation, *Our Fair City,* (Vanguard Press, 1947), that Boston is "a center of Coughlinism, of Curleyism, and America Firstism. The hatreds they sow have made Boston a fruitful case study in anti-Semitism for the Harvard Psychology Department."

Contemporary Boston sees almost none of this bitter and even violent interreligious discord. Boston today is a calm city—with the calmness of a society and a culture under unchallenged dominance from Lake Street. Protestants and Jews may chafe at this reality. Now and then their spokesmen do so publicly. Patronizing brushoffs or thunderous verbal blasts greet these expressions of dissent. Then the gracious city along the Charles resumes once again its surface calm.

Interreligious tensions in the Boston area are subtle. Under the web of surface politeness and traditional New England reticence there is more than aloofness. Rabbis are welcomed into Protestant-led ministerial associations here and there in Metropolitan Boston, but some Christian home owners and realtors impede the movement of Jews into certain suburban residential areas. Occasionally, an explosion results, as in Milton, Massachusetts, in 1949, when a packed Town Meeting heard sharp opposition to the projected erection of a Jewish Center (now Temple Shalom of Milton). Milton's Jewish population has advanced from sixty to more than 800 families in the decade since and the open animosity has disappeared. This same pattern has been repeated to a lesser degree in other parts of suburbia.

However, the Immigration Restriction League which

sprang from New England soil has left its mark upon attitudes toward the sons and daughters of Eastern European immigrants. The "new races," as the League inaccurately calls these (Jews, Italians, Armenians, etc.), are under constant trial.

While Protestants in Massachusetts have been generally inclined to blink at issues like public transportation of parochial school pupils, the dynamics of change in suburban school boards—with Roman Catholics increasingly in the majority—spur discontent. For the Horace Mann influence on public schools is a matter of deep pride in Massachusetts. Still recalling that the early schools were Protestant parish schools and the early schoolmasters were Protestant clergymen, many Protestant groups have, in modern times, fought hard to resist Catholic intrusions into the public schools. Now to see the destinies of the old Yankee school systems in the hands of Roman Catholic school committeemen, many of whom send their own children to parochial schools, is galling to many Protestants. As they watch the Catholic sector of the population mounting more rapidly than the non-Catholic, Protestant apprehension carries over from the public schools into public services. Protestants do not necessarily complain, but they at least observe with malaise that such agencies as Division of the Blind, Aid to Dependent Children, Child Guardianship, and Public Welfare are manned largely by Roman Catholic personnel.

As the suburbs lure commuters from central city, Roman Catholic churches seem to flourish wherever they are erected. Protestants, on the other hand, are more inclined to maintain their affiliations with the "downtown churches," long dear to their families, despite their own removal to the suburbs. Hence, the Protestant suburban churches do not always find the quick acceptance enjoyed by the Catholic churches.

Protestant churchmen point out also that younger Protestants and Jews tend to leave Massachusetts to make their futures, whereas Roman Catholics are more inclined to live out their lives in "Catholic Boston." Population studies confirm this trend.

Cooperation between Protestant and Jewish leaders in Boston is continuous, firm, and cordial. The mantle of champion of civil rights and civil liberties is still worn by Protestantism, but the robe is large enough to admit the vibrant Jewish community. The Massachusetts Council of Churches views the Massachusetts Board of Rabbis as partner in many enterprises, and the Race Relations Department of the Massachusetts Council of Churches works as a team with the Jewish Community Council of Metropolitan Boston on a great range of issues affecting minority groups.

The one serious divergence in views in such relationships appears in the firm support of released time religious education by the Protestant Council in marked contrast to the Jewish community's emphatic dissent from this type of week-day religious instruction.

In addition, Protestant leaders, energetically conducting a year-round campaign against organized crime and gambling, note that rabbis seem too preoccupied with other items on their agenda to share Protestant enthusiasm for the war on bookies, race tracks, and other forms of gambling.

Still and all, you may obtain a handy reference pocket

calendar from the Council of Churches, bravely marking off Pesach, Rural Life Sunday, Feast of the Ascension, Purim, and Maundy Thursday on one side while educating with regard to "The Problem of Organized Gambling" on the reverse, with effective quotes from George Washington, Harry Emerson Fosdick, Cardinal Cushing, and Rabbi Roland Gittelsohn.

In the same connection, Protestant persistence in the war against crime is reported to have attracted Cardinal Cushing's support, following a rare official visit by the executive head of the Massachusetts Council of Churches to the Chancery Office. And it is noteworthy that Cardinal Cushing has opposed a state-sponsored lottery, a proposition branded as "one of the most pernicious types of organized gambling" by the Committee on Organized Gambling and Crime of the Massachusetts Council of Churches.

The religious organizations have a less positive record on other social problems. Boston has a long history of civic and political corruption. Decades of corruption have permeated City Hall; public works have enriched contractors and milked the public of millions; bribery has been commonplace; and all forms of vice have flourished freely. With the exception of opposition to gambling, all three religious communities have, until recently, been curiously silent about this situation and all must share the responsibility for it.

Gambling was the subject of a fiery row in the fading weeks of 1961. The entire nation had been treated on November 30 to an extraordinary glimpse into the state of civic morality in Boston as a result of a nationally televised program by CBS entitled "Biography of a Bookie

Joint." The cameras caught the Swartz Locksmith Shop flourishing in Back Bay, Boston, with ten Boston policemen among those dropping into the busy place for unexplained visits. Rising to the defense of Boston, and especially of Boston cops, was Cardinal Cushing who did so to the accompaniment of thunderous cheers from a jammed Boston Police Relief Association ball at Boston Garden shortly after the television bombshell had fallen. Asserting that Boston had been "betrayed," the Cardinal said: "Gambling exists everywhere. And no one can deny it. The United States Army wouldn't be a sufficient law enforcement body to stop people from gambling. In my theology, gambling itself is not a sin any more than to take a glass of beer or hard liquor is a sin. It's the abuse that makes gambling evil or drinking intoxicating liquor evil." Indicating that he had not seen the film and had no desire to see it, the Cardinal insisted that "whoever is behind it owes an apology to the city of Boston."

On the other hand, Protestant clergymen hailed the exposure and sharply disagreed with the Cardinal. A group of nine ministers meeting at Emmanuel Protestant Episcopal Church said, "The city was exposed by television and not betrayed." They called on Governor John A. Volpe to clean up Boston.

The city's Protestant clergymen were almost unanimous in challenging the Cardinal's statement. Typical was the reaction of Rev. Francis W. Hensley of the Massachusetts Baptist Convention: "I am concerned lest Boston lose its finest opportunity for house-cleaning that has been presented in many years."

Observing the interreligious tempest, a veteran group relations worker in Boston noted wryly: "This old town is rocking over this thing. First time in all the years I've been in Boston that I've seen Protestant ministers go to the mat with the Cardinal and say, 'Hey, mister, you're wrong.' "

The daily press—so frequently the gadfly and first point of pressure for civic betterment—is notoriously weak in Boston. With the exception of the *Christian Science Monitor,* the newspapers—quite aside from their mediocrity—have blandly accepted the status quo. Not until recent years have their voices rallied the moral leadership of the community of all faiths to do something about Boston's political cesspool and to save the city from decay.

One powerful segment of Boston opinion-shapers has reared a cult of interfaith banquetry and headtableship as a charm for warding off any suggestion that relationships are less than harmonious. Boston has not one, but two leagues of Christians and Jews. A New England office of the National Conference of Christians and Jews churns away at the traditional educational approach to tolerance. At the same time, a "Massachusetts Committee, Catholics, Protestants, and Jews" conducts a localized and independent program. Until recently, the second group was the front runner in the contest for bigger and more spectacular good will banquets. But now the National Conference has perked up its annual program with a banquet and the customary good will citations.

The presence of two competing bodies in the interfaith field confuses many a newcomer to Boston. Indeed, even an old-timer, a proper Bostonian bearing a most famous name, illustrates the honest bewilderment which results by listing himself in *Who's Who in America* as a member of the executive committee of the "National Conference, Catholics, Protestants, and Jews."

This amplitude satisfies the need of a number of good people seeking a way to prove their amiability. Some devote endless hours to the tedious minutiae of banquetship. But few of them, when invited to fight for the passage of anti-discrimination legislation or to try to smash the Jim Crow armor of the Boston Red Sox (accomplished in 1959 without them), seem ready to accept such realistic challenges. Klieg lights and flashbulbs are more to their liking than the demanding, unpopular, onerous undertaking of breaking through the color line, or smashing housing discrimination against Jews in Wellesley or Winchester, or reducing anti-Catholic bigotry in election campaigns.

How far those annual flashbulbs throw their beams can be symbolized, perhaps, by a flashback to the good will banquet conducted by the Massachusetts Committee, Catholics, Protestants, and Jews in May, 1955, when then-Governor Theodore R. McKeldin of Maryland (according to *The Boston Post*) "launched his plea for tolerance and understanding after unfurling a miniature flag of his native state, with the cross of Christ atop the mast and announcing to his audience he brought it to be presented to that beloved bishop, the Catholic leader of this community, Archbishop Cushing." Not all Protestants and Jews in the audience shared the enthusiasm of the Governor.

The relationships between the Roman Catholic church and the organized Boston Jewish community are compounded of cordiality and conflict, set in a framework of peculiar ambivalence.

Even among Roman Catholic prelates, Cardinal Cushing is an unusually vigorous anti-Communist. His small handbook, *Questions and Answers on Communism,* with its pointed defense of Senator Joseph R. McCarthy, is vigorously promoted. The Cardinal's initial endorsement of the frenetic John Birch Society was, however, checkmated by a forthright attack upon the Birchmen by *Pilot* editor Msgr. Francis J. Lally. Cardinal Cushing's April, 1960, letter to a Los Angeles correspondent—"I unhesitatingly recommend him [Robert Welch] to you and endorse the John Birch Society"—lost some of its punch in the Birch Society arsenal when the *Pilot,* in October, 1961, took sharp aim at Mr. Welch. Shortly after the latter had made a "long-range guess," during a rally in Garden City, Long Island, that one-half of one per cent of all U.S. Catholic priests are "comsymps" (Communist sympathizers), Msgr. Lally editorialized Mr. Welch into the corner of no return by offering to print the names of the leftist priests if Welch would supply them. The figure, Mr. Welch admitted, was "simply pulled out of a hat." Meanwhile, Msgr. Lally had won wide approval by satirically hinting that in Mr. Welch's book, Pope John might well be listed as a "comsymp" and by wistfully commenting: "If you see any red under a Roman collar, be careful! It may be a Communist—or on second thought only a monsignor." In November, 1961, the Roman Catholic bishops issued a strong and solemn warning against right-wing extremists.

Late in 1959 Cardinal Cushing authored a series of articles in *The Boston American.* In addition to some shocking McCarthy-like attacks on the United Nations, the American Civil Liberties Union, the United Auto Workers, and others, which raised hackles all over Boston, several of the articles came as a pointed body blow to the Jewish community.

The columns made painful reference to "International Bankers," erroneously asserted that Leon Trotsky's real name was Leonard Bernstein, and recommended to readers such books as John Beaty's offensively anti-Semitic *Iron Curtain Over America*. Don Lohbeck, former editor of *The Cross and the Flag*, the vicious Gerald L. K. Smith publication, was listed as an author to consult; and Alfred Lilienthal's violently anti-Zionist *There Goes the Middle East* and *What Price Israel?* were prescribed for further reading. The series also urged the perusal of "all issues of the *American Mercury* during the past two years," a period in which publisher Russell Maguire is said to have lost several of his right-wing editors who apparently could not stomach his penchant for publishing anti-Semitic drivel.

When a dignified but firm protest was made by the Jewish Community Council to Cardinal Cushing, his response was prompt and unequivocal. He apologized humbly. He explained that the offensive articles had been written by others during his own confinement to the hospital, but he did not shirk his responsibility. He stated that he had ordered all copies destroyed, and ended, "I am truly very sorry. Please believe me."

Cardinal Cushing has publicly recorded his gratitude to many of Boston's most prominent Jewish philanthropists for including his projects among their regular contributions. "No man could have my faith concerning Christ," he once said, "without loving him and loving the people who produced him, the Jews."

Boston's Roman Catholic prelate has cooperated cordially with Jewish community organizations on many occasions. In 1945 he helped the Jewish Labor Committee establish the Massachusetts Labor Committee Against Intolerance and also spoke at a meeting of the Newton, Massachusetts, Ladies Auxiliary of the Jewish War Veterans. In 1946 he was guest speaker at the annual good will meeting of the Brotherhood of Temple Ohabei Shalom in Brookline. He spoke at a General Assembly of the Union of American Hebrew Congregations. He is a friend of Brandeis University.

The Jewish community's positive response to these cordialities was expressed early in 1959, when the *Boston Jewish Advocate* designated Cardinal Cushing as recipient of its second annual "Man of the Year" Award, citing him for his contribution to interfaith understanding, civic progress, and human betterment. "His social thinking has given him place among the most vigorous prelates of the world," the *Advocate* stated.

This award raised eyebrows within the Jewish community itself as well as in Protestant circles. For the edge of ambivalence which has cut across Catholic-Jewish relationships in Boston is sharp and on the record. Knowledgeable members of the community were distressed when, late in 1957, Cardinal Cushing accepted the Oriel Society Peace medal from J. Russell Maguire, chairman of the board of *The American Mercury,* the same sheet which was to cause him embarrassment two years later, as already noted.

This same ambivalence is revealed clearly in the relationship between Lake Street and ex-priest Leonard Feeney, who has constituted, in a real sense, Boston's successor to Fathers Coughlin and Curran. For more than seven years, Father Feeney and his "Slaves of the Immaculate Conception," ranging in numbers from 60 to 100, marched on to Boston Common with malice toward all, including the archbishop, but with special contumely for the Jews of Boston. Recently, the Feeney band disposed of its Cambridge holdings, abandoned its Sunday afternoon anti-Semitic forays, and melted into the bucolic reaches of Still River, near Ayer, Massachusetts, in the Worcester diocese.

But it is noteworthy that a New York *Herald Tribune* writer, interviewing Cardinal Cushing at the time he was awarded his red hat late in 1958, queried him about the Feeneyites, who had been frequently and sharply condemned by him. At the urging of the Cardinal, Pope Pius XII is said to have excommunicated Feeney in 1953. He quoted the new cardinal as saying, "They've been very good in the last few years." Sophisticates blanched when they read this, knowing well that *The Point,* the Feeney house organ, was still being mailed to nearly 3,000 readers. They wondered whether the cardinal would dismiss thus lightly, the issue of *The Point* (February, 1959) sent forth from the new retreat in Still River, only an hour from Boston. In the summing up of seven years of publication, the Feeneyite editors asserted, "One topic especially has occupied *The Point's* attention during the past seven years: the problem, in its many aspects, of the Jews. . . . Why this emphasis? Because we think it is imperative that American Catholics wake up to the fact that the Jews, as an organized force, are the implacable, declared enemies of Christianity—of its tenets, its traditions, its moral code, its very culture."

Some Jews in Boston were disturbed in 1955 by Arnold Toynbee's references to Judaism as a fossilized museum-piece. It was only natural that rabbis and the Jewish press would speak out. *The Pilot*, official archdiocesan weekly, in commenting on Jewish reaction, stated that its editors were "not unfamiliar with the nervous sensitivity" engendered by minority status. But *The Pilot* was quite annoyed to note that Rabbi Roland B. Gittelsohn, in a sermon on Toynbee, had said he found the key to him in the fact that Toynbee is a Christian fundamentalist.

The Pilot's defense of Toynbee offers an illustration of that type of criticism of Judaism considered objectionable by Jews: "He (Rabbi Gittelsohn) points out that Christian theology teaches that the 'whole historic purpose of Judaism was to serve as a preparation for the appearance of Jesus.' This, in Christian teaching, was surely an important part, perhaps *the* important part, of the role of the Jews in history and while it is inaccurate to say that Judaism 'should have laid down quietly to die,' as the rabbi suggests, it *should* have accepted the Messiah and been part of the flowering of faith that was foretold by the prophets and fulfilled in Jesus. If Toynbee believes this, he does no more than all other informed Christians who on that account surely may not be accused of anti-Semitism."

Social discrimination against Jews in Boston parallels that of other American cities. Some real estate dealers will not sell to Jews in a few areas. Most country clubs and the more exclusive downtown clubs alike maintain a rather firm barrier against Jews, with the result that the Jewish country club pattern has in recent years proliferated.

In one suburb, with a Jewish population of 22 per cent of the total, not until recently was it practicable for the Rotary Club to admit Jews since the Rotarians held their luncheons at an old-line country club which refused to have Jews there even as luncheon guests. Now the club management, in effect, looks the other way when Rotary meets; and Jewish members of Rotary thus gain the dubious privilege of breaking, not 80, but bread at the country club.

In the changing suburban pattern, the location of synagogues and Roman Catholic churches plays a vital role. With no thought of discriminating, some real estate dealers direct newcomers to a suburb close to places of worship. Thus, it is not unusual for a Catholic realtor to be occupied with finding homes in a given parish while a realtor of another faith may spend much of his time seeking homes for Jews conveniently located near temples.

Protestant-Catholic relations are shot through with deep-seated animosities, at times irrepressible. Now and then the calm of Boston is shattered by the eruption of interreligious conflict on an institutional level.

When he was president of the Federal Council of Churches (now the National Council of Churches), Bishop G. Bromley Oxnam spoke at an ecumenical service in famed Trinity Church in Boston, March 27, 1946, and accused the Roman Catholic church of "practices that we believe constitute a threat to religious freedom." He said, "Pressures on newspapers, radio, and other sources of public information, together with political activities that constitute a grave threat both to political and religious freedom, give Protestants grave concern."

Bishop Oxnam then asserted that when Harold Laski tried to get time on the air to comment on the Vatican's attitude toward Franco Spain, efforts were made to keep his speech off the radio, and others who participated in the anti-Franco meeting were threatened. Then Bishop Oxnam added, "It was left to Americans who are Roman Catholics to point out that the Pope—who is a king as well as a religious leader, a head of a state as well as a head of a church—is subject to criticism for his political activities just as any ruler, and that such criticism is not an attack on the church."

The archdiocesan newspaper, *The Pilot,* struck back with an editorial significantly headed: "In Accusing the Church, Bishop Oxnam Accuses Christ." Reasoned *The Pilot:* "The essence of Bishop Oxnam's criticism of the Catholic Church is very old. The Church is 'too political.' Well, Christ himself was accused as 'an enemy of Caesar . . . .' In sincerest fraternal charity, can't Bishop Oxnam understand what we're driving at? Heresy is a sin. . . . If Christ had not come, if there had been no divine revelation, then Bishop Oxnam's guess about eternal realities might be as good as anybody else's. But Bethlehem is an historical fact! The Gospels, the Acts of the Apostles, and the various Epistles are historical documents! And these reveal that the birth, the death, and the resurrection of Christ were designed to end religious speculation and debate. . . . Is 'one religion as good as another'? If that's true, then one religion is as false as another. And the death of Christ is made void. . . . At the heart of Bishop Oxnam's objection to the Catholic church is his unwillingness to acknowledge the divinity of Christ."

One Catholic spokesman—Msgr. John J. Wright, now

Bishop of Pittsburgh—saw in Bishop Oxnam's "attack" the conclusion that "Protestantism is dynamic, democratic, and consistent with liberty, whereas Catholicism is static, hierarchical, and authoritarian." And, added Bishop Wright, since "the mood of the hour is progressive and democratic, Catholicism stands condemned as reactionary and Fascist."

The winter of 1947-48 witnessed a sharp exchange between Archbishop Cushing and Rev. Emery S. Bucke, editor of *Zion's Herald* and one of seven Protestant churchmen making up a delegation visiting Yugoslavia. Archbishop Cushing branded the report on the state of religious freedom in Marshal Tito's nation "infamous and monstrous" and charged the Protestant group with a "campaign of misrepresentation and malice." The Protestant group had reported finding no religious suppression in Yugoslavia.

Periodically through the years, this kind of interchange has bloomed in Boston newspaper headlines. In June, 1953, for example, Methodist Bishop Lord saw what he called the reflection of "a deep-seated prejudice held by the Roman Catholics" in Archbishop Cushing's observation that Harvard, Boston University, and Northeastern University "have too many professors who are destroying the faith and Americanism of Catholic students." Retorted Bishop Lord, "The Archbishop assumed that, had these students been educated at Catholic institutions, they would have retained their faith and Americanism."

Deep and persistent differences divide the religious groups in Boston on a broad range of public issues. Frequently, these issues are fought out in the pulpits, the pages of the denominational press, the city council, and the halls of the state legislature. Not infrequently, these issues are of an explosive nature and give vent to deep emotions on all sides. In most public issues, Protestants and Jews, at least on the level of leadership, find much common meeting ground. On other issues, such as complete separation of church and state in the public schools, the organized Jewish community frequently finds itself nearly isolated and embattled. What of the man in the street? He rarely knows, even more rarely cares, about such issues in Boston.

In child adoption cases, as perhaps in no other single issue, have relations between the Catholic and Jewish leadership of Boston been marred in recent years. The continuing, seething controversy reached its apogee in the widely-discussed Hildy McCoy, or Hildy Ellis case. Hildy was born in February, 1951, to a Catholic student nurse, Marjorie McCoy, said to have been unmarried. Records indicate the court had ascertained that the father of the child, an intern, was Protestant. With the oral consent of the young mother, Hildy was placed by her physician, Dr. Herman Sands, with a Jewish couple, Mr. and Mrs. Melvin Ellis of Boston.

When Hildy was five weeks old, the mother, who later married Mr. McCoy, claimed she had learned for the first time that the adoptive parents were not Catholics and that both had been divorced previously. Under church pressure, she began proceedings for Hildy's return. There followed a long battle in the courts, climaxed in February, 1955. The Supreme Judicial Court of Massachusetts ruled in favor of Marjorie McCoy. The Ellises, defying the court, fled Massachusetts with Hildy. Legal finis was written to the case May 23, 1957, when Governor Collins of Florida turned down an extradition request from Massachusetts. The Ellises thus have not faced Massachusetts charges of kidnapping. Periodic feature stories in the press through the years have portrayed Hildy's apparent happiness with her adoptive parents.

Boston's Msgr. Francis J. Lally, reflecting on the Ellis case in *America* (June 8, 1957), referred to what he called the "heavy cloud of silence which enveloped the official Jewish spokesmen" in the Ellis case. "It is easy to understand their embarrassment in the face of the manipulations of those who set out to make the Ellis case hinge on the religious issue. The clear Jewish record in the famed Finaly and Beekman cases* would, however, have led us to believe that such spokesmen might have properly been counted upon here to stand on the side of the law and the rights of a mother. For a people with a keen sense of justice, and not notably reticent in the past in bringing their cause to public notice, their silence in this issue was woefully eloquent. Catholics would have felt a brother's embrace if what was readily admitted in private had been willingly made public."

In the Ellis case and others, the Roman Catholic

---

* The former in France, the latter in the Netherlands, both cases involved struggles by Jews to have children returned to them by Roman Catholics who took the youngsters during World War II, saving them from the Nazis.

Church has stoutly defended that section of Massachusetts' adoption law which states that, wherever practicable, the judge shall place a baby with adoptive parents of the same religious faith as the natural mother. It is to be expected that, almost without exception, "wherever practicable" equals "mandatory." Officials of the Massachusetts Council of Churches and many in the Jewish community strongly oppose the religious-placement aspect of the Massachusetts child adoption law as a violation of the church-state separation principle.

However, *The Pilot*—returning again and again to the Ellis case for comment—has been quick to reject such claims and has even gone so far as to accuse a Boston radio station disc jockey of "thinly-veiled anti-Catholic prejudice" when he made so bold as to offer his comments on the Ellis case.

Religious tensions in the Boston area come into sharp focus also when birth control is mentioned. Massachusetts and Connecticut are the only two states in which it is illegal for doctors to prescribe contraceptive care to parents, even for the protection of life or health. The Planned Parenthood League of Massachusetts has twice attempted to change the law by referendum. In 1942, the referendum lost by a vote of 683,059 to 495,964. In 1948, a similar 7 to 5 ratio in the voting saw the referendum defeated, 1,085,350 to 806,829.

In both campaigns, as in the course of other efforts to further the cause of planned parenthood, the community has felt the abrasion of feelings between the two dominant religious groups. Protestants, in attacking the law (enacted by Protestants in the Comstockian days of 1879), marshal the strength of well-known Harvard

Medical School names along with other independent-minded crusaders, while the Catholic church, per se, through such able attorneys as the late Mayor Frederick W. Mansfield, mobilizes support so much stronger that the law stays on the books and probably will continue there.

The Planned Parenthood League, indeed, maintains that down to this day, "fear of stirring up the opposition" is such that, even at the Harvard Medical School, the students who go to all parts of the world to practice are given no instruction in the techniques of contraception.

The sharpness of the birth control controversy was revealed in a memorable exchange between the Methodist *Zion's Herald* and Bishop John Wright. The editor of *Zion's Herald* had accused Archbishop Cushing of making "an unfortunate expression of bigotry" in referring to proponents of birth control thus: "It is saddening to see Fifth Columnists in the Gethsemane of the Christ whom they profess to serve." Bishop Wright wrote *Zion's Herald* (which *The Pilot* once suggested should be named "zionist Herald"), calling the editorial "bad tempered." In his letter, Bishop Wright insisted that "the fight against marriage perversion [his term for birth control] is no such thing as a Catholic-Protestant fight. The deliberate effort on the part of some sections of the Protestant clergy to represent it as such is unworthy of their office," he observed.

Church-state relations create perennial problems everywhere and Boston is certainly no exception. Cardinal Cushing has been highly critical of those who oppose released time programs and, on occasion, of those who do not want state aid earmarked for sectarian education.

In 1947, the Catholic leader branded as "phony" the plea of conflict between church and state when raised with reference to "questions of school buses, emergency school subsidies, and other democratic aids to education."

Protestant and Jewish organizations alike resent Cardinal Cushing's use of clichés about "godless" education and educators. Religious tensions mounted late in 1955 when the Cardinal said: "Let us oppose with all our energy the attempts of educators trained in godless tradition to maneuver our schools and colleges into a position of helpless subserviency to iniquitous state control."

"Religion has been banished from private and public life," Archbishop Cushing commented at Christmas, 1945. "Even in our own land, one of the last ramparts of freedom, there is little room for the Christ. The unity we had in days of destruction and death has fallen asunder on the threshold of peace. . . . Officially, we may talk of religious tolerance and respect for everyone's religion or creed. Yet in the daily routine of our relations, how much discrimination exists, based on racial and religious prejudice and even hatred for a fellow man because he happened to be born a Jew, a Protestant, or a Catholic."

Each December, crèches and other symbols exalting Jesus appear on Boston Common in testimony to the almost unconscious breaching of the church-state separation principle. Mayor John B. Hynes referred to the city's yearly Christmas Festival on the Common as "one of the most gratifying accomplishments of my administration." Only in monolithic Boston, among America's major cities, do such practices go virtually unchallenged.

Boston public schools have a "normal" share of sectarian religious practices. Bible reading has been required by law in Massachusetts for more than 100 years; New and Old Testament passages are used. Christmas observances are part of the school routine. In the *Boston Herald* of April 10, 1952, there appeared photos of artwork done by boys in the James P. Timilty Public School: "Christ Carrying His Cross to Calvary" and "Sorrowing Mary Waiting at Tomb of Jesus," both painted on window panes.

How sensitive to even gentle inquiries about the singing of Christmas carols a community may be is well illustrated by an incident which occurred in December, 1949, in Chelsea, a Boston suburb. A Jewish couple respectfully petitioned the Chelsea School Committee for a chance to appear before that board to present views in reference to the singing of Christmas carols and the presentation (in public schools) of religious pageants. A simple, private audience was sought, but one member of the school committee insisted that the hearing be open to the public. Mere announcement of this intention set off such a ruckus in Chelsea that (1) the hearing was never held; (2) the petitioning couple received so many menacing phone calls and letters that they sought sanctuary in another suburb of Boston; and (3) a Jewish merchant bearing the same name as the petitioners took paid space in the Chelsea *Record* to make it clear that he not only disapproved of the petition but didn't even know his namesake.

The Massachusetts Council of Churches continues zealous in its insistence that the American principle of the separation of church and state be maintained. "We are unalterably opposed to the efforts of any religious body to secure political, economic, or any other special privilege from the state, including the use of taxes for the direct or indirect support of private or sectarian schools," a recent resolution adopted by the Church Council sets forth.

Late in 1950, the Massachusetts Council of Churches referred to its Board of Directors, without a vote, a resolution protesting the "unfortunate appointment" by Governor Paul Dever of Msgr. Cornelius T. H. Sherlock, diocesan supervisor of parochial schools, as a member of the State Board of Education. The Council did not question Governor Dever's legal right to make the appointment nor did the Council question Msgr. Sherlock's personal abilities. Msgr. Sherlock's position as the superintendent of parochial schools in the Boston Roman Catholic Archdiocese "disqualifies him from serving on a board charged with the control and direction of the public school system of the state," the Council reasoned. In opposing the resolution, a council member pointed out that two Protestant clergymen—both prominent private school educators—were already members of the same state board. Msgr. Sherlock eventually became chairman of the State Board of Education.

Representative of an element of Protestant thought in the community is Rev. Harold J. Ockenga, pastor of the 150-year-old Park Street Congregational Church. Dr. Ockenga wrote in 1951 to Attorney General Francis E. Kelly to question whether the Commonwealth had the right to turn over the Bradley W. Palmer mansion (a part of the W. W. Palmer State Park) to the House of Good Shepherd, Boston, for the summer months. "What are the terms of the gift?" Dr. Ockenga inquired. "Does this mean that it will soon be sold or given to the archbishop? A little elucidation would be appreciated."

International tensions between Protestants and Roman Catholics come to sharp local focus in Boston in situations embedded in history. Untarianism's seed bed was in Boston. Hence, it is natural that the Beacon Press, maintained by the American Unitarian Association, should be located in the Hub. Again, it is natural that the Beacon Press should publish such provocative books as Paul Blanshard's *American Freedom and Catholic Power* and *God and Man in Washington*. This led to the inevitable expectancy that *The Pilot* should find frequent occasion to protest Blanshard's views. It has done so, charging Blanshard and his followers with anti-Catholic bigotry.

In Catholic eyes, the *Christian Science Monitor,* a national institution housed in Boston, expresses animus towards Catholicism. The *Monitor,* according to *The Pilot* (October 22, 1955), "has managed for many years to scatter through its editions a generous portion of stories with a notable anti-Catholic slant."

Returning to the attack on April 13, 1957, *The Pilot* declared: "It is not by chance that the notice of the Protestants and Other Americans United for Separation of Church and State meeting, like so much of POAU news over the years, was featured prominently in a two-column story in the *Christian Science Monitor*. Even the post-office box was given for interested readers to follow up the promotion of POAU. This does not surprise us and should not surprise readers of *The Pilot* who have learned to expect this anti-Catholic bias in the pages of the *Monitor*."

Along with the *Christian Science Monitor* and Bishop Oxnam, the American Jewish Congress is a special target of *The Pilot*. Early in 1958, taking issue with an American Jewish Congress memorandum on "The Display of Crosses, Crucifixes, Crèches, and Other Religious Symbols on Public Property," the Catholic paper insisted that the Congress "seems to push us toward a totally secular state, which makes an absolute separation where there should be friendly cooperation." Two months later, disappointed in the Census Bureau decision not to include questions of religious affiliation in the 1960 survey, *The Pilot* noted that "by the time AJC's Leo Pfeffer arrived at the Bureau in Washington with his portfolio in hand the case was won." In sadness, the editor concluded that the Congress had won, not a victory for religious liberty, but a propaganda victory.

Censorship in Boston is fed by streams of both Protestant and Roman Catholic history. As stated above, it was Anthony Comstock who inspired the creation of the Watch and Ward Society, and in modern times, it is the Knights of Columbus and the Holy Name Society which show most vigorous interest in keeping "offensive" literature at a minimum in Boston. Until recently, Massachusetts lawmakers with deep Yankee commitments to civil liberties could be depended upon to strike down frequently-proposed censorship bills in the General Court (State Legislature). But their ranks are thinning, and tensions between Catholic leaders on the one hand, and Protestants and Jews on the other, appear to be rising over this issue.

When the General Court in 1958 set up an Obscene Literature Control Commission requiring the governor to appoint representatives of the three major faiths, the organized Jewish community protested publicly against the law on the ground that it established official partnership between commonwealth and churches and synagogues. Rabbi Zev Nelson did accept appointment as a member of the Attorney General's Committee. This elicited a considerable amount of controversy within the Jewish community itself, between those who felt that no such recognition should have been given to the committee and those who felt that the legislation was so drawn that if a responsible religious leader did not represent the Jewish group on the Attorney General's committee, someone less concerned with civil liberties would have been appointed. The Massachusetts Council of Churches, too, was reluctant to cooperate with the governor on the same grounds.

More than 50 per cent of Boston's Roman Catholic children attend public schools, but Catholics have found it necessary to build more and more parochial schools in order to provide religious training. (Figures for 1959 indicated 197,477 children enrolled in public schools in Metropolitan Boston and 125,305 children enrolled in Roman Catholic parochial schools in the same area.) Whenever possible, Catholics have joined with non-Catholics in Boston's released time program. Jews, too, joined in such a program from 1942 until 1949. *The Pilot* refused to accept the Jewish community's departure from the released time program on the stated principle of deep conviction after careful deliberation. "Jewish non-participation in Released Time," it insisted (March 23, 1957), "is less a matter of principle than of present policy."

In the explosive issue of public funds for parochial

schools, Cardinal Cushing has often been regarded as a spokesman of the more liberal wing of the Catholic Church. Indeed, in December, 1955, the then-Archbishop told Catholic audiences in Boston in unvarnished terms:

> We are not looking for any federal or governmental aid to build schools. I would absolutely refuse the offer for I cannot see how any government or state would build schools without expecting to control them in whole or in part. . . . First of all, we could never get such aid. Historically, and under the constitution as it has been interpreted, we could not receive such aid. . . . Today, as it becomes increasingly difficult to maintain and develop our schools, let us never make the mistake of assuming an attitude of hostility toward our American system of government as such, merely because certain of its policies may affect us adversely, or because we may suffer injustice in the distribution of governmental funds and subsidies. . . . (*U.S. News and World Report,* December 23, 1955.)

However, the Cardinal's position seemed to harden over the years. In March, 1961, he was one of the signatories to the ringing declaration by the Council of Bishops which was widely interpreted as an ultimatum that if President Kennedy's aid to education program were not extended to parochial schools, the Bishops would fight it. Later that year, when some angry public post mortems, on the death of the President's education bill, accused the Church of at least complicity in killing the program,

Cardinal Cushing cautioned his coreligionists to use persuasion and not coercion to achieve purposes they felt were justified.

THE MIDDLE EAST

Late in October, 1954, *The Pilot* sharply criticized publication of a full-page advertisement in the *New York Times* signed by Eddie Cantor and directed to the Secretary of State's policies in the Middle East. "We will make no comment on the propriety of a professional funnyman being used as the agent for strictly political propaganda," *The Pilot* declared, and then proceeded to tick off grievances against Israel (anxiety over Christian shrines, internationalization of the Holy City of Jerusalem, the alleged exiling by Israelis of Palestinian Arabs, and alleged defiance by the Israelis—and not the Arabs!—of U.N. directives).

Catholic-Jewish tension has frequently been caused by *The Pilot's* barbed attacks on the State of Israel and upon American Jewry for its support of the Jewish state. *The Pilot* editorials have bristled with such loaded language as the following: ". . . the most predatory type of modern nationalism" . . . "nationalistic intoxication" . . . "Israel, like a child playing with firearms. . . ." Happily, Jewish leaders noted a moderation in *The Pilot's* views on Israel beginning in late 1960.

A *Pilot* editorial of June 2, 1956, questioned whether the American Jewish Congress' protest to the State Department against restrictions on Jews, including Jews in U.S. uniforms, by Arab states was not "too provocative and emotional." What the Congress was asking, *The*

Pilot commented, was something that could hardly be "reconciled with the realities of the world situation."

THE PATH AHEAD

The fight for better race relations has helped pull Boston religious leaders together. The Hub's comparatively small non-white population has found champions in the Council of Churches, among Roman Catholic archdiocesan leaders, and in Jewish groups seeking to make civil rights more secure. Massachusetts has been a pioneer in modern civil rights legislation. In the past five years, suburban Fair Housing Practices Committees have been formed in more than a score of suburbs, often cutting across church and synagogue lines and uniting men and women of all three faiths in a determination to see new neighbors welcomed regardless of origin. Cardinal Cushing's enrolment as a life member of the NAACP has stimulated this determination.

The interreligious skies are frequently brightened by individual example. Thus, discerning Protestants and Jews in Boston credit Father John S. Sexton, Stoneham, Massachusetts, with great contributions to the cause of human understanding and interreligious amity. In recent years, the temperate and friendly voice of Father Robert F. Drinan, S.J., dynamic young dean of the Boston College Law School, has done much to ease religious tensions in the Hub area. Enterprising in civic activity, where representatives of the three major faiths work together with increasing harmony, articulate and accessible, Father Drinan has offered Boston a model of disagreement expressed agreeably. His article in *America* on "Religion and the ACLU" was an excellent example of his ability to wheel into a highly controversial arena, state his point of difference, and depart with the respect and affection of those criticized. In this instance, he praised ACLU for its efforts on behalf of religious minorities, yet concluded that ACLU is partisan on some religious questions (notably on parochial bus subventions by the state and on off-the-school-premises released time programs).

In Boston, as in many other communities, when men of understanding assemble to see how best the American principle of acceptance of religious diversity may be advanced, regret is often expressed over lack of communication. Protestants and Jews try to bridge the gap by strong participation in civic activities, some of which seem to thrive best when headed by Roman Catholics. Occasionally, a Catholic voice is raised as if in answer to unuttered questions of non-Catholics. Late in December, 1958, for example, John Cogley, widely-known Catholic layman, speaking at the Catholic Information Center on Beacon Hill, called upon Catholics to "forsake picket lines, power plays, and letter-writing campaigns in favor of intellectual exchange with non-Catholics." Catholics are "far too clannish for their own good," he stated. "They have huddled too much." How many times have Jews been similarly challenged!

An example of Protestants reaching out in concern and courtesy for dialogue with Roman Catholics in the Boston area was an all-day conference, November 3, 1958, on morals, marriage, education, and politics, under leadership of both Protestant and Catholic clergy. "It was a lively meeting," according to *Christian Out-*

look, official organ of the Massachusetts Council of Churches. The *Outlook* noted frankly that "with the steady growth of Roman Catholic population in the small town and country areas of Massachusetts, many Protestants face for the first time the challenge of living in Christian love and peace with those who do not agree with them. In less than a generation, in many small towns, Protestants have become a minority group after generations of being the only organized religious group in town."

A few weeks before the conference here referred to, Msgr. Francis J. Lally, editor of *The Pilot,* Rabbi Robert W. Shapiro, and Dr. Myron W. Fowell of the Massachusetts Congregational Christian Conference had discussed social issues similarly at Framingham. More recently, Rabbi Roland Gittelsohn of Temple Israel spoke on Jewish theology to a group at Boston College, a Catholic institution of higher learning.

The interreligious climate of Boston became no more feverish in the fall of 1960 as the local popularity of John Kennedy, even among many Protestants, muted the religious issue somewhat. In heavily Catholic Boston, most folks muffled their anxiety about a Roman Catholic in the White House. But when a prominent rabbi wrote to several leading Protestants to suggest a joint statement against bigotry in the election, he was surprised at the awkward silence which resulted. Pride and "tribal loyalty" solidified the Catholic community; the Cardinal maintained a discreet and cautious reserve. In the Jewish community, troubled fears about Joseph Kennedy's alleged anti-Semitism and about Jack Kennedy's failure to support censure of McCarthy ("he should have gone on crutches") finally gave way to the traditional Democratic-liberal pull. Kennedy carried Boston by storm, chalking up a 5 to 1 vote in heavily Jewish wards and an even higher margin among Catholics. A Republican Roman Catholic of Italian origin swept into the governor's office.

In Boston, a few more people are beginning to come into the hall. And the acoustics are improving. There is hope that more Bostonians will accept the sage advice of Timothy Tingfan Lew, a Chinese missionary: "We must agree to differ but resolve to love."

CLEVELAND
City without Jews

That boast is by all odds the best-known "commercial" in the Cleveland area. For years industry and newspapers have made it the central theme for promoting Ohio's metropolis. And though the slogan was designed to highlight the geographic and industrial advantages of Cleveland's central location, workers in the field of human relations have tended to adopt it as their own. With justifiable pride (as many Clevelanders believe) or with unjustified smugness (as others are quick to point out), the claim is often made that Cleveland is the best location in the nation in terms of good community relationships.

Some fairly impressive evidence can be mustered to support the contention. Cleveland has perhaps the richest variety of ethnic and cultural groups of any city in the country. Here is America's largest settlement of Slovenians, and one of the leading centers of Hungarian life; Slovaks, Czechs, Poles, Germans, Irish, Rumanians, and Italians have all been attracted to Cleveland in large numbers by the city's heavy industries—but no one ethnic group predominates. Four consecutive mayors in recent years were of British, Slovenian, Irish, and Italian backgrounds.

The city's white population is almost equally divided

between Catholics and Protestants (about a third of a million each), and the Negro population of 250,000 is among the highest of northern cities in percentage terms. The Jewish community of 85,000 (in the county) is probably the sixth largest in the country.

Not a single major outbreak of religious or racial violence has resulted from this colorful mingling. Cleveland has had no race riots or cemetery desecrations. Schoolboy fights along religious or racial lines and "swastika incidents" have been rare enough so that they shock the community conscience. There has been little hostility or even ill-tempered joining of issues in the local religious press.

Cleveland was the third city in the nation to pass a municipal FEPC; it has been cited frequently by various national organizations for its outstanding record in human relations; it has elected three Negroes to judicial posts; it accepted matter-of-factly the selection of a Jew as chairman of the board of lay advisers (Board of Trustees) of the local Catholic university. It is probably the only city in the country with a Negro as the (elected) president of the Board of Education and a Jew as superintendent of schools. Visitors to the city are often taken on a tour of the Cultural Gardens, where twenty-seven nationality and religious groups have developed attractive centers of ethnic culture, honoring the contributions of poets, statesmen, and scientists to their own culture and to mankind. All military figures are strictly excluded.

But slogans are not reality, and a visitor who decides to study Cleveland in depth, rather than being contented with a surface (though undoubtedly significant) show of amity, will have no difficulty in discovering that the picture is not all rosy. The most casual observation will, for example, reveal a strong tendency toward self-segregation by most of these ethnic groups.

The Jewish community is merely the most classic example of an almost universal tendency. Since the turn of the century, five neighborhoods have been centers of Jewish settlement—each progressively further east from the center of the city. (The western half of the city has never had more than 500 Jewish families.) When these neighborhoods have been left, they have been totally abandoned, to the point where today, perhaps uniquely among American cities, Cleveland proper is almost literally a city without Jews. (At a recent Jewish affair a candidate for state office remarked not-so-facetiously to the mayor of Cleveland, "What in hell are *you* doing *here?*") Over 90 per cent of the Jews of Cuyahoga County, in which Cleveland is located, live in the suburbs and only two of the twenty-five synagogues are still in the city itself. Of the estimated 1000 Jewish graduates of public high schools of the county in June, 1961, a maximum of half a dozen received diplomas from Cleveland's schools—and the number will soon disappear almost entirely. Only some 250 of the 140,000 children attending Cleveland's public schools are Jewish. All but three of the Jewish service agencies are located in the suburbs.

Moreover, the concentration within certain specific suburbs is remarkably high, even though housing restrictions against Jews have all but disappeared everywhere. The Jewish density in a few middle and upper-middle class suburbs is probably just as high as it was fifty years ago in the downtown, rundown districts, when the Jewish community was overwhelmingly immigrant and first generation and had yet to be "accommodated" to the general culture. One suburban street, surrounded by homes that are quite new, is irreverently known as the "Rue de la Pay-ess"* because it contains so many Jewish institutions, particularly Orthodox ones. Economic status has little effect on the tendency to cluster; those who purchase homes in the $50,000 class tend to concentrate in Jewish neighborhoods about as much as those on the $20,000 level. And a 1961 Yom Kippur census indicates that the concentration continues *within* the suburbs. Two older suburbs are well on the way to losing their Jewish population completely; another is becoming almost completely Jewish.

Although the "mother city" has completely disappeared, the line of Jewish settlement runs in an unbroken rough crescent, swinging north and then east through eight contiguous suburbs. One of the suburbs is primarily the home of newly-married or relatively young couples and another tends to have somewhat more status than the rest, but the similarities among the suburbs are far greater than their differences. Jews continue to think of themselves as a single community rather than as a series of separate neighborhoods. Attempts by national agencies to organize along distinctive suburban lines are frequently resisted.

The Roman Catholic community has had a somewhat similar history since the end of the Second World War.

---

* Payyos are the ritual earlocks worn by some groups of Orthodox Jews.

The population of the local diocese has grown in unprecedented fashion, but the number of Catholics in the city proper is about the same as it was in 1945—a third of a million. *All* the rapid growth has been suburban, with the result that less than half of the diocesan population now lives in Cleveland proper, whereas only thirteen years ago more than two out of three Catholics lived in the city. And the outward movement of Catholics is far from complete. "The Catholic diocese is not *following* the shift to the suburbs," its paper points out. "It is ahead of it. It owns twenty-five properties in rural areas for future expansion." It is worth noting, however, that though the Catholic growth has been all suburban, Catholics have, unlike the Jews, held their own in the city.

The astonishing recent growth of parochial schools —almost all of them suburban—is another harbinger of things to come. The post-war years have been a period of swift increase in the child population, and it is therefore not surprising that the parochial schools have increased in numbers.

But the increase has been vastly greater than the normal growth expected for the period. The percentage of Roman Catholic children in the diocese who attend Catholic schools has risen from 50 per cent to 67 per cent, so that the diocesan school system now numbers over 125,000, making it the largest school system in the state except for the Cleveland public schools. The goal of "every Catholic child in a Catholic school" may be soon substantially within reach, thus contributing to the growing tendency of public schools to be one-group, racially and religiously.

The birth rate for Catholics in the diocese is thirty-three for each 1,000 people, as contrasted with twenty-four for non-Catholics, and it is therefore probable that the future will bring an even heavier Catholic concentration in the county than the present 34 per cent.

Easily lost sight of in the wide attention given to these highly visible Jewish and Roman Catholic migrations outward is the fact that the *first* group to move to the suburbs was the old line, long-established Protestant. Almost without exception, every suburb was developed and settled by Protestants, and the problems of suburban accommodation (to be spelled out in some detail later) are to a major degree the result of the impact of Catholic and Jewish (and just now beginning, Negro) out-migration upon conservative, middle-class, long-established Protestant communities.

Who then is left in the central city? The fact is that in the past twenty years, during a time of dynamic population growth, the central city has actually decreased in numbers. All the dramatic increase of population has been suburban. As a matter of fact, the white population of the city has in the past ten years dropped dramatically despite the recent markedly increased birth rate, the significant immigration of southern whites to help man Cleveland's heavy industry, and the fairly substantial migration from overseas following World War II, all tending to increase the white population of the city. The places of the whites have been taken by the Negro community which has grown during this period from approximately 85,000 to close to 250,000.

In summary, then, as contrasted with 1940, the central city has far more Negroes; it is almost completely emptied of Jews, and its white population is somewhat more Catholic since the out-migration of Protestants to the suburbs has been at an even more rapid rate than has been the case among Catholics.

One obvious result of these changes can be seen in the political life of the city. Negro political awareness has grown markedly, with the Negro newspapers on almost a weekly basis stressing the need to elect Negro candidates. (As one editorial pointed out: "Particularly if they are well qualified.") The major concrete result of this militancy has been the steady increase of Negro councilmen in the central city to the point where there were, in 1961, eight Negroes (out of thirty-three) as contrasted with two at the end of the war. In each case but one, the addition of a Negro to council has been at the expense of a Jewish representative, and at a recent election the last remaining Jewish Cleveland councilman was defeated, thus ending an era when Jews played an outstanding role in Cleveland's political life.

Somewhat the same process can be seen in the (elected) Board of Education where the single remaining Jewish representative has served for almost three decades and will undoubtedly be the last Jewish member to serve on that important public body. When the Board of Education considers released time proposals or the city council considers legislation enforcing Good Friday closings, it makes a difference that not a single Jew is involved in the debate and—even more important— that the Jewish constituency has been completely eliminated. And policies arrived at in the central city often have a powerful effect on suburban schools and councils.

Religiously speaking, the decisive influence in Cleveland's political life in recent years has been Roman Catholic. For more than two decades, Cleveland has had only Catholic mayors and it seems unlikely that the foreseeable future will change this pattern. Religion has in practice if not in theory become a test for high office in the city. During the same period of time there has never been more than a handful of white Protestants among the city's thirty-three councilmen, and city council at present is almost exclusively either Catholic or Negro.

The dominance by Roman Catholics of the Democratic party machinery has its effect on certain county elections as well. The delegation to the State Legislature from Cuyahoga County is for all practical purposes chosen at the Democratic party primaries from a long list of names, often over 100 in number, largely of political unknowns. Party endorsement and a "good" name therefore become crucial, and the result has been that the delegation has been almost solidly Catholic. In 1961, for example, not a single Negro or Jew held any of the twenty-three places, and white Protestant representation was limited to one.

However, county elections involving national office, where candidates are far better known, present a significantly different picture. Cuyahoga County's four Congressmen in 1959 included two Republicans—both Protestant and both from the suburbs—and two Democrats—both from the city proper and both Catholic. This would seem to reflect rather accurately how the population movements of recent years have affected political patterns in the city and the county: Cleveland is overwhelmingly Democratic and elects Catholics. The county outside the city is (though far less decisively) Republican and elects Protestants.

Religion had a strong effect upon the 1960 election in Ohio. Many observers attributed Senator Kennedy's loss of Ohio to the "Catholic issue." In Cuyahoga County (Cleveland) itself, the Democratic standard-bearer ran up a majority of 150,000 but this was 75,000 below expectations. A precinct breakdown suggests that Kennedy scored strongly among Roman Catholic, Jewish, and Negro voters; and Nixon was overwhelmingly ahead in Protestant areas. Despite the stratification of voting along faith lines, religious tension was not markedly overt in the campaign, perhaps because evangelical Protestantism is weak in Cleveland. Considerable anti-Catholic literature poured in from out-of-town but no organized campaign of bigotry developed in Cleveland. The Catholic archdiocesan newspaper reported, more in sorrow than in anger, the incidents of anti-Catholicism in other parts of the country. At no time was Kennedy endorsed. Even after his victory, Roman Catholic leaders permitted no gloating to disturb the serious dignity with which they met the test of the strange and historic campaign of 1960.

The intense concentration of Jews in certain of the suburbs has led only slowly to the assumption of political responsibility. Although Jews constitute 70 per cent of the population in one of the eight suburbs in which most of them live, and form more than a majority in two others, there has never been a Jewish mayor in any community. With two exceptions, there is no more than a single Jew on any Board of Education. In the suburb where Jews have lived for the longest period of time—since before the First World War—there has never been a Jewish councilman who came to office originally through election. Both present representatives on city council, as well as their few predecessors, were appointed to fill vacancies by the administration in power—and have subsequently been elected as "members of the team." The only real breakthrough has been in the past two years when the suburb with the highest Jewish density finally elected Jews to the majority of councilmanic posts. It may be significant that this community, as will be indicated below, subsequently almost split into two sections, with the non-Jewish section seeking through a long process to secede from the northern "Jewish" section.

In general, the "old settlers" retain a firm grip on the administration of suburban communities, and the incoming Jewish group makes inroads, if at all, slowly and fearfully, with a constant desire to include non-Jewish candidates on any slate that appears to be too strongly Jewish. The point of view of the newcomers (mostly Jewish) tends to be liberal and Democratic; the original group (mostly Protestant) tends to be conservative and Republican. No wonder tensions develop! The best symbol of the determination of the entrenched group to hold on to the machinery of power is to be found in the various appointive bodies which often remain almost completely Christian even in communities that are overwhelmingly Jewish. Not a single Jew serves on the Zoning Commission and only two of seven on the Library Board—both appointive—of the suburbs with the largest Jewish population, although, particularly in the former case, they make decisions which vitally affect Jewish institutions.

On the other hand, it is common to find Jews leaning over backward not to assume positions of responsibility too hastily. P.T.A. officers, for example, tend to remain overwhelmingly or predominantly Christian long after the school population has become mostly Jewish. In two instances, an unwritten rule is observed: one year a Christian president, the next year a Jewish one—and all without public discussion. It is simply understood that such topics are for the closed conference of top leadership, not the public platform of general debate.

The few suburbs that have, even more recently, become predominantly Catholic, reflect no comparable reluctance to assume power. Roman Catholic mayors and councilmen are frequent in these circumstances.

Ethnic patterns often reinforce religious segregation. A recent survey of mailing addresses of local foreign language newspapers revealed that the movement out from the original nationality islands has not gone haphazardly into the suburbs. Particular ethnic groups—almost all Roman Catholic—move to specific new settlements. In Cleveland, if you name your ethnic background, it is not difficult to venture a well educated guess about where you live and into which suburb you are likely to move. But unlike Jews, the nationality groups do not totally abandon the old neighborhoods. Usually, they spread outward from a home base that remains identifiably and substantially Hungarian or Polish or whatever; the Jewish withdrawal is total and rapid. A Jewish leader recently took his children to see the house he lived in until the late thirties in what was then an overwhelmingly Jewish neighborhood. There was not a single Jewish family left on the entire street. Italian or Slovenian parents who have moved out of the old neighborhoods have no need to take their children on nostalgic tours of the past. In most cases, grandparents—or an uncle—or cousins newly arrived from the old country still live in the original family home.

Even within suburbs with strong Jewish or Catholic components, there is nearly always a clustering in certain areas rather than a general dispersal into the new neighborhood. A recent Yom Kippur survey of one of the suburbs, for example, revealed that of its ten elementary schools, four had Jewish populations well in excess of 90 per cent while two had virtually no Jewish students. Real estate agents accept as a perfectly normal part of their daily operations that Catholics will want to settle only near new suburban parochial schools, Jews around the many new institutions they have built, and Protestants in "their" neighborhoods.

Certainly, the pattern of housing and voting, both in the suburbs and in the central city, makes any claim that Cleveland has solved its interreligious problems seem shallow and incomplete. Conflict is rare, but so is integration, no matter how one interprets that all-inclusive term.

THE NEGRO COMMUNITY

Increasingly, a kind of high level irritation with problems of Negro-white relationships breaks through the overlay of good feeling. The dramatic migration from the South in recent years of rural Negroes (and whites) unprepared for city living has resulted in a growing number of crimes of violence. One paper, reviewing 1958, reported that 55 per cent of all convictions for crimes in the Common Pleas courts of the county involved Negroes.

Much lively discussion has resulted on the question of group responsibility. Who should "educate" the newcomers? Does the Negro community as a whole have any responsibility for colored malefactors? Negro leadership rejects any such idea. It stresses that both Negro and white newcomers to the city are victims of inadequate housing and schooling and services. The problem is one for the total community, they claim.

Liberal white leadership agrees, but a sensational murder or rape by a Negro inevitably raises anew the question in the press, on the air, or in private conversation: "Why don't they (Negro leaders) *do* something about conditions?"

Negro irritability and militancy also seem to be growing. A recent widely-heralded, privately-financed urban renewal project turned sour when the rents—$105 a month—proved too high. A "rent strike" flared up and the neighborhood was rocked by demonstrations. A reporter who interviewed the tenants found massive resentment of white owners, despite an inability to point out a single specific ground for complaint. Significantly the most bitter charge was: "They treat us like boys. We want to be treated like men."

Negro-Jewish relationships are particularly complicated. Every morning at the bus stops in the central city, there are knots of Negro women waiting for buses to transport them from their ghettos to suburban homes

—often Jewish—where they spend the day making white homes clean and comfortable. At the same hour, dozens of Jewish businessmen will be passing them going the other way—from the suburbs to all sorts of business establishments in the city that serve the Negro trade. A substantial share of housing in the Negro area—with all the attendant irritations—is owned by Jews, partly because the neighborhoods are largely formerly Jewish.

Mistress and servant—storekeeper and client—landlord and tenant. Some of these relationships can be and are warm and creative. But the tendency is the other way. There are no peer relationships, few opportunities for meeting as equal to equal.

The picture is radically different, however, on the leadership level. The NAACP and the Urban League have always worked in close association with various Jewish agencies, in addition to the fact that a substantial number of Jews belong to both. There are few community relations questions where the leaders of the two minorities do not work together with considerable harmony and mutual respect. But this holds true only on the leadership level. Three new Negro organizations have come into being in the past two years sharply challenging the NAACP, Urban League, and the churches for being too "soft." There is every reason to believe these groups will grow in influence, with an inevitable unsettling of Negro-white relationships.

In addition, a few Negro professionals and businessmen have succeeded in making the leap into the suburbs. In almost every case, it has been a leap into a Jewish neighborhood. One Negro social worker put it, "I wouldn't think of moving anywhere except into a Jewish suburb. It's the only place I'd feel safe." Despite the official positions adopted by Protestant and Roman Catholic churches, and although fear and prejudice against the Negro is a Jewish as well as a Christian phenomenon, the Negro feels he has a far better prospect of acceptance in a Jewish neighborhood than anywhere else.

So the Negro-Jewish pattern is a strange mixture. Negro anti-Semitism co-exists with feelings of warmth toward Jews. The immediate symbol of the white hostile world too often happens to be a Jewish merchant or landlord, but at the same time, the opener of closed doors in employment or housing is also likely to be Jewish.

At least equally complicated is the feeling of Jews towards Negroes, compounded as it is of active support and understanding of a fellow minority, and uneasiness at the constant pressures on each successive neighborhood to which Jews move. The entire relationship presents a tremendous challenge to sober and objective social, economic, and psychological study.

INTERRELIGIOUS

What of religious relationships?

On the formal level a rather good report could be made despite such irritations as the exclusion of Jews from the higher Masonic degrees and a few other status organizations. The annual drives of the Catholic Charities, Jewish Welfare Fund, or the YMCA's attract contributions from individuals of all groups. Bequests are frequently reported designating as beneficiaries the charitable institutions of all three faiths.

There are projects on which the three religious communities—or more precisely, their leadership—work closely together. The Cleveland Committee on Immigration, for example, is primarily composed of representatives, official and semi-official, of the three religious faiths.

All three faiths are on record as being profoundly concerned with problems of housing for minorities (euphemism, for the most part, for Negroes). The Auxiliary Bishop of the Roman Catholic diocese and a Presbyterian minister have won civic awards and many kudos for their joint efforts in rehabilitating parts of the community. This Catholic-Protestant partnership has been highlighted regularly in news items; it is a rare enough occurrence to warrant feature treatment. Two tense neighborhood situations that developed because of the first purchase of a home by a Negro in a hitherto all-white neighborhood resulted in all three religious groups working actively to secure acceptance of the new neighbors by their constituents.

Hearings on civil rights proposals nearly always feature a Roman Catholic, Protestant, and Jewish spokesman, and some kind of secular instrument is usually formed for interreligious consultation. It is significant that such secular instrumentalities are necessary for this purpose.

These kinds of cooperation, however, are a long way from creating strong and permanent bonds of association. Particularly in the case of the Roman Catholic community, activities are likely to be on a "separate but equal" basis. In each of the housing situations described above, there was no joint statement or shared program of attack on the problem as between the Catholic and the other two religious groups. Contact with the parish priest resulted in his undertaking to interview certain key parishioners and to speak on the problem at Sunday services. Attempts by the other two groups to involve Catholic leadership in an ongoing program of interpretation and consultation were fruitless.

Similarly, although the vast majority of refugees from abroad have been Roman Catholic, there has been a strong tendency by Catholics to view modification of the McCarran-Walter Act as a "Jewish" interest primarily. When Jewish representatives on the city's Immigration Committee decided not to continue in the role of prime leadership, there was no assumption of responsibility by the Catholic groups. This was evidently not an issue that "counted." Despite strong official backing by the Roman Catholic bishops of the state for FEPC, almost all the planning and activity for city and state campaigns for legislation (and proper enforcement after a bill was passed in 1959) was the result of the cooperation of Protestant and Jewish organizations with interested secular groups. Almost never has there been more Catholic involvement than the appearance of a spokesman at a hearing. Representation from Protestant churches and from synagogues and other Jewish organizations has not been paralleled by comparable support from Catholics. They are rarely "on the team." Even a television program on "The Moral Viewpoint" could be initiated only with the understanding that Catholics would have their exclusive hour every third week with the rabbis and ministers joining to produce together the other two programs.

Deeper than the contacts in the area of community relations are the relationships that have developed in the health and welfare field. Cleveland has a reputation for being a highly-organized (or over-organized) community. Certainly, the innumerable committees of the Community Chest and the Welfare Federation of Cleveland with its six councils (for hospitals, children's services, group work services, case work services, problems of the aged, and area councils) provide almost daily opportunities for staffs and lay leadership of various agencies, religious and non-sectarian, to work together on problems of services and finances in which they are all mutually involved.

The links between the Welfare Federation and the Jewish Federation are particularly close. The same building houses both agencies; the staffs hold joint meetings on regular occasion; Jewish health and welfare agencies place a high priority on work in their respective welfare federation councils. The immediate past president of the Community Fund was simultaneously a vice-president of the Jewish Community Federation.

The Area Council movement has its origin in Cleveland and is probably more fully developed there than anywhere else in the country. It seeks through its seventeen councils to bring together organizations and individuals in a given neighborhood to work on problems of immediate local significance—traffic control, liquor control, zoning, lighting and policing, juvenile delinquency, and general neighborhood improvement. Churches and synagogues are basic members of these organizations and important interreligious cooperation has at times developed out of the shared absorption in common problems. Three councils have given considerable importance to intergroup relations problems, and colorful intercultural programs have been held, featuring the cultural diversities in the neighborhood. Unfortunately, area councils have had the least success in the sophisticated suburbs, and since the Jewish community has largely withdrawn from the central city, there is a decreasing impact of Jewish organizations and individuals on this important grass roots development.

Other formal interreligious contacts are moderately frequent. In addition to the program of the National Conference of Christians and Jews, which is of course based on equal formal representation from the three faiths, exchanges of pulpits between rabbis and Protestant ministers occasionally take place and neighborhood interreligious Thanksgiving celebrations have become more common. The annual Institute on Judaism sponsored by a local congregation results in a fine attendance of Protestant ministers. The Catholic university has in recent years become more of a center for consideration of intergroup relations problems.

There is considerable question, however, as to the depth of many of these contacts. The Ministerial Alliance is exclusively Protestant and there is no medium of any kind for regular exchange of views by the clergy. Indeed, except for the leading figures, rabbis and ministers scarcely know one another. On the lay level, however, the staffs of the Church Federation, the over-all Protestant group, and the Jewish Community Federation consult frequently and are part of an over-all clearing house in intergroup relations that meets monthly and involves all agencies in the community—except the

Roman Catholic ones. The women's organizations have a forum involving official representation from all three groups, but they are constantly bedeviled in program planning by the problem of addressing themselves to questions that are within the scope of all. A recent institute on housing, originally sponsored jointly by the Protestant, Jewish, and Catholic women's organizations, led to the somewhat embarrassed withdrawal of the last group on instructions of church officials who felt that matters of faith might somehow be injected into the programs. A subsequent program on religious music of the various faiths was "unsponsored" by the Orthodox Jewish women as well as by the Catholic group.

Vital interreligious relations seem to result *least* out of directly religious concerns. They would seem to grow —if at all—from sweating out the numerous problems of daily living—housing, education, employment.

What are the formal issues that divide the community religiously? A reading of the religious press would indicate that they are chiefly Sunday closings, the campaign against "indecent" literature and films, and problems of separation of church and state. The most space given to any single local issue during the past two years in the local diocesan paper is the need for some control of the mass media. "Art theaters and condemned movies are spreading like crabgrass in Cleveland," pronounced the Roman Catholic bishop recently, and it is certainly true that, in an industry which has been generally depressed, the art theaters have shown remarkable vitality.

In the summer of 1958 a parish priest in a Catholic neighborhood announced to the general press that he had "lost all patience" with attempts to persuade the owner of an art theater in a Catholic neighborhood to modify his booking policy, and he was therefore instructing his parishioners that they must refuse to attend all movies at the theater until the owner agreed to conform more closely to Roman Catholic standards of decency. Ironically, the week he issued the statement the theater was playing *Peter Pan*. The boycott announcement led to a lively debate in the general press, but there is no indication that such official pronouncements have had much effect one way or another on the attendance at the offending theater. Although the organized Jewish community has refrained from adopting any position on the boycott issue, there can be no doubt that the fact that almost all the theater owners in question are Jewish injects a religious irritation into the situation.

Ohio was one of the last states to be forced by court decisions to abandon pre-censorship of films. The Roman Catholic diocesan papers of the state have for the past four years led vigorous campaigns in the Legislature to recreate an Ohio Film Censorship Board. Although token support has been given by the Protestant church women, no position of any kind has been adopted by the Jewish group, with the result that the campaign remains almost exclusively Roman Catholic.

Recently, attention shifted to attempts to police literature in drug stores and similar establishments. A *Committee for Decent Literature* was established on both the local and state level and considerable prominence in the Catholic press is given to any Protestant or Jew who joins the movement or publicly stresses the need to combat "smut and obscenity." Considerable impatience is displayed with the American Civil Liberties Union or any other organization that raises questions as to the wisdom of censorship or the means by which it can properly be exerted. In general, civil liberties—as contrasted with civil rights—get little or negative attention in official Roman Catholic organs.

The leadership of campaigns to enforce Sunday closings has primarily been Protestant, with active support from the Catholic community. Unlike New York and many other states, Ohio enjoys full Sabbatarian rights and Jewish store owners in communities that enforce the state's blue laws are given the option (which sometimes is an advantage) of closing Saturday or Sunday. Partly for this reason and partly because of the sensitivity of the issue, the Jewish leaders of the state, including Cleveland, have chosen not to participate in the campaigns for (or against) enforced Sabbath closings of business, although in principle their position is opposed to that of Catholics and Protestants. On these two issues —censorship and Sunday closings—Jews officially tend to be on the sidelines about as completely as the Catholics are when civil rights are involved, with this difference: Jewish leaders feel strongly they should be in the battle *opposing* censorship and Sunday closings, but are often not prepared to pay the price of opposition. Catholics feel mildly they should be in the battle *for* civil rights but usually are not sufficiently interested to enlist with enthusiasm in the various campaigns.

The real drive behind recent activities aimed at enforcing the state law on Sunday closings that has for years been unobserved is, however, economic rather than religious. More and more places of business, particularly in the suburban areas, have opened on Sunday and have begun to cut seriously into the business of the large downtown stores. In retaliation, an organization has been formed called "Sunday, Inc.," which is an unusual combination of business and religious leadership. Its president has stated, "We have not approached this problem on religious lines. We have as our common bond a desire to keep merchants from doing unnecessary business on Sunday. The laws are on the books." But the same article announces the officers of the organization: a number of key businessmen, the executive director of the Cleveland Church Federation "representing Protestants," a leading Catholic official "representing Catholics," and a Jewish businessman "representing Jews." Here again almost all of the "offending" merchants are Jewish. Religious tension sometimes results, but as in the case of the art theaters, there would seem to be relatively little mass support by their constituencies of the official stands taken by the authoritative Christian groups, if one is to judge from the volume of Sunday sales in many neighborhoods that are certainly not Jewish.

EDUCATION

Problems of church-state relationships occur most frequently in the public schools. This is an issue that strikes home. Every Christmas season the irritations break out with renewed vigor—in Jewish neighborhoods.

On the one hand there is the organized Jewish community, committed to the separation of church and state, determined to resist tactfully but firmly the annual Christological invasion of the schools. On the other hand, there are the Christian parents, some seeking to "put Christ back into Christmas," others outraged that there should be resistance to "the perfectly beautiful celebration our children always enjoyed so much until. . . ." Still others warn of the terrible and certain dangers of juvenile delinquency and even Communism "if religion is banished from the classroom."

Some liberal Christians are firm separationists and others plead the case for using the season for joint understanding. To complicate matters further, there are many Jewish parents who cheer every introduction of Chanuko despite the stern warnings of Jewish leaders. In a mixed suburban school, a teacher's lot is not a happy one in December; many dread facing the annual problem of just *what* they are supposed to do anyway. In one overwhelmingly Jewish school, a parent violently objected to her son's bringing home a red-striped candy cane because it was a religious symbol while another parent gathered money to buy the school an electric menorah!

Separation in general seems to be a fluid concept capable of a variety of meanings—sometimes strangely contradictory. At a conference in the Church Federation office, a brochure was prominently displayed stressing the need to preserve separation of church and state by actively campaigning against an ambassador to the Vatican. The conference itself was devoted to the desire of the Church Federation office to conduct a religious census of school children under public school auspices. In one case separation was proper and "good"; in the other it was irrelevant and "bad."

A Roman Catholic official vigorously denounced separation as a "shibboleth" when Christian celebrations in the public schools were being opposed on that basis; but when a Methodist minister told Protestant students at a high school that they had no obligation to keep a promise to raise children as Catholic if they intermarried, he commented, "Considering separation of church and state, is it proper for a minister to go into a public school even to conduct a counseling course?" The YMCA holds a position of official status in many public high schools, and at least one priest has forbidden his parishioners to join the Y, since it is a means of spreading the Protestant position.

Jewish community organizations, unlike some Jewish parents, have consistently adhered to a strict separationist policy. As a result, school superintendents in the suburbs with significant Jewish enrollments have, in recent years, become sensitive to problems of Bible reading, prayers, grace before meals, and scheduling of school events on religious holidays. The rapid turnover of faculty in the elementary schools, and the need during the desperate shortage to import teachers from small communities where religion is accepted as an unquestioned part of the curriculum have, however, led to repeated classroom intrusions of religion despite official attitudes of the administration. One superintendent raised the interesting question as to whether the school calendar, which is obviously designed to accommodate Christian holidays, ought not to be revised to avoid conflict with Jewish observances since the community has become primarily Jewish. Although Jewish parents and the community insist upon the right of children to observe religious holidays, they avoid carefully any suggestion of tailoring school calendars or procedures along "Jewish" lines.

All these issues, however, paled in 1961 in comparison to the struggle over federal aid to parochial schools. Here is a real "bread and butter" issue that the local Catholic diocese has begun to feature far more than any other. The Protestant church for once was united; every spokesman has vigorously opposed such aid. A number of Orthodox rabbis for the first time broke the solid Jewish "separation front" by endorsing government aid, but the Federation overwhelmingly repeated its traditional support of the separation principle. There can be little doubt that this will for years to come constitute the most controversial of interreligious issues.

OTHER ISSUES

Problems which in other cities seem to raise interreligious blood pressures, have made little impact in Cleveland. Warm expressions of sympathy for Israel from the Christian clergy are not too frequent, for example, but on the other hand there is an almost complete absence of hostile comment, even when the Middle East situation is tense. Occasionally, newspaper stories will feature disputes arising out of adoptions across religious lines, but at no time has any real controversy developed. The general bland attitude toward issues in this area may well be a reflection of a certain absence of emotion connected with issues in general. Civic problems, war and peace, recession and recovery, are often conversation pieces, but rarely lead to stirring debate. Even the attitude toward the local baseball team is remarkably low pressured in recent years!

Considerably greater emotional involvement is seen when the issues touch home directly, rather than being concerned with philosophical differences. Almost any Jewish institution seeking to build for the first time in a new suburb is likely to encounter resistance. Twice in the past decade, cases involving the right of synagogues to build in suburban areas had to be carried to the Ohio Supreme Court.

One of the cases had an ironic ending. For years, counsel for the suburb fought through three courts with unprecedented tenacity to prevent the building of a synagogue. Despite all sorts of guarantees and assurances, it was alleged that the town would suffer from increased traffic problems, difficulties in providing services, and other similar situations. But the temple was hardly completed when the city fathers, faced by a desperate shortage of public school facilities, requested (and were granted) space in the new synagogue's school until a new public school could be built.

Religious exclusions practiced in a number of the suburbs by the company that developed the area were broken in the mid-fifties only after a bitter campaign and threats of taxpayer suits that would have depressed land values considerably. One suburb enforces a complicated 25 per cent quota on Jews, and the northern section of a suburb that is half-Jewish has developed a neighborhood compact that has succeeded so far in keeping out all but a single Jew. One community was almost torn apart by a campaign for a second high school, which many contended was motivated primarily by the desire of the northern half of the community (strongly Christian) to have "their" school, while resigning the original high school to the southern, "Jewish" section. In another suburb, an election was held on the question of dividing into two villages, one overwhelmingly Christian, the other just as strongly Jewish. Both efforts failed—but only after bitter campaigns. Permission to build a Jewish community center in a suburb was secured only after a long struggle, although a Lutheran high school was approved far more easily on an adjoining parcel of land.

In each of these cases there were more factors involved than religious differences. But no one who attended the various meetings of zoning commissions, city and village councils, or neighborhood town halls could escape the conclusion that, although problems of zoning and traffic and taxes were involved, religious hostility or unfriendliness were also powerful determinants of attitudes. Few situations present "clean" examples of bigotry; there is almost always a complicated intermingling of economic, sociological, psychological, and religious interests.

Sometimes, hostile attitudes are expressed crudely and in the unmistakable accents of the bigot, as in the case of the man who wrote in explanation of why neighborhoods run down: "In the first instance the Negro follows the Jew in housing; no Jews, no Negroes to follow. . . . The Jew is too greedy when it comes to the almighty dollar. You will think this man is prejudiced and biased who is writing this letter, but I am not! These are the facts; it is food for thought."

Much more significant and typical, perhaps, is the attitude revealed in a tribute in the Roman Catholic diocesan paper to a converted Jew who had just died. "Dad always saw to it that we children did not miss mass on Sunday," the daughter proudly writes. "If we were reluctant, Dad would threaten, 'All right, then, we will go to temple.' You never saw children hurry to church as we did." That homely vignette reveals an attitude that may well be just beneath the surface of much of the "tolerance" that is so wide-spread.

Sometimes neighborhoods change so completely as to create religious problems where there is no bigotry at all. One worried Christian mother, whose daughter attended a junior high school that is overwhelmingly Jewish, described in a thoroughly rational and unpunishing manner how her child was treated with perfect fairness and friendship during school hours, but was increasingly excluded from the social contacts that were becoming important to her. The family subsequently and regretfully moved from the neighborhood since dating possibilities had become virtually impossible for the daughter!

Despite the occasional highly dramatic cases where Jews have achieved top leadership in various civic roles, the community as a whole is, in a quiet and undramatic fashion, divided along religious lines. Cleveland has an FEPC, but evidence indicates that perhaps one out of every four job orders filed with private employment agencies is discriminatory against Jews. Perhaps equally significant is the increasing self-segregation in employment. A leading utility in Cleveland, which had been closed to Jews for years, changed its policy and freely accepted Jewish clerical help. The local Jewish Vocational Service soon found itself encountering substantial difficulties in filling job orders, because the girls wanted to work in places "where they could meet Jewish fellows"!

Any observation that social life in Cleveland tends to follow rather closely along religious lines is often greeted with indignant instancing of various parties and gatherings of Jews and non-Jews. Nevertheless, these are overwhelmingly the exception and the so-called "5 o'clock shadow" is clearly visible in the community's social life. Jews socialize for the most part with Jews; Catholics with Catholics; Protestants with Protestants.

In 1958 the executives of two well-established women's civic organizations requested help in increasing Jewish participation in their work. The fact that these organizations contained few Jews could not be ascribed to discrimination; both have been eager for some time to expand their Jewish membership. Why, they asked, do Jewish women join so enthusiastically in the work of Hadassah, Council of Jewish Women, Sisterhoods, the Welfare Fund Appeal, and many other Jewish organizations, but are often so hard to interest in non-sectarian groups? Surely Jewish women are civic minded; surely they have much to contribute.

An easy—and truthful—answer would be that opportunities for advancement to top leadership are best in one's "own" organization. But like most easy answers, that explanation is only part of the truth. Over and over again, leaders of Jewish organizations described their impatience as they sat at meetings of a number of non-sectarian organizations, where the issues being discussed were "piddling"—a budget item of a few dollars or a minor, unexciting program detail. The really successful Jewish organizations, they claim, present far bolder challenges. What is to be avoided at all costs is dullness. And, they conclude, those non-sectarian organizations that are truly—not perfunctorily—open to all women and that grapple with basic community needs *do* attract Jewish women. Unspoken is what may well be the most important factor: Jewish women in Cleveland are more comfortable with Jewish women. But in any case, the fact remains unchallengeably true that the overwhelming majority of Jewish (or, for that matter, Catholic and Protestant) women are "club ladies" within their own religious groups.

Although the world of business necessarily involves more contact across religious lines, it is nevertheless true that the husbands, too, eat lunch (when there is no business appointment), play golf, and attend committee meetings most frequently with men who are of the same religious faith. If they are Jewish, they are very likely to have a Jewish insurance man, a Jewish lawyer, a Jewish doctor—except in the case of specialists. And, with variations, the same generalizations could be made about the other religious groups.

SUMMARY

In summary, then, interreligious relationships in Cleveland might be characterized by the following generalizations:

1. Little overt conflict exists, and there is a pervasive atmosphere of avoiding tension situations. As a result, there is little "dialogue" among the religious groups, and the price of relatively little conflict is relatively shallow interreligious contacts. Blandness is the key everywhere.

2. Close interreligious cooperation, where it exists, is rarely on specifically religious projects. It is more likely to occur on civic, philanthropic, and business levels.

3. The Roman Catholic community is the most iso-

lated of the three major faith groups. The Archbishop explains the withdrawal: "Our inferiority complex reveals itself even today in the tendency to isolate ourselves from the community as a whole." There is only now, with the beginning of an interreligious dialogue, faint stirring toward increasing participation. These efforts are sparked by Catholic laymen.

4. Each religious group has issues in which it is primarily interested: the Catholic priority is increased policing of the mass media and gaining support for their schools; the Protestant, changing neighborhoods; the Jewish, church-state relationships. Closest cooperation exists, particularly between liberal Protestants and Jews, in the area of civil rights.

5. Almost all areas of daily living reflect an increasing sifting down into religious compartments. Churches and synagogues have become more central institutions; schools, housing, and social satisfactions are likely to follow religious lines. Even employment and (to a lesser degree) business patterns have increasingly an element of religious self-segregation. Weekly ads in the diocesan paper seem to symbolize the strange ways of this apartness: "Low cost hospitalization," it emphasizes in large headlines, *available only to Ohio Catholics.*"

6. The white population of all three religious groups is becoming increasingly suburban. Despite the growth of religious institutions and the separateness that has been described, religious issues and values seem to count less than the absorbing interest in material satisfactions that characterize all three groups. The "things" of suburban living outweigh religious values or differentiation.

Is Cleveland, then, the best location in the nation? If

the negative test of absence of conflict is applied, the boast can be very largely made good. But if the aim is a culturally diverse community where creative living of cultural groups is balanced by full and easy communication across religious lines, Cleveland, like most cities, still has a long road to travel.

LOS ANGELES
Exploding Metropolis

TO EXAMINE LOS ANGELES IS TO LOOK THROUGH A SMOG-clouded kaleidoscope. It is a giant, gaudy, improbable city in frantic motion. It is a variegated patchwork of a "hundred neighborhoods in search of a city." It is a way of life—vibrant, yeasty, and exploding—spiced with such ingredients as the Dodgers and the Angels, Disneyland, Hollywood, kidney-shaped swimming pools, faddists, and jammed freeways. It is the fastest-growing city in the fastest-growing state of the Union. California is now the second most populous state and is roaring, like a rocket gone awry, to the top of the heap. In the north, San Francisco, cool in its hills beyond the high Tehachapis, maintains its staid, stolid grace, grandly aloof for the most part to the feverish turmoil of the City of the Angels. But Greater Los Angeles, with its bustling industries and bustling chauvinism, with its raucous materialism and flood-lighted artificiality, is a city on the go—and on the make.

Within the immense amalgam of sixty-seven separate municipalities and 31,144 square miles, live more than 6,000,000 people. By 1970, this figure is expected to reach eight million. Mushrooming minority groups now represent almost a quarter of the booming population. Of these, some 500,000 are of Mexican extraction—comprising the largest such group outside Mexico itself.

The Negro community has sky-rocketed from 70,000 in 1940 to some 500,000 in 1960, constituting the largest Negro group outside of New York and Chicago. The Jews number 425,000, a 21 per cent increase since 1951 and double the size of the Jewish population in 1941; Los Angeles is the largest American Jewish community outside of New York. In addition, there are approximately 50,000 Japanese and 15,000 Chinese, constituting the largest Oriental group in the United States outside of Hawaii. Some 15,000 Indians represent the largest urban assemblage of the earliest Americans in any American city. Mix it all together, add the special yeast of the new frontier, flavor freely—and you have Los Angeles.

Metropolitan Los Angeles is in constant movement. Like other major areas, expansion flows outward, the center of the city steadily becoming predominantly low-income, transient, and commercial. As restrictive covenants break down, Negroes, Japanese-Americans, and Mexican-Americans find greater housing opportunities in new neighborhoods.

As in other metropolitan areas, it is largely the Protestant churches which feel the full impact of changing neighborhoods. Many Protestant churches have followed their congregations to the suburbs. Others have been rendered hollow shells as their congregants have moved. Often such churches were sold to Negro Baptists who had become the next migrating wave.

Roman Catholic churches, on the other hand, have usually remained fixed and represent a strong force for the integration of all who would join the local parish. Parochial schools, church membership, and church activities are thrown open to people of all races. Despite changing neighborhoods, Catholic churches invariably refuse to sell and move, but rather build new parishes to accommodate the suburbanites. The Church stands as a rock in the shifting tides of urban change.

Los Angeles is one of the few large cities not predominantly Roman Catholic. Nor is the center of the city markedly Catholic in population. Many eastern cities include among their low-income labor force sizable blocks of East or Central European nationalities, or Irish, dominantly Catholic in religious outlook. Such East European nationalities are less numerous in Los Angeles. The large Negro population is heavily Protestant in background, while the Mexican-American group, though Catholic, is somewhat cut off from the mainstream of Catholic activity and dogma. The result is that, while Protestants are slowly losing their strong foothold in central Los Angeles, fundamentalist Negro Protestant, and independent churches are almost as numerous as Roman Catholic churches. The pressure of reorganizing, rebuilding, or shifting bases keeps most Protestant ministers busy with their own affairs, while often their congregations commute long distances, maintaining affiliation with the mid-town church for a period, but finally shifting to a more convenient suburban affiliation.

Synagogues face the same challenge of mobility, augmented by the sharply rising number of Jews in-migrating to Los Angeles each year. Some of the temples have moved westward or into suburban San Fernando or San Gabriel Valley. Soaring enrollment and budgets enable an enormous variety of synagogue-sponsored programs for recreation, education, and community activities. Supervising this expansion both financially and programmatically has kept many a rabbi with his nose to the grindstone of organization. At the same time, many synagogues have opened their facilities to community non-sectarian groups. A number of synagogue sisterhoods have tried conscientiously to share programs with nearby Protestant churches.

In Los Angeles' boisterous development, the racial pot has boiled over more than once. The bloody "zoot suit" riots of 1943, involving cadets at the Naval Armory and Mexican-American youths, touched off so much violence that the entire city was once placed off limits to Navy personnel for a week. Mistreatment of Japanese before World War II and their mass relocation during the war still haunt the conscience of the sprawling metropolis. And Negro-white clashes sometimes accompanied the waves of population change.

But Los Angeles, at the end of World War II, launched a crash program to straighten out its human relations and prepare for the bright future. The nation's third largest city has done a creditable job of easing racial tensions and enlarging opportunities for all. A key to the progress was the development of the Community Relations Conference of Southern California which began with ten agencies and has grown into a network of sixty-five. Called by some a "United Nations of community organizations," because of its diversity, the County Conference has been directed since its birth in 1947 by George Thomas, a devoted Negro lawyer and church worker.

While the Conference and its member organizations have welded a sense of cooperation, and notable improvement in race relations is manifest, "Angelenos" tend to turn to superlatives to describe their race relations. A rather breathless series of articles in the Los Angeles *Examiner* in February, 1960, declared that, "it is universally agreed that Los Angeles is the pride of the nation, head and shoulders above the other great sister cities, some of whose very names—New York, Chicago, Detroit—conjure up nightmares this community has fought to avoid." Modestly characterizing Los Angeles' program as "the greatest mass effort to establish good group relations the world has ever seen," the newspaper pointed out that "no great urban area except Los Angeles has been able to do this." Purple adjectives and hyperbole apart, Los Angeles has attacked its racial problems with zeal and spirit.

Community problems have led to the strengthening of the Welfare Planning Council, which, with the Community Chest, shares the task of charting the social, philanthropic, and welfare needs of the skyrocketing city. In turn, the Council has reached out to the city's many suburbs, setting up area subcommittees which have helped to bring together neighborhood leadership and agencies to take a more comprehensive look at their own problems.

On yet another level, a Federation of Coordinating Councils, serving more than ninety-six local coordinating councils, works closely with county and city as well as social agency personnel to help deter delinquency through improvement in education, health, recreation, and other areas. Common to the Coordinating Council, the County Conference, and the Welfare Planning Council movements is a search for conscientious citizens whose help is needed to cope with the back-breaking urban problems which Los Angeles faces daily in absorbing new migrants and providing social services to its residents.

THE RELIGIOUS FACTOR

But what of the interreligious relationships in this euphoric city? Beneath the smog and the glamor and the vista-vision, how do the people get on? Do Protestants, Catholics, and Jews live happily together forever after, like characters in a Hollywood romance? Or does Los Angeles, too, suffer the strains and stresses which afflict lesser cities?

Without describing the vast internal efforts whereby Jewish, Roman Catholic, and Protestant groups strive diligently to meet their own expanding needs, suffice it to say that religious leadership, especially clerical, is rarely available to serve the broader community welfare. Each religious group is preoccupied, understandably but regrettably, with its own problems and rapid growth. Moreover, religious lines are tightly drawn denominationally.

One natural result of this preoccupation is a certain amount of self-segregation, particularly evident in the Jewish community. A considerable percentage of Los Angeles Jewry resides in neighborhoods which are predominantly Jewish in character. Beverly Hills and Beverly-Fairfax are typical of this phenomenon. In the latter neighborhood over 95 per cent of all students are absent from school on Jewish holidays. Beverly Hills was referred to by a Christian minister, in a not unkindly fashion, as "Hebrew Hollow." Synagogues, delicatessen stores, social centers, and Jewish cultural institutions have helped to solidify the Beverly-Fairfax ghetto and to attract in-migrants who wish to live among their core-ligionists.

As a result of activities in Jewish cultural, educational, social, and religious institutions in this area, and because of many Jewish families who frown on bringing non-Jewish teen-agers into their homes, thousands of Jewish children grow up in denominationally sheltered environments. At the same time, the non-Jewish minority frequently withdraws from neighborhoods where their own children appear to be either isolated or boycotted.

Aware of the concentration of Jewish voters in his district, one politician visited Israel a few years ago and upon his return made endless appearances before Jewish groups of all types. When election time came around, his campaign literature stressed his pro-Israel sentiments to the virtual exclusion of issues more relevant to his district and to the public office which he was seeking. This type of campaign tactic was severely criticized in responsible Jewish circles, and one Anglo-Jewish newspaper charged editorially that the candidate "virtually wrapped himself in the Israeli flag, charging across the Sinai desert."

In spite of some tendencies toward Jewish self-segregation, Jewish residents participate fully in non-sectarian fund drives for educational, cultural, and charitable causes, especially for the Community Chest.

Among Protestants there is considerable suspicion that Roman Catholics in Community Chest circles are concerned only with the work of Catholic agencies which benefit from Chest allocations. Protestant leaders who are familiar with the Chest and Welfare Council operations insist that the leading old families of Los Angeles are Protestant in tradition, dedicated to community service, and motivated by a personal commitment to civic welfare which requires no label of religious affiliation. On the other hand, according to these Protestant observers, Catholic leadership is increasingly being harnessed to archdiocesan aims and objectives, with interreligious contacts held to a minimum.

The most controversial and influential religious leader in Los Angeles is Francis Cardinal McIntyre, spiritual leader of more than one million Roman Catholics. Catholic participation in interreligious activities has virtually ceased under his administration, with priests unavailable for interfaith panels, archdiocesan representatives unwilling to sit on the stage with other religious leaders at community affairs, and clerical leaders of the Roman Catholic faith absent from virtually every level of community planning, from the neighborhood Coordinating Council to the county-wide agencies in the social welfare and human relations fields. Protestant and Jewish leaders keenly resent such a policy of isolation.

Los Angeles Protestant ministers are generally more active in community affairs than are either priests or rabbis. Social welfare attracts Protestant participation. Social action movements trail badly, and direct interreligious programs are virtually non-existent. Conversely, it is Jewish clergymen who seem to evince the most interest in interreligious and social action programs, while participating less in social welfare projects outside their own religious institutions.

On the top echelons of the Welfare Planning Council, two priests and one Catholic nun play prominent roles. The sister, in fact, heads the important Child Welfare Division. The two priests are full-time representatives of the Catholic Youth Organization and Catholic Welfare Bureau, rather than parish priests. On the various area levels of organization (the Welfare Council seeks to secure greater neighborhood participation through subregional clusters) no comparable Roman Catholic clerical participation exists, so that the Protestant minister who participates has no chance to meet his Catholic counterpart regarding welfare and social problems common to their immediate community. A top Welfare Council spokesman acquainted with a similar gulf between priest and minister in other communities felt that "stringent hierarchical structure" within each archdiocese determined whether the parish priest was kept internally preoccupied or freed somewhat for broader community responsibilities.

While Jewish-Christian relationships are generally good on a superficial level, there was serious misunderstanding of the Jewish community when it stood virtually alone among major religious groups in its opposition to a bill, introduced in the State Legislature, calling for compulsory Bible reading in the public school classroom. Catholic and Protestant groups favored the bill, which was reintroduced during several legislative sessions until the Attorney General ruled that the proposal was unconstitutional.

The campaign in support of the bill was so strong that many Protestant clergymen, who privately opposed the measure, refrained from voicing their conviction. Only some Seventh Day Adventists, humanists, and Masons joined the Jewish community in opposing the bill publicly. Fundamentalist spokesmen stood on the undisguised platform that this is a "Christian nation," and that "god-lessness" was at the heart of our current plethora of immorality and crime.

Had it not been for the strong opposition to the bill by teacher groups, the legislature would probably have passed it. The bill died in committee each time, but every hearing was tinged with innuendos of prejudice against non-Christian and "godless teachers." Though these controversies shook relationships between leaders of the Jewish community and the Protestant clergy, no bitterness lingered after the defeat of the bill and friendly understanding continued.

However, the relationships between Protestants and Catholics are strained, have definitely not improved over the past decade, and in the eyes of some, are worsening. Leading Protestants were asked their views in the course of this study. Not one held that Catholic-Protestant relationships were good. Most of those queried pointed to the absence of year-round contact with Catholic clergy as a major factor. Few community welfare projects exist, they said, where "we ministers work side-by-side with our Catholic colleagues on long-range objectives. Thus, we only get to know them rather superficially when we sit next to them at public luncheons and dinners."

One of the few conscious areas of interreligious cooperation has been the University Religious Conference, founded by leaders of Protestant, Catholic, and Jewish groups in 1928 at the University of California at Los Angeles (UCLA) to foster greater religious understanding and commitment among UCLA students. In a jointly-owned building to which all denominations contribute financially, courses in religion and culture are taught by the religious advisers of each faith, while other activities are encouraged by the full-time staff which includes Methodist, Lutheran, Episcopal, and Presbyterian, as well as Roman Catholic and Jewish representatives. The "Panel of Americans" was conceived at UCLA by the Conference as a way of promoting greater interreligious respect and understanding. Panels of an interfaith and interracial nature have for years visited high school and community institutions to make dramatic pleas for inter-group understanding. But in recent years, denomina-tional leaders have concerned themselves more with their own denominational programs, less with interre-ligious programs. Recently, Catholic participation in the Panel of Americans was curtailed, apparently on orders from the Chancery. A real interfaith forum in the earlier years of its operation, the URC building seems to be rapidly compartmentalizing, with less and less sharing of activities.

Intergroup relationships, especially in the religious field, require not merely good will gestures and occa-sional exchanges of pulpits, but rather a common ground on which clerics and laymen can work side by side for common objectives. What part does interreligious coop-eration play in attempts to solve the major problem areas of community life in Los Angeles?

More than sixty civic groups, belonging to the County Conference on Community Relations, include as part of their programs an emphasis on good human relations. These sixty include all the minority groups: Jewish, Negro, Mexican-American, Nisei, etc. They also in-clude the YWCA, organized labor, and many of the Social Action departments of Christian churches. In the history of the County Conference, only one small Roman Catholic group (a devoted group of women with no official church status) has ever been a member of the organization. As a forum for working on common problems, the County Conference has cemented Protestant-Jewish relationships and has given leaders in both groups a sense of solidarity and of unity in action.

While the staff services and financial support of Jewish community relations agencies have loomed large in making the work of the County Conference effective, Protestant groups have played a larger role in its support than they play in other cities. Among the foremost are Baptist, Congregational, Episcopal, Methodist, and Presbyterian church groups, many of them represented by clerical leaders.

Protestant leaders, active in the County Conference, have high praise for the important role played by Jewish human relations agencies—through staff and lay leadership—in the County Conference. Frequently, they express the wish that their own denominational groups would be as active in the field of race relations as is the leadership of the Jewish community. They are equally impressed by the Jewish Community Building where most Jewish organizations maintain their offices and where meetings of the County Conference are often held. This modern and impressive building, the nerve center of Los Angeles Jewry, is located at 590 North Vermont Avenue. It has become a symbol of Jewish unity, Jewish dedication to racial equality, education, and philanthropy. Jews sometimes poke sly fun at the building—usually in a friendly spirit—calling it the "Jewish Pentagon."

The interplay of agency leaders on the broad problems of intergroup relations has carried over to ad hoc committees, created by the County Conference, acting in such specific areas as revision of U.S. immigration policy, fair employment practices, and housing, with a good degree of involvement by Protestant and Jewish clergy and lay leaders in these fields. With notable exceptions, Roman Catholic priests have not participated.

The absence of a real interreligious relationship between Roman Catholic clergy on the one hand and Protestant and Jewish clerics on the other, does not mean that race relations programs have necessarily suffered. The Roman Catholic archdiocese includes many Mexican-Americans, and a large number of churches have entirely Spanish-speaking membership, although they are usually served by "Anglo" priests, mostly Irish. The Catholic attitude toward the Negro and toward racial integration is markedly positive, with parochial schools integrated along with the parish churches in mixed neighborhoods. Absent is the technique for cementing a better working relationship between churches and social agencies in transitional neighborhoods. Yet the Roman Catholic Church has unquestionably been a positive force for racial justice.

Loyola University, a Jesuit institution, has sponsored a summer workshop on human relations for several years, to which teachers, social workers, law enforcement officers, and community leaders have been invited, and which also draws priest-novitiates and nuns. As part of the intensive six-week course, community and religious leaders of all faiths have been invited to present the views of their groups on race relations, civil rights, and social justice. On occasion, Baptist, Methodist, Episcopalian, and Presbyterian ministers, both Negro and white, have been guest speakers. The workshop itself is not sponsored by the archdiocese, but stems from the concern of Jesuit priests and Catholic lay leaders.

A word needs to be said about the National Conference of Christians and Jews, which makes interreligious cooperation its chief objective. Its Committee on Interreligious Organization has clerical representation from Protestant, Jewish, and Greek Orthodox groups, but it includes virtually no Roman Catholic representation except occasional laymen or Jesuits. The archdiocese eschews cooperation with the NCCJ. The National Conference of Christians and Jews evokes widely varying reactions among those concerned with interracial and interreligious problems. A labor official once denounced it for "selling brotherhood for $25.00 a plate" while others were putting brotherhood into action. Other observers commend the NCCJ as a bridge of interfaith communication. On the board of that organization and among its sponsors are many noted citizens, but the organization has not yet succeeded in fashioning a close working relationship among the leaders of the major faiths.

In 1960 an ad hoc group was organized to commemorate World Refugee Year, and to plan a reception for Dr. Elfin Rees, international WRY director, on his visit to Los Angeles. Top Protestant clergymen were extremely active in the program planning, as were leaders of Jewry. After one meeting, the clerical representative of the archdiocese pleaded his inability to attend, leaving the Catholic Family Movement, a lay group affiliated with national Catholic welfare activities, as the sole Roman Catholic group within the committee.

CHURCH-STATE RELATIONS

In Los Angeles, Christian-Jewish understanding is perhaps more fragile and fraught with tension in the area of church-state separation than in any other. Yet the Christian community itself is far from united on this issue, with deep underlying cleavages which divide liberal from conservative Protestants, and Protestants from Catholics. A 1958 state-wide battle over tax exemption for private and parochial schools further deteriorated the relationships between Protestants and Catholics.

Typical of the anti-Catholic campaign tactics employed was a pamphlet captioned "Is Your Religion Counterfeit?" It stated:

"On Page 112 of Book Three of the standard high school text, LIVING OUR FAITH, used in Roman Catholic high schools of California, appears the following declaration:

> COUNTERFEIT RELIGIONS. The material, size, and shape of the paper and metal money in the United States is determined and authorized by the government. No other money is legal tender, and any other agency issuing such money is guilty of counterfeiting. *In the same way, non-Catholic methods of worshipping God must be branded counterfeit.*

"On Page 237 of the same volume this appears:

> In the words of Pope Pius XI: 'It is evident that both by right and in fact the mission to educate . . . belongs to the Church.' . . . Teachers should be Catholics and, wherever possible, religious. Textbooks in every branch of knowledge and on every level of education, from the first grade to the end of university training, should be Catholic publications when they are available.

"This un-American, intolerant philosophy of religious choice is taught in the tax-exempt Roman Catholic schools of California—and *you, of whatever faith,* are paying to have it taught.

"It teaches that all of the Protestant, Jewish, Christian Science, orthodox religions, except the Roman Catholic, are 'counterfeit.'

"Divisive teachings are bad in a democracy, but are particularly dangerous when taught to small children in school—at the taxpayer's expense!

"Under the American system we can't seek to have this kind of teaching stopped in such schools—but we *can* eliminate such schools from the benefit of tax exemption!"

California editors characterized the election as the foulest in the 108-year history of that state. The following spot radio announcement urged passage of Proposition 16 in the California campaign:

> Californians! Don't pay the blackmail tax. Let parochial and private schools pay their own taxes. Vote "Yes" on Proposition 16. Parochial schools in California say if you don't pay our taxes we will flood the public schools with our

students. Don't you believe it. Parochial schools in California have existed for over 100 years. For the past five of these years you have paid their taxes and during this five-year period these schools have increased by 258 per cent. Don't let the threat of blackmail stop you from voting "Yes" on Proposition 16. Make private and parochial schools pay their own taxes on November 4. Vote "Yes" on Proposition 16. "Yes" on Proposition 16.

Not all Protestant leaders opposed tax exemption for parochial schools. Several prominent Protestant clergymen, headed by a leading Episcopal minister, sided with Roman Catholic and other groups in opposing repeal. Many of these denominations, Lutheran, Baptist, and Episcopalian, operated their own full-time parochial schools which benefited from the exemption. Others believed that taxation of private and parochial schools was unfair and imposed financial burdens on schools which were already having a difficult time trying to cope with pupil enrollment and building programs.

Even where Protestant and Catholic clergy were on the same side, however, interfaith associations rarely resulted. The public campaign favoring retention of the tax exemption was directed by a public relations firm very close to the Chancery office. An imposing letterhead was drawn up, on which not a single Roman Catholic of prominence was listed. Catholic church activity against the repeal was prodigious but it went parallel to the efforts of others. It led to no new interfaith bridges.

While the tax-exemption measure was on the ballot,

Attorney General Edward "Pat" Brown, a Catholic, was candidate for governor. He was pitted against Senator William Knowland, a Protestant. In the closing days of the campaign, literature was circulated "predicting" that Brown, if elected, would close the public schools.

Brown was elected by an overwhelming majority and the fear that the state administration would be dominated by Catholics has not been justified. The governor's appointments have been of generally high caliber, with Protestants and Jews placed in key positions along with Roman Catholics.

Controversies of this type tend to create an uneasy feeling among those concerned with separation of religion and the state and with improving relationships among the various religious groups. It shows itself in a variety of church-state issues, ranging from religion in the schools, through tax exemption for religious institutions, to outright state subventions (money, use of property, etc.), to religious pageants and programs. On each of the issues, deep anxiety seems to grip one or another of the religious groups, often leaving the others cold. Depending on which issue one talks about, animated reactions come forth revealing a suspicion of clergy of other faiths for failing to understand, or what is worse, actively breaching the principle of church-state separation. Obviously, the church-state principle is understood differently by each of the faith groups.

For understandable reasons, preoccupation with all facets of the church-state relationships is most intense in the Jewish community. Most of the encroachments are Christological in character, provoking reaction from Jewish groups. Most frequent are Nativity scenes or plays in schools, perennial legislation which would make Bible reading in classrooms compulsory, released time proposals, Easter Sunrise services, and other worship rites on public property.

Jewish opposition to such practices has frequently led to incidents which aroused serious Christian counter-reaction. One of the most memorable of such brouhahas in recent years popped up in Sierra Madre, a Pasadena suburb. There the request of a Jewish parent for cessation of the school-sponsored Christmas Nativity play led to an emotion-packed series of public meetings, harsh anti-Semitic utterances, and sharp demands by Christian clergymen for the traditional Christian program and, later, for released time. (This in turn was rejected by the Board, leading several clergymen to vow they would defeat those members of the Board of Education who made the decision.)

Public schools approach the December festivals with trepidation. In areas with a large number of Jewish students, the response of educators has varied from eliminating the December assembly program altogether to matching a highly Christological Yuletide program with one where Jewish students, wearing skull caps, symbolically light the Chanuko Menorah. In one school, the religious festivals were separated, with the Jewish program on one day and the Christmas program on another day. Jewish parental reactions are mixed. Some want all religious emphasis eliminated. Others are prepared to settle for a symbolic performance about Chanuko to balance the Christmas program. In one school, a parent who arrived early, spotting a small Chanuko Menorah alongside a towering Christmas tree, put in an emergency call to a nearby rabbi. After a frantic search, the rabbi presented an antique Menorah several feet in height, giving a semblance of parity to the Yuletide-Chanuko festival, pacifying Jewish parents, at least until the December crisis the following year.

Jewish opposition to religious practices in schools has been laced at times with such expediency, including the willingness of some rabbis to speak at school baccalaureate services, to urge presentation of Chanuko programs, and to demand that public schools not open on a Jewish High Holy Day.

Efforts to involve Jewish and Christian leaders in serious discussion of separation of church and state have invariably fallen flat. It has been hard for Christian leaders to see why this issue has prime importance. Conversely, rabbis and Jewish lay leaders have been less concerned with such matters as diplomatic recognition of the Vatican, alleged suppression of religious freedom in Spain and Latin America, and Roman Catholic efforts to secure tax exemption for parochial schools, issues which alarm most Protestants.

Anxiety by Protestant leaders about Catholic attitudes toward church-state separation carries with it little personal acrimony toward the priest around the corner. But there is strong fear among Protestants of the rapidly expanding parochial school system of the Catholic archdiocese. Because of this, Protestants have felt increasingly defensive about public education and its alleged neutrality toward religious commitment. Despite the fact that half the Roman Catholic children in greater Los Angeles (110,000 at latest count) attend parochial schools, the number of Catholic children taking advantage of released time in the public schools is almost double the Protestant attendance figure. And this, notwithstanding the fact that the Protestant Council of Churches has been the main advocate of such programs! In suburban communities, a much higher percentage of all children take advantage of the released time program. In metropolitan Los Angeles, however, Protestant released time programs are generally ineffective, of doubtful instructional quality, and hence a sore point with churchmen who seek ways to effectuate greater religious education programs through the public schools. It should be noted that Los Angeles Jewry does not participate in the released time program.

SCHOOLS UNDER ATTACK

The charge that public schools are "godless" evokes differing responses from Protestant and Roman Catholic religious leaders. Foremost among the critics of public schools for alleged indifference to religious values is Cardinal McIntyre. Repeatedly, he has raked modern education for failing to inculcate a belief in God, a sense of religious values. Public schools, charges the Cardinal, fail to distinguish the moral qualities of right and wrong, but rather attempt psychologically to explain the "why" of wrong-doing instead of condemning it. His diatribes have been so repeated and so bitter that some of his own friends within Roman Catholic leadership began to plead with him to stop his attacks lest they backfire against the church.

Local Protestant leaders bristle at the McIntyre charges, which they regard as less calculated to improve public education than to appeal for the expansion of his rapidly-growing parochial school system. But the Protestants' defense of public schools is weakened by their own misgivings as to the role of public education in the religious area. At the University of California at Los Angeles, the University Religious Conference is urging accreditation by the university of sectarian religious courses taught off-campus by each denomination, under its auspices. Many rabbis and some ministers have opposed this proposal which is calculated to get around protests against the university teaching such denominational courses on the campus itself.

The volatile Protestants and Other Americans United (POAU) has little strength in Protestant church circles of greater Los Angeles, though a few prominent ministers, including a Methodist bishop, have joined in POAU-sponsored programs and have endorsed some of its views. Most sober Protestants regard POAU as having overstated its fears of the Vatican and of Roman Catholic policy in America. They avoid affiliation with POAU as a consequence, regarding it as anti-Catholic in motivation rather than affirmative in its defense of the separation of religion and the state. But almost nowhere do the difficult problems of church-state relations, especially as they impinge on public schools, come in for interreligious discussion on an objective basis.

Public support of public education has been less than effective until recently, despite the harbingers of crisis involved in the ultra-reactionary putsch which several years ago caused the ouster of Dr. Willard Goslin from his post as school superintendent in Pasadena, and the domination of the Los Angeles schools by an anti-United Nations clique. A recent study by the Carnegie Foundation of public attitudes toward the United Nations found the greatest hotbeds of hostility to the UN in Houston and Los Angeles. In probing these attitudes, the Carnegie study found that strong anti-Semitic and anti-foreign feelings dominated the UN critics.

Problems of social action in the Los Angeles metropolis are well symbolized by the magnitude of the task of restoring sanity and popular representation to the Los Angeles Board of Education. This vast school system serves more than a half million students. Its citizen-voters total more than a million, and, in the past, a 20 per cent vote was enough to decide who should serve on the school board. The Los Angeles *Times* habitually dominated the decision by its endorsement of candidates.

The painstaking job of mobilizing public opinion to defend public schools against pressure groups brought Protestants and Jews together along with teachers, civic and labor leaders, and spokesmen for various ethnic groups. The herculean task of alerting a million voters to an understanding of the issues, and replacing incumbent board members with a new slate, was aided in great measure by interreligious cooperation and joint action by synagogue and church. Indeed, the 1957 school board election became historic because it spelled defeat for two ultra-reactionary incumbents who had been backed by the entire metropolitan press and much of the Who's Who of society and industry.

The Committee for Better Schools, which conducted the campaign, was headed by youthful Methodist Bishop Gerald Kennedy, while Congregational, Baptist, Episcopal, Lutheran, as well as Methodist ministers, pitched in to get out the vote. To many of the Protestant leaders interviewed for this study, the crash program of interfaith cooperation between Protestants and Jews in school board campaigns of the past few years stood out as one of their proudest recollections.

Roman Catholic participation in these efforts was limited to lay men and women, with virtually no contact with the clergy. Archdiocesan coolness to the committee's activities was based partly on alleged POAU leanings by individual committee members, and partly on the fact that the archdiocese itself favored a deeply-conservative 3-R approach to education as against "modern" pedagogical methods.

More recently a repeat performance by the Committee for Better Schools (this time including a liberal Roman Catholic among its slate of four) was marked by less suspicion on the part of the Catholic clergy. Developments during the bitterly-fought parochial tax exemption battle partly reassured the Catholic leadership that public school teachers, Protestant clergy, and other friends of public education were not necessarily hostile to parochial education. Many non-Catholic leaders hope that public school elections, a biennial social struggle of mounting proportions, will win Catholic cooperation, just as previously the same issue had drawn Jewish and Protestant leadership together. It appears that the social goals of public education have proved the greatest common unifier for citizens and religious leaders of varied backgrounds in Los Angeles. Los Angeles continues to be bedeviled by that baffling, chronic, and dangerous disease which has afflicted its public school system. In 1961, the Board of Education was badgered by right-wing super-patriots who demanded the banning of a number of films which they deemed to be subversive and Communist propaganda. (Example: "The Face of Red China," CBS-TV documentary.) The wild charges of the ultras were amplified by the sensational *Los Angeles Herald-Express*. When the Board of Education refused by a vote of 5 to 2 to capitulate to know-nothing pressures, the Hearst newspaper carried a large front-page headline which shrieked: "L.A. SCHOOL BOARD KEEPS RED PROPAGANDA FILMS." A steady stream of hysterical letters to the editor indicates that the "film" issue may be merely an opening round of a new effort by the super-patriots to gain control of the public schools.

What makes Los Angeles so susceptible to cranks, crackpots, and super-patriots? Why is Southern California the most fertile ground for such bizarre groups as the Minute Men, private guerillas who have acquired arms and are preparing for the apocalyptic worst; and bands of grim-visaged warriors against fluoridation of water, polio vaccine, NATO, income tax, and mental health? Why do so many residents of Los Angeles feel constrained to put signs on their automobile bumpers, advertising that they are not Communists? There are many hypotheses. No doubt the invasion of elderly retired folks, living on small incomes, has given the community a conservative tone. A restless, unstable community (one in four Los Angelenos changes his address each year) tends to demand conformity and is responsive to the skills of mass communication, which characterize Los Angeles. Los Angeles newspapers—two of which went down the drain in early 1962—have shown little readiness to act as guardians of civil liberties or as shapers of cultural maturity and civic responsibility. Moreover, as Bruce Bliven has pointed out (*Reporter*, January 18, 1962): ". . . there is a natural westering tropism for crackpots; these human tumbleweeds keep drifting toward the setting sun until they are finally halted by the ocean."

The ubiquitous problem of censorship takes a variety of forms in Los Angeles. In the city called the motion picture capital of the world, the cynosure of pressures for decency in films is the National Legion of Decency. As a major production center for radio and television, Los Angeles is the cockpit for the feverish efforts of self-appointed censorship groups. The constant threat of boycotts has been a problem not only because of religious pressures, but also because of charges of "pro-Communism" by the American Legion and other groups. Two examples of recent years include the failure to show Charlie Chaplin pictures and hesitancy to show the *Martin Luther* film in Los Angeles.

In public schools, fierce pressure was brought to bear against the teaching of controversial issues, including the United Nations, human relations, and sex education. In the latter case, semi-official Roman Catholic pressure was directly responsible for the withdrawal of teaching materials on the high school level, making effective teaching of this subject a test of ingenuity or courage on the part of the individual teacher.

More recently, drives against comic books and paperbacks sold by retail stores have received renewed impetus. Pressures have been notably successful in suburban areas with the initiative usually taken by Protestant ministers, often acting officially through ministerial alliances and enlisting P.T.A. and other communal groups in virtual ultimata aimed at the retail merchant.

Historically, Roman Catholics have relied on their clerical leaders to indicate the improper books, films, or other media programs which they might not read or view. Thus, the National Legion of Decency, the National Organization for Decent Literature, etc., have been official or semi-official arms of the Catholic Church. As against this approach by Catholic clerical authorities, Protestants have eschewed banning of books or films, relying instead on working positively for higher standards through the Protestant Film Commission and other church agencies. Freedom to read, to be exposed to controversial issues, and to make up one's own mind as a matter of individual conscience are deeply imbedded in Protestant tradition. But recent events have seen shifts in this pattern, with Protestant ministers officially leading the crusade against "smutty" paperbacks and magazines in several Los Angeles suburban communities. Significantly, the Broadcasting and Film Commission of the National Council of Churches has spoken out with increasing severity against violence and sex in motion pictures. Jewish groups in Los Angeles, while officially disdaining censorship or boycott, have worked closely with motion picture producers toward the avoidance of anti-Jewish stereotypes. There has been some Protestant and Catholic resentment at the reluctance of Jews to join in campaigns against "indecent" literature.

No public battle has taken place in Los Angeles over birth control, as it has in New York. On the other hand, Planned Parenthood is not a member of the Welfare Planning Council, which includes all social, philanthropic, and welfare agencies in its program. Nor are divorce laws or procedures a cause of interreligious friction. California legal procedures take a year, but are relatively liberal regarding grounds for divorce. For those who are impatient, Nevada divorce mills grind them out in six weeks, with little protest by California religious or legal bodies.

Interreligious marriage is a more serious problem. As a top Protestant cleric put it, liberal Protestant ministers try not to condemn such marriages, while counseling prospective couples of different faiths regarding the need to examine both faiths and perhaps to be united in either one. To such advice, Roman Catholic clerical leaders are opposed, refusing to sanction marriages unless both parties accept the Catholic faith or, at least, are married by a priest. Not all Protestant ministers will conduct an interfaith marriage ceremony. With one or two exceptions, none of the rabbis will conduct such a marriage unless the non-Jew has accepted Judaism beforehand. Sammy Davis, Jr. and Elizabeth Taylor have been perhaps the most spectacular converts to Judaism in Hollywood. Since adamant stands occur most often in Catholic-Protestant marriages, some resentment exists against the Roman Catholic position in liberal Protestant circles.

No state laws compel business establishments to remain closed on the Sabbath. The only existing "Blue Law" restrains boxing on Sundays, but does not restrict any other sport, including legalized gambling at race tracks. Efforts have been made to establish voluntary business codes calling for closing on Sunday but few of these have gained the fervor of a crusade. So long as no legislation exists, the decision to open or close on Sunday has been largely an internal problem of individual business groups, such as auto dealers, retail stores (largely food markets), service establishments, and amusement centers. Some groups of retail merchants have decided to close on Sundays, but in many cases major proprietors continue to remain open, and such practices, therefore, are not uniform. On the other hand, many business establishments thrive on week-ends, including resorts, amusement centers, food markets, realtor and housing tracts, and restaurants. In California's dynamic economy, it is doubtful if the profit motive will long be curbed by moral scruples about the Sabbath unless businessmen come to the conclusion that remaining closed one day a week can best be done on Sunday without competitive disadvantage.

Religious issues played a role in the cliff-hanging election contest waged in California in 1960. In contrast to the public charges and counter-charges which enlivened the 1958 campaign, the religious issue in 1960 was mostly underground and carried on through hate pamphlets, whispering campaigns, and parlor conversations. While a segment of the Protestant community worried about the spectre of a Roman Catholic in the White House, there was little jubilation at the chancery about such a prospect. "I don't like it," a high-ranking prelate confessed to a non-Catholic friend after the nomination of Senator John Kennedy. One Catholic clergyman, troubled by Kennedy's statements on religious liberty in *Look* magazine, expressed the fear that such views will "loosen" Roman Catholics from the teachings of the Church. Yet, in the election, a substantial majority of the state's Catholic voters obviously plumped for Kennedy, while a crucial segment of the Protestant community expressed anti-Catholic fears in the polling booth.

Jewish voters maintained their strong, traditional Democratic loyalty, even though many of them nursed their disappointment about Adlai Stevenson. Indeed, because of a widely-felt antipathy to Nixon, among other reasons, the Jewish vote in California was overwhelmingly pro-Kennedy, reaching 90 per cent in some heavily Jewish neighborhoods of Los Angeles.

Southern California has always been a happy hunting ground for crackpots, political extremists, and zealots of the left and right. Los Angeles has become one of the unofficial centers for "radical right" forces, marching under the twin banners of anti-Communism and super-patriotism. The *New York Times,* on October 29, 1961, reported evidence that "some Protestant and Roman Catholic organizations and churches and segments of business are behind the proliferation of these right-wing clusters" in Los Angeles. The so-called Christian Anti-Communist Crusade, which had eclipsed the John Birch Society in popularity in Los Angeles, drew 12,000 persons to the Hollywood Bowl for a mammoth "anti-Communist rally." Many of the brightest lights of the Hollywood galaxy participated in the three-hour extravaganza, which was carried by 33 television stations in six states to some 4,000,000 viewers.

The *New York Times* also reported "a strong indication that the anti-Communist forces are linking forces appeared in the October 6 issue of *The Tidings,* official weekly publication of the Los Angeles Archdiocese of the Roman Catholic Church." Three pages of a four-page supplement in *The Tidings* were devoted to an article by Father Cletus Healy of Marquette University, on "Our Moral Obligation to Oppose Communism." The remaining page of *The Tidings* listed some twenty-seven recommended anti-Communist books and thirteen bookstores where the books could be secured. It appealed to its readers to join Christian Resistance, an ultra-conservative local group, and urged subscriptions to such publications as Robert Welch's *American Opinion,* the *Dan Smoot Report,* and the *Network of Patriotic Letter Writers,* an organization with headquarters in Pasadena. The supplement also urged support of several "patriotic business firms," including one that "sponsored" *The Tidings* supplement; and appealed for wide distribution of the controversial film, "Operation Abolition." In addition to the 112,000 subscribers to *The Tidings,* some 200,000 reprints of the supplement were distributed upon request and through "pro-American" bookstores.

By 1962, the "radical right" had become a potent and unpredictable force in Southern California social and political life. While Democrats were under harassment from the ultras, the venomous civil war for control of the Republican Party of California threatened the very future of the party as a responsible political agent. The raw thrust of the extremists also had its not inconsiderable impact upon Los Angeles religious life. The vast majority of the Los Angeles clergy have spoken out against the new wave of witch-hunting which has swept the community. In more placid communities, to preach against the Birch Society and other extremists was to be "on the side of the angels" and was akin to hailing motherhood or brotherhood. In the supercharged atmosphere of Los Angeles, attacking the Birchites evoked some of the same swift reprisals which ministers in the South must expect when they touch the tender nerve of white supremacists on the racial issue.

Methodist Bishop Gerald B. Kennedy is a good example. Bishop Kennedy had been outspoken in his condemnation of right-wing extremists. He was promptly smeared as a "Communist" or "Communist sympathizer."

At a five-day anti-Communist rally—held in April, 1961, at the Shrine Auditorium under the sponsorship of "Project Alert" (a highlight of this parley was a proposal by a Marine colonel that Earl Warren should be hanged)—a pamphlet was distributed entitled "Bishop Gerald Kennedy's Public Record—How the Bishop Fights Communism." The pamphlet opened with the statement: "Bishop Kennedy has long been a member of the Methodist Federation for Social Action. . . . It is not known of his ever denouncing its program of social action and study, which is a perfect blueprint for the destruction of America." The pamphlet then proceeded to "prove" the Bishop's "Communism" by citing his opposition to the House Un-American Activities Committee, his participation in the Los Angeles school board contest, his activities against the McCarran-Walter Immigration Act, his criticism of Senator McCarthy, and a review he once wrote about an anti-Franco novel.

Los Angeles right-wingers find their primary clerical support in James Francis Cardinal McIntyre and Dr. James W. Fifield, Jr., minister of the First Congregational Church. Fifield's large church was a temple of arch-conservatism long before the most recent upsurge of Birchism in Southern California. Fifield is the guiding spirit behind the so-called Freedom Club which on January 11, 1962, rented the Sports Arena to present General Edwin A. Walker to a breathless public. The minister is a formidable ecclesiastical warrior against such "menaces" as UNESCO, and shares the Cardinal's view that UNESCO "would commit the United States to socialize its education."

It was possible in 1962 to discern the mounting signs

of community recoil in Los Angeles. Most people were shaken by the bombings of the homes of two Christian ministers in February, 1962, while they were addressing an anti-Birch rally in a local synagogue. Thoughtful Californians were disturbed and embarrassed that the distinguished educator, Dr. Buell Gallagher, was so viciously hounded by the vigilantes of the right that he had thrown up his job as chancellor of the State College System in California, after only a half year, to return to the relative sanity of his former post as president of City College in New York City. These and other dark incidents lent fresh urgency to the words of warning which President Kennedy had chosen to utter in Los Angeles: "There have always been those on the fringes of our society who have sought to escape their own responsibility by finding a simple solution, an appealing slogan, or a convenient scapegoat. . . . They find treason in our finest churches, in our highest courts. . . . Let us not heed these counsels of fear and suspicion. . . . Let our patriotism be reflected in the creation of confidence, rather than in crusades of suspicion."

The balmy climate of Los Angeles is in sharp contrast to the gray climate of interfaith relations. The ugliness which attended the campaign against Pat Brown, the excesses of the tax exemption fight, the inscrutable behavior of thousands of Californians in the Kennedy election, the deep religious rifts over public education and on church-state questions, the dangers posed by extremists and super-patriots—all these should jar Los Angeles religious leaders into more forceful action in building freeways of cooperation.

MUNCIE
Middletown in Slow Motion

"MIDDLETOWN, U.S.A." IS MUNCIE, INDIANA, AN INDUS-
trial city of 70,000 people, located about fifty miles
northeast of Indianapolis. Surrounded by rich farming
land, it is an important shopping center for many farmers
and other small towns in eastern Indiana. Muncie gained
the title *Middletown* as a result of the study made by
Professor Robert Lynd and his wife, Helen Merrill Lynd,
in 1926, and the follow-up of *Middletown in Transition*
in 1934. The Lynds specifically denied that Muncie was
a "typical" American community. Yet their studies held
up a perceptive mirror to an important aspect of American life. Typical or not, what is true of Muncie is true, in
different measure, of many communities in the Midwest
and the South. Thus, a glimpse at the character of interreligious relationships in Muncie, Indiana, may be both
interesting and revealing.

Muncie has many large industrial enterprises, including two General Motors plants, a Borg-Warner Corporation gear plant, a glass factory, a packing plant. West-
inghouse has built a new transformer plant in Muncie
which may well become the most important industrial
unit in Delaware County. Early in 1962, the city was
rocked by an unexpected announcement that Ball Brothers Company was discontinuing its glass-manufacturing
operations in Muncie. Although Ball will maintain its

zinc rolling mill, machine repair work, and other operations, the elimination of glass-manufacturing threw some 600 persons out of work—a major dislocation in a town like Muncie. Ball State Teachers College, with a total enrollment of over 8,000 students, is one of the important cultural and economic institutions in the city.

The population is native American, with very few foreign-born beyond an occasional war bride or refugee who has come to Muncie. The statistics tell the story: native white, 91.6 per cent; foreign-born white, .79 per cent; Negro, 7.53 per cent; other, .08 per cent. A large segment of the laboring force has migrated to Muncie from Tennessee and Kentucky.

There are about 5,000 Negroes in the community who are concentrated in two rather distinct residential areas. Questions of recreation and economic opportunities for Negroes have created the most severe tensions in Muncie. This was particularly evident when the city government opened the municipal swimming pools to all people regardless of race, color, or creed. As Negroes began to use the pools, there were several incidents which could easily have developed into riots. Tempers and emotions ran so high that it was difficult for the police to prevent mob violence.

The city is predominantly Protestant, with a sprinkling of Catholics and Jews. There are about 61,000 Protestants, 5,500 Catholics, and 175 Jews. Muncie has 87 places of worship, of which 67 are Protestant, 2 are Catholic, 1 is Jewish, and 17 are of miscellaneous denominations.

Rated as Indiana's eighth largest city, Muncie's population has been increasing at a rate of about 1,500 people per year. In recent years the city's growth has been slightly below the national rate of increase. The Negro population has been growing somewhat more rapidly than the total population. This has been due in part to migration from the South. In the past thirty years the Catholic population has been increasing at a more rapid rate than the Protestant. It was estimated in 1929 that there were roughly 15 Protestants to 1 Catholic. Today the ratio is closer to 11 to 1. The Jewish community is tiny, declining in relation to the total community, and almost completely middle class.

There is a compulsive urge not to be religiously offensive in Middletown. People want respectability, and it is not respectable to be publicly intolerant toward Jews, Catholics, or Protestants. As a result, there are few openly expressed tensions among religious groups. Muncie is rather proud of its breadth of toleration toward religious groups. However, tolerance, like a river, can be a mile wide and an inch deep. For example, an atheist seems to be outside the pale, and may be made uncomfortable indeed if he is outspoken and is at all sensitive to public pressures. Religious tensions do exist in Muncie, and they are real. Undoubtedly, the most serious tensions are in Christian-Jewish relationships. Tensions crop up in housing, social and service clubs, and in church-state relations.

HOUSING RESTRICTIONS

One of the most sensitive problems in interreligious relationships involving the Jewish population is the restriction of certain residential areas to people of "Caucasian descent" or the "pure white race." The restrictions have been generally interpreted to mean only white Christians. Neither restriction would technically prevent Jews from residing in these areas and the courts will not enforce these restrictive covenants. Nevertheless, these limitations have been effective in making many areas white Christian preserves.

At least eight residential developments on the "West Side" have restrictive clauses that either directly or indirectly exclude Jews. But only four have made any real attempts to keep them "racially pure." They are the rather wealthy districts of Westwood,* Westwood Park, Kenmore, and Westwood Heights. A new prestige residential development, Gatewood, does not have anti-Semitic restrictions.

Undoubtedly, the most exclusive residential developments in Muncie are Westwood and a recent extension, Westwood Park.The people who have lived there have "arrived." This area is bounded on two sides by Ball State Teachers College, but the other two sides of this wealthy area are faced by more modest upper-middle-class developments. Several Jews who have been successful in the business and professional world have built or bought homes just across the street from these exclusive areas. Apparently, if Jewish families cannot live in "paradise," they can, like Moses of old, look at the Promised Land from afar.

---

* Westwood—"The ownership and occupancy of lots and buildings in this addition are forever restricted to members of the pure white race. No Negro, mulatto, Chinese, Japanese, or person of any race, or mixture of races, other than a person of the pure white race, shall acquire title to any lot or building or part of lot or building in this addition. . . ."

Recently, a Jewish family bought a house in Kenmore, another silk-stocking district with "Caucasian race" restrictions. The lot was bought from the developer by a Christian contractor and then sold to the Jewish family. The realtor indicated that he had had some protests from the neighborhood.

Gatewood, which joins Kenmore on the west, has no anti-Semitic restrictions. The developer sold a lot to a prominent Jewish family, and apparently there have been few complaints from the neighbors. These are among the rare breaks in the "white Christian barrier" in the exclusive residential developments on Muncie's West Side.

Several methods have been used to enforce the "unwritten law" which excludes Jews from these residential sections. First, the real estate developers have refused to sell directly to Jewish families. At times there have been blunt refusals, and at other times somewhat more subtle means have been used. But in either case, the results have been decidedly effective. One influential Jewish businessman found a lot in one of the restricted developments for sale. He contacted the legal representative of the developer, and they agreed upon the price. The prospective buyer agreed to have the cash the next day when the sale would be completed. Later in the day the prospective buyer received a call, informing him that the seller was sorry but the lot had already been sold. Ten years later the lot was still for sale—to persons of "Caucasian descent."

Direct pressure and coercion are used upon Jews who have bought a lot or have an option to buy a lot in these areas from a second party who was not the developer.

Threats of legal suits or of anti-Semitic repercussions in the neighborhood have convinced the Jewish families that it would be better to look elsewhere for homes in which to rear their children.

Real estate agents have refused to show houses for sale in these areas to Jewish families who are looking for homes. One prominent realtor said that at times he had calls from Jewish families asking about homes for sale in the restricted developments. His first step was to tell them that there was an "unwritten law" that this area was not open to Jewish families and that "you wouldn't want to live where they don't want you, would you?" If the Jewish family persisted, he would tell them that they could contact the seller directly, that he would withdraw from the transaction, and that he would not accept a commission because he wanted no part in the sale. He said, "I will not be a party to violate the conditions under which the other home owners bought their homes (i.e., no Jews permitted). This is purely business. I have no dislike of the Jews and would not object to having one as a neighbor. I do not restrict them from buying in my new developments. But this is a purely business matter. If I played a part in selling a house to a Jew in one of these areas, the people would be mad as hell at me, and I would not have a chance to get clients in these areas again.

"It is just like selling a lot to a man that I knew was going to build a pre-fabricated house. Many people would be mad at me for doing this. There are also some Christians that I wouldn't sell houses to in this area because the neighbors would not like them and that would not be good business. I am not anti-Semitic, but if there were several Jewish real estate businesses in Muncie and they were giving me a tough time in my business, I might be anti-Semitic."

The Jews have not seen fit to test these restrictions in court. Many of the Jews in Muncie are engaged in retail business. There is a feeling that if the issue were taken to court, it might have an adverse effect not only upon their own businesses but also upon those of their Jewish friends. Coercion and threats of legal action were used to prevent one Jewish family from building in a restricted area. The head of the family said, "I could have won my case and lost my customers." Talking with Jewish families in Muncie indicates that psychological insecurity, a fear of the kind of social abuse they and their children might have to face, is also a potent factor in the reluctance of Jews to press their right to live in previously restricted neighborhoods.

What is the background of this anti-Semitism in housing? In 1923, when Westwood was platted, Muncie was a center of Ku Klux Klan power, with its strong streak of anti-Catholicism and anti-Semitism. Because of the enthusiastic reception of the Klan in eastern Indiana, Muncie has been called the "Atlanta of the North." A realtor was trying to raise money to develop the sixty-acre tract in this age of militant Protestantism. An outstanding Jewish leader in Middletown, a good friend of the realtor, told him that, if he wanted to avoid failure, he must not sell to Jewish people. This incident, which is alleged to have taken place some thirty years ago, is still a source of occasional dispute, particularly among Jews. Some insist the "friend" spoke in jest. Others say the friend was a self-hating Jew. Others insist the entire incident is apocryphal. Most agree, however, that the hoary incident still serves as a handy rationalization for anti-Semitic realtors to justify continued anti-Jewish discrimination.

Exclusiveness is not limited to Christians. One incident was reported in which a Jew objected to a Negro's purchasing a home in an all-white residential area. The details were reported by the seller of the property:

"Appearing one afternoon at our door, he introduced himself, mentioned where he lived (several blocks away), then proceeded to launch his appeal in approximately these words, 'I'm the last person in the world who should be coming to you with objections to the sale of your house to a minority-group family, for as a Jew and thus a minority-group member myself, I have personally experienced similar restrictions in this very city. Thus, I realize only too well that I can offer no ethical basis for coming to you with this request, but can only ask you to consider the economic self-interest of the other property owners in this area and, therefore, to refuse to sell to the Negro family.' We expressed our agreement regarding the lack of ethical grounds for his request, then indicated our doubts that even the economic objections could be validated by research findings but pointed out that even if they could, this would support his request *only* if one were willing to place property rights above what we considered basic human rights. The ensuing discussion explored in more detail the exclusions he had experienced in the course of seeking a home in various parts of northwest Muncie, and the decision finally to settle in the area from which he was now seeking to have another kind of minority-group member excluded. As you can see, the interview ended with full accord on virtually everything but the issue which had occasioned it! On that, we were as far apart as ever; the logic of extending to racial minorities the ethic our visitor had long sought to have applied to himself as a member of a religious minority was now, for him, superseded by the logic of 'protecting' property values!"

Social and Service Clubs and Charitable Organizations

Exclusive memberships in the Delaware Country Club and in the Muncie Club pose sticky problems of inter-group relations. Annual dues and membership fees are expensive enough to eliminate all but the more prosperous business and professional men, or those who find it necessary to belong for business and professional reasons. Jews are excluded from these clubs. Exclusion applies only to membership, since members may take Jewish friends to either of the clubs.

An industrialist in town, a member of the country club for several years, attempted in vain to get his Jewish son-in-law into the Delaware Country Club. He had aided several of his executive staff to become members. Although his son-in-law held an executive position in the organization, he was refused membership. He resigned from the country club along with his executive staff, but even this drastic action was not sufficient to gain membership in the club for a Jew.

This exclusiveness, too, seems to go back to the militant Protestantism of K.K.K. days. A board member of the Delaware Country Club rationalized the discrimination. He recounted an incident in which two Jewish members of the club invited about 100 Jewish friends from "all over the state" to a day of golfing and a picnic in the evening. "They didn't replace divots or let others through; were noisy; scattered refuse from their picnic; and did several hundreds of dollars in damage to the golf course." At a board meeting of the Delaware Country Club, all Jews were excluded except one. Since the death of this Jewish man several years ago, no Jews have been members of the club. The newer Muncie Club, a stag social group, has followed the earlier country club pattern of discrimination.

About a decade ago several Jewish leaders and others in the community decided to organize a second country club. It was the dream of some of the leaders to provide social and recreational opportunities to those who were excluded from the Delaware Country Club for financial and ethnic reasons. It was also recognized that Muncie was large enough to support another club. Green Hills Country Club was organized and financed almost exclusively by Jewish families. Today, its members include most of the Jewish families in Muncie, along with teachers, college professors, and a liberal sprinkling of factory workers and labor leaders. To many, it is affectionately known as the "poor man's country club." Yet, the double-edged character of discrimination shadows even this "liberal" club, which was obviously organized as a counter to discrimination against Jews. The club bars Negro memberships. This has embarrassed a number of the club's Jewish members who recognize the duplicity of their position but use "economic necessity" as a defense against their own personal and ethical sensitivities.

For some years the president of the club was Jewish,

but more recently a Roman Catholic lawyer has held that position. Free golfing memberships are given to all the ministers in the county. At present, the vast majority of the members are Christian.

Another spawning ground for religious conflict has been the Muncie men's service clubs, or "knife and fork" organizations. While all club charters avow their allegiance to "the American way," religious freedom, and the Constitution, few in Muncie have seen fit to include Jews in their membership and none admits Negroes. Apparently there has been some retrogression since the Lynds wrote in *Middletown* that "Jewish merchants mingle freely with the businessmen in smaller business clubs, but there are no Jews in Rotary."

There are still no Jews in Rotary. There are now two "synagogue attending Jews" in Kiwanis, none in the Exchange Club. The Lions Club has four Jewish members. Some years ago, a personable and capable young rabbi challenged the "exclusiveness" of the clubs. He applied for membership in the newer of the two Kiwanis clubs. He stated that the only way to find out if there is exclusion of Jews is to give the clubs a chance to indicate their true feelings. His application was delayed for many weeks because it was not "properly filled out," but ultimately he was admitted. Three other Jews were later admitted to the Kiwanis. In many middle-sized and smaller American communities rabbis are admitted to otherwise-restricted groups, if they are willing to join. The rabbis are then used as "Exhibit A."

According to leaders of the United Fund, by 1961 there had been no Jewish member on their Board of Directors. Neither were there any Jewish members on the preceding Community Fund Board of Directors, and only in the first year of its existence (1925) did the earlier Community Chest have a Jewish board member.

For many years, the treasurer of the National Foundation for Infantile Paralysis of Delaware County was a Jew. The Delaware County chapter of the Red Cross has had a Jewish president for the past year. The fact that these items are so often mentioned is significant.

Until recently, no Jew had ever served on the Board of Directors of the Muncie Chamber of Commerce, although the membership includes some Jews who have received state and national recognition for their contributions to business and the American way of life. In 1960, a prominent Jewish businessman was appointed to fill the unexpired term of a member who resigned. When his term expired, he was asked to allow his name to appear on the slate for election to the new board. The election is conducted by secret ballot from the membership. He was not elected. Some member agencies of the United Fund have Jewish members on their boards. The anti-Jewish situation is severe in the men's fraternal and service organizations. The local Elks Club, which has excluded Jews for decades, made an advance in 1961 which, for Muncie, was almost revolutionary. Some of the younger members of the club made an issue of anti-Semitism and launched a campaign, against bitter opposition, to admit a popular and civic-minded Jewish businessman. They succeeded.* This action is cited as a liberal "victory" in some Muncie quarters, as is the initiation of several Jews in the Masonic Lodge. By contrast with many other American communities, however, it seems doubtful that

---

* Other Jewish members have since been admitted.

Muncie has made any substantial progress in these regards in the last thirty years.

The women of Muncie appear to be more tolerant of minority groups than their spouses. Recently, the Ladies Auxiliary of Ball Memorial Hospital elected a capable Jewish woman to their Board of Directors. The membership list of the Hospital Auxiliary Board reads like the Blue Book of Muncie. One Jewish mother said membership on the Ladies Auxiliary Board for a member of their group "could not have happened ten years ago." Recently, the Auxiliary Board was planning a tea. When they discovered that the chosen date conflicted with a Jewish High Holy Day, they changed the date so that their Jewish board member might attend and participate in the social function. This reflects an attitude not widely prevalent among the men's organizations in Muncie.

One of the leading women's service organizations, the Business and Professional Women, has had several Jewish women in the club, and the American Association of University Women has Jewish members on its roster. Red Cross has had Jewish women on its Home Service Committee, and about five years ago a Jewish lady from this committee became a member of the Red Cross Board of Directors. She became a member, it was pointed out, "not because she was a Jew but because of the fine contribution she had made to Red Cross."

SCHOOLS

In Muncie the most inflammable problems in the area of church-state relations seem to center around sectarian teachings and the observance of traditional Christian holidays in the public school classrooms. The most serious religious tensions are likely to arise at the Christmas season. The administrators of the Muncie public schools have wisely chosen the Easter vacation as the week before that Christian holiday, thus avoiding Easter celebrations in the schools. It was explained by a top administrator in the Muncie public schools that this was done deliberately to avoid conflicts between Roman Catholics and Protestants and between Christians and Jews during this important Christian holiday, as well as to avoid embarrassment to any youngster in the public schools, whether Christian or not.

However, the Christmas season still plagues Jewish families with children in public schools. Songs about the baby Jesus, Christmas window decorations, the Nativity scene, and Christmas presents help to create confusion in the minds of Jewish students and parents alike. Jews resent Christian prayers and hymns, like "Jesus Loves Me," in public school classrooms.

At Christmas a thorny problem has developed in some Jewish homes about the giving of Christmas presents. Undoubtedly, the Christmas spirit with all of its glamour has influenced many devout Jewish parents to make Chanuko a time of giving gifts to their children that are equal to those that their Christian friends receive. One Jewish father protested that his interpretation was that only *small* gifts should be given. His wife strongly disagreed. Since Chanuko occurs during the time when Christian neighbors are celebrating their Christmas holidays, she felt that Jewish parents should try to make their observances more impressive and appealing. They should seek to satisfy the yearning of their young for gifts, cheerful lights, and pageantry.

Questions were also raised about the teaching of moral and spiritual values in the public schools. One prominent Jewish leader in "Middletown" said, "The teaching of moral and spiritual values in the public schools is good in principle, but the teacher is usually Protestant and the students get a distorted view. In principle, I approve, but most elementary and high school teachers do not have the broad training necessary to do an objective job. Therefore, I would raise some questions, not about the good intentions, but about the ability of the teacher to present a rounded, unbiased point of view."

Another active member of the temple said, "I am opposed to the teaching of the great religions, including Judaism, in the elementary school even on a comparative basis because the teachers are not well trained in this area."

One liberal and broad-minded school principal who has a large number of Jewish students in his school said, "The idea of being good because of being a Christian is wrong, but we should be good because that is good. Our major task is to teach Christians to be Christians. The Jewish parents and students have been very tolerant. The Jews have leaned over backward in being tolerant to the Christians."

In general, the Jewish community has refrained from bringing pressure to bear upon public school administrators. But all Jewish families do not have the same set of problems. From one Jewish mother came a statement about Muncie public schools: "School is a painful experience to many Orthodox Jewish youngsters." A Jewish father said, "The schools are Protestant-oriented and are really Protestant parochial schools." Yet, he continued, he himself had been educated in the local public schools and that he felt no ill effects from his experience. In fact, he felt there was real value in learning about other religions if the home and the temple provided a firm basis for the youngster to get his own spiritual bearings. But this would put a special responsibility on the Jewish families and their synagogue to begin preparation for public school before their youngsters are ready for kindergarten and to continue that training during their whole public school experience.

In order to relieve misunderstanding and to combat prejudice, the Sisterhood of Temple Beth-El has in past years invited public school teachers to a tea at the temple. There the Sisterhood attempts to explain the problem of the Jewish child in a public school and to give some explanation of Judaism and the principal Jewish holidays. These teas are well attended, and an excellent rapport has been established between the public school teachers and the mothers of the Jewish community.

For several years the Gideons International, a fundamentalist Protestant missionary society, has been attempting to give the King James version of the Bible to all fifth graders in the Muncie public schools. Their aim is "to win men and women for the Lord Jesus Christ," and there have been suggestions that this is an answer to the problem of juvenile delinquency. This has stirred questions about separation of church and state in the minds of many local school administrators. Rules for distribution laid down by the school officials stated that the Bible would be given only when the parents signed a slip granting permission for their child to receive a King James version of the Bible. The Gideons' representatives protested that these Bibles were being handed out as "literature," and there should be no restrictions. One principal reportedly said: "Then why not let us give them out for you as literature, because we do not believe that it is fair for you to distribute the Bibles and give a sales talk to a captive audience. If the objective is to give Bibles even as literature, all right, but let's not give a song and dance."

The Gideons refused to give Bibles under the conditions laid down by the public schools. Protests against distribution of the Gideon Bible came from both Jewish and Universalist parents. Apparently, the Roman Catholic clergy and laity have raised no protesting voice as have Roman Catholic representatives in other communities.

It seems to some that, in the eyes of pupils and their parents, the public schools have placed their stamp of approval upon this distribution and, in fact, upon the Gideons' King James version of the Bible itself. A state official of the Anti-Defamation League reported that the Gideons had stopped distributing Bibles because of an unofficial ruling of the Attorney General of the State of Indiana that such distribution was illegal. It was believed that the Attorney General's decision was based upon an important 1953 decision* of the Supreme Court of New

---

* *Bernard Tudor* vs. *Board of Education of Rutherford* states, "We are here concerned with a vital question involving the very foundation of our civilization. Centuries ago our forefathers fought and died for the principles now contained in the Bill of Rights of the Federal and New Jersey Constitutions. It is our solemn duty to preserve these rights and to prohibit any encroachment upon them. To permit the distribution of the King James version of the Bible in

Jersey which reversed a resolution of the Board of Education of the Borough of Rutherford permitting the Gideons to distribute their Bibles in the public schools. The court there held that such distribution was unconstitutional.

Four public elementary schools in Muncie have a "released time" program conducted in cooperation with the Delaware Council of Churches. Apparently, very little dissatisfaction has been expressed about this program. One Protestant minister is opposed to the idea because it puts pressures upon children who may have no desire to participate. He feels it may force them to do things they don't want to do because of a fear of being different from the other youngsters.

A high percentage of the students enrolled in these schools are participating in the released time program. The participating school patrons are almost "pure Protestant." A representative of the Ministerial Association said that to his knowledge there were only three Catholic children and no Jewish youngsters enrolled in their four public schools. At present, the program is maintaining a "holding operation" until the committee of teachers working with Protestant ministers and laymen can determine whether to expand the program or to "set up a curriculum which the school teachers can do themselves."

Most Jews are opposed to the teaching of religion and the use of religious symbolism and pageantry in the public

---

the public schools of this state would be to cast aside all the progress made in the United States and throughout New Jersey in the field of religious toleration and freedom. We would be renewing the ancient struggles among the various religious faiths to the detriment of all. This we must decline to do."

schools. As a minority group, they feel that at best their children will receive watered-down religious instruction based on the Judeo-Christian ethic, and at worst they will have a Protestant orientation toward moral and spiritual values. The Muncie Jewish Community Relations Committee opposes the observance of Chanuko as well as other religious festivals in the public schools.

Recently, five or six teen-agers from Muncie's West Side made a series of obscene telephone calls to several Jewish families. The contents of these telephone coversations were reminiscent of the virulent anti-Semitism of the Nazis. Ironically, one of the boys involved had been dating a daughter of one of the Jewish families receiving the calls, and another Jewish boy was looked upon as a regular member of this group of teen-agers. It was hoped that the offending boys could be put on a year's probation and that, as a condition of the probation, they should be required to cooperate in a study to be conducted by a professor of one of the state universities. Unfortunately, none of the Jewish families would press charges that might have made possible a searching socio-psychological study of the causes of their anti-Semitism.

In predominantly Protestant Muncie, neither Jews nor Roman Catholics play a significant role in the community. There have been few overt conflicts between these two minority groups. In fact, beyond a rare mixed marriage, members of the two groups have almost no contact, except for casual business relationships.

Jews in Muncie are rather well accepted in the business world, but they are not generally accepted after six P.M. Jews are not afraid of violence in this community. One Jewish leader said, "Thank God nothing has happened in

Muncie (i.e., bombings, violence, etc.). Our Jews are no longer afraid in Muncie. They are now secure in their faith, and they are not too worried about being excluded."

But they may be overly-sensitive to the opinions of the Christians. In general, Jews, comprising less than half of 1 per cent of the community, have been most careful not to ruffle the feathers of the majority groups in the community. There is a strong desire among the Jewish population to conform and to be good, if not the best, Munsonians. This drive to cooperate and to conform to the general cultural pattern of Muncie has led to charges of docility and submissiveness. A Jewish leader from outside the city said: "Muncie is the least integrated and the most segregated Jewish community in the state both before and after six P.M. Jews have accepted self-ghettoization. Muncie Jewry has removed itself from the mainstream of Jewish life in America. We cannot solve problems on a local community level. They (Muncie Jews) have no real backbone in matters of principle. For some time, they have had no full-time religious leader. We need someone to point out what is moral and what is ethical. Sometimes you must stake your profession, your career, and your hopes on a principle. If you do not, then you are much lower than the angels."

This is a harsh judgment—perhaps too harsh. Given the history of Muncie and its hate-ridden past, the fears of the minuscule Jewish community have been understandable. In 1946 a state-wide meeting of Jewish representatives was held in Muncie at the home of a distinguished Jewish leader. It was a torrid summer day; the temperature was in the 90's. As the meeting opened, several of the Muncie representatives bustled about the house, closing windows and nervously pulling down the shades. Then the meeting proceeded.

This climate of anxiety has undoubtedly lifted considerably in the intervening years. Muncie Jewry has provided valuable leadership to state and national Jewish and non-Jewish causes. In recent years, the Jewish community of Muncie has been increasingly willing to oppose religious intrusions in the schools. The smallness of the community, its lack of professional and spiritual leadership, the pervasive pressures of the general community—these factors are significant and must not be discounted.

CATHOLIC-PROTESTANT RELATIONS

One of the most surprising changes in Muncie during the last thirty-five years has been the advance from the bitter anti-Catholicism of K.K.K. days to the relative quiet of the present. One might think that the Klan would have left deep wounds which would continue to cause bitterness. The fuel which powered the Klan in Muncie was anti-Catholicism.

Since the Depression there has been a large migration of Roman Catholics to the more prosperous West Side, which had previously been a Protestant preserve. In the past two decades, the West Side Parish has increased from about 500 members to almost 2,800. This has been due to the emergence of the Roman Catholics from their immigrant status and the achievement of higher economic and educational status by many of their group. There are many Catholic lawyers, doctors, and public school teachers in Muncie, as well as several Catholics who hold elective offices in the city and county governments.

Some school administrators and teachers have complained that the Roman Catholic parochial schools send their "problem" children to the public schools. One principal charged that a Catholic sixth grade teacher put up religious posters in his room that were "based on the Catholic value system."

BINGO

"Police Chief James P. Carey has banned bingo games among churches and other groups. A bingo game has been held weekly at St. Mary's Catholic church during the past year, but when a crowd arrived for a bingo session Monday, the pastor, Father Edgar J. Cyr, announced that the games must be stopped. Carey later confirmed that a police order resulted in halting of bingo games sponsored by religious and social organizations."— *Muncie Evening Press,* September 18, 1958.

The facts behind this newspaper story caused a furor in staid Muncie. Protestants supported the Chief of Police —but continued to raffle off new cars, motor boats, golf clubs, and TV sets for their churches and for civic causes. Roman Catholics showed an unusual display of courage in attacking both the action of the police and the reaction of the Protestant community. The incident died quickly.

In local politics, many Roman Catholics have been elected to office. In 1951, a blind Catholic attorney, who had been a city judge, ran for mayor. A vicious whispering campaign broke out against him. During the campaign an active member of the Methodist Church was told by another member of his church that if he were going to support a *Catholic* and a *Democrat* for mayor,

132   *A TALE OF TEN CITIES*

he should resign from the Methodist Church. It was not certain which one of these "sins" was the more damnable and heretical to the Methodist Church member. One Catholic leader expressed the belief that the blind attorney was not beaten because of religious intolerance but because of his handicap. He said that he might have remained as city judge for years because the traditional symbol of justice is blind, but the mayor of a city is supposed to be able to see holes in the streets and to keep an eye peeled for open sewers.

There has been no apparent discrimination against Catholics in any social area, in the service clubs, or in any professional or business areas, and only relatively mild tensions have erupted in the political arenas in recent years. A student of Muncie, who has watched the community closely from the vantage point of the faculty of Ball State Teachers College, warns: "We should not be deceived by the decline of overt anti-Catholicism in the community. We are sadly mistaken if we underestimate the depth and extent of latent anti-Catholic feeling among the middle classes of Muncie, including Protestants located in pivotal positions within the school system, business enterprises, industry, and the Protestant churches. A few Jewish residents have also expressed obvious anti-Catholic prejudices."

There is little doubt that religious issues played an important role in the final results of the 1960 presidential election in Muncie. Two important Democratic officials estimated that up to 5 per cent of the voters switched to the Republican ticket for religious reasons. A more conservative estimate would be that the over-all impact of the religious issue would be between 1 and 2 per cent. This was important enough in Delaware County to give all but one local office and three state offices to the Republicans. A strong Democratic candidate for governor, Matthew Welsh, carried Delaware County by 1,619 votes, while Kennedy lost the county by 2,900 votes.

The impact was much more significant south of the tracks. This is the residential area of the majority of the laboring men of the city. To be successful in an election, it is necessary for the Democrats to win by a significant majority in this area. In the past few years there has been a heavy migration of laboring families into Muncie from Tennessee and Kentucky. Undoubtedly, their traditional fear of Catholicism had a significant effect upon their vote.

Some anti-Catholic literature circulated in Muncie. Apparently most of it came from sources outside of Muncie. Relatively little of the anti-Catholic campaign came out in the open. Most of it was subtle and never found its way into the mass communication media. Nevertheless, it was quite effective. Anti-Catholic jokes were popular during the campaign, and prejudices and fears were passed from person to person.

Some Catholics who normally vote Republican shifted to Kennedy. However, many Catholics in Muncie continued to vote the Republican ticket in 1960. Apparently, the Jewish group voted even more strongly Democratic than normally.

Anti-Catholic feeling is strongest among the people from Tennessee and Kentucky who have recently settled in Muncie. According to a priest, many of these ill-educated newcomers believe that the Catholics "worship idols, pay the priest to pray the dead out of hell; that the Catholics can commit any sin they want at will because the priest will forgive them at confession." Salacious stories about priests and nuns who break their vows of chastity are particularly popular among many of these people. As one priest put it: "Protestants are woefully ignorant about the Catholic Church. People from Tennessee and Kentucky have some of the wildest ideas about Catholics." Religious tensions are caused because "we don't understand each other, and we judge superficially. Intelligent people of good will can't be intolerant."

Why the decided reduction in anti-Catholic tensions in Muncie during the last three decades? One priest said he believed it was "better communication" between the Catholics and non-Catholics. He continued: "There are more social and business contacts between Catholics and others, and also the emergence of the Catholics from immigrant status has helped to reduce suspicions and fear about Catholics. The World Wars, where Catholics, Jews, and Protestants all contributed to the defense of their country, have helped. No group has a monopoly on patriotism.

"Many mixed marriages in my parish," he added, "act as a leaven in better relations between the various church groups. Anti-Catholic feeling is no serious problem in Muncie." One spiritual leader estimated that half of all Catholics in the St. Lawrence Parish have at least two Protestant grandparents. It might be added that Muncie Catholics have been exceptionally fortunate in having outstanding leadership from their clergy. Also, many Catholic laymen have taken an active interest in, and have given capable leadership to, many civic, charitable, governmental, and community projects.

However, Roman Catholic priests do not belong to the local Ministerial Association. In accordance with Catholic teaching, they believe they belong to the only "true faith" and they cannot compromise as they might be asked to do in a group with many different beliefs. In addition, as one priest said, "We are too busy with our own affairs."

AREAS OF COOPERATION

Perhaps one of the best examples of cooperation among religious groups has been the Muncie Youth Advisory Council which is appointed by the mayor on a non-partisan basis. Catholics, Jews, and Protestants have worked together to increase youth services and to combat juvenile delinquency. The group has made useful contributions to the community in helping to obtain a full-time professional recreation director for the city of Muncie. The city and the Muncie public schools have cooperated in paying the costs. The Youth Council has also helped initiate an in-service training program for the Muncie police force, particularly the Juvenile Aid Division. Several regular police officers have been sent to police training schools, and every member of the Juvenile Aid Division of the police force has attended at least one training school to sharpen his understanding of the problems of youth. The captain of the Division spent ten weeks at a school held at the University of Minnesota, and another member of the department attended a three-months' session at the University of

Southern California. The Council, under the leadership of a capable Protestant minister, has pleaded for a juvenile detention home so that boys and girls will not be placed in the county jail with hardened criminals.

Each year the Jewish congregation invites the Ministerial Association to an all-day session in their temple. An outstanding Jewish speaker is brought in to address the group. These fellowship seminars have been well attended, and both Protestants and Jews believe they have been helpful in the direction of creating an atmosphere of good will and understanding.

A few years ago a group of liberal religious leaders in Muncie organized a "Human Relations Association," and the Association has conducted a series of meetings and workshops on human rights for minority groups. Their major objective has been to establish equality of opportunity for the Negro and other minority groups. Most of these efforts have been devoted to finding additional job opportunities for the Negroes. Attempts are being made to substitute reason, education, and understanding for ignorance. The organization is composed primarily of Jews, Negroes, and some liberal white Protestants who believe in the "social gospel." Few, if any, Roman Catholics have attended meetings, and none has taken an active part in the Association.

The areas of cooperation among religious groups have not been numerous in Muncie. Organized religion has done little to solve the social problems of the community. Unfortunately, the pulpit in Muncie has given little real leadership in attempting to alleviate the problems of anti-Semitism, "Catholic-baiting," or anti-Protestantism. Nor, for that matter, has the community indicated that it would be ready to accept religious leadership in the civic area. At present, there seems to be a slightly enhanced sensitivity to some of these issues among the more liberal members of the clergy, and there is a possibility that some action may be taken by them in the not-too-far-distant future.

HOPES FOR THE FUTURE

For the past decade or two, there has been some progress in the removal of discriminatory practices against Jews. However, there is a much different story regarding the Roman Catholic community. There seems to be relatively little overt anti-Catholic behavior at the present time. However, if the Catholic population continues to increase at its present rate, there may be some fears raised about the growth of Catholic power in Muncie.

Muncie has come a long way since the dark and ugly period of Ku Klux Klan dominance. The rapid changes in the outside world have impinged in a measure upon Muncie as well, bringing some improvements in human relations. But Muncie is what it is—a quiet, prosaic town in the midwestern heartland of America. No great sense of urgency impels it. Dramatic and spectacular strides are not to be anticipated. Unfinished business waits in Muncie, as it waits in every American city, but it will not be completed soon. A few imaginative and sensitive men and women—Protestant, Catholic, and Jewish—will have to continue, patiently and with ever-increasing determination, to touch the slumbering conscience of this slow-moving American town.

NASHVILLE
Athens with an Achilles Heel

"THIS IS THE CONFEDERATE UNDERGROUND. WE HAVE just dynamited the Jewish Community Center. Next will be the temple, and then any other nigger-loving place and nigger-loving person in this community. We are going to shoot down Judge Miller in cold blood and then your husband. . . ."

Pearl Silverman rushed to tell her husband. Rabbi William Silverman called the Jewish Community Center; a police sergeant confirmed the fact that it had just been dynamited. Within minutes, F.B.I. agents were speeding to the home of Judge William E. Miller, the Federal jurist who had ruled that the local schools must desegregate.

The date: March 16, 1958. The time: 8:27 P.M. The city: Nashville, Tennessee, the "Athens of the South."

*　　*　　*

The grocer and his customer picked up copies of the leaflet just tossed through the open door of the small store. They saw a picture of Negro men kissing and fondling white women. Together they read the shrieking print:

LAST DAYS OF PEACE
BETWEEN
NIGRA AND WHITE RACES

RACE RIOTS FEARED!
WHITE CITIZENS SAID TO BE ARMING!
Enemies of the White Man in Nashville
. . . You Name 'Em:
1. Broad-bottomed, pot-bellied Politicians
2. Communists (NAACP and other Reds)
3. Most Preachers
4. Jewspapers, most Radio-Television
5. Vanderbilt-Fisk-Peabody-A&I Race Haters

LET'S GO, WHITE MAN. "Load your shotgun to defend your wife and home . . . be prepared for the worst race riots, hangings, anything. That's what Uncle Benny's School Board wants."

The grocer crumpled the paper into a ball, tossed it into his garbage box, wiped his hands on his apron. "Crap," he said.

"Sounds crazy," said the customer, "but where there's smoke there's fire. Never can trust a Jew."

Three weeks later, a professionally-prepared dynamite charge destroyed the Hattie Cotton School. It had a few Negro children in its first grade.

The date: September 11, 1957. The city, Nashville, Tennessee, the "Athens of the South."

* * *

A group of executives of the state gathered over coffee a week before the 1960 national election. Political excitement was alive in the discussion. Which candidate had drawn the largest crowd and what was the effect of the weather on those crowds? How were the newspapers reacting to Kennedy's speech on labor-management relations? What had the downstate press said about Nixon's forthright talk on integration? How did it all look anyhow?

"Let's quit the baloney, boys," said the deputy commissioner as he lit a formidable cigar. "There's only one issue in this town and in this state. Kennedy's religion, that's the question."

John F. Kennedy did not carry Tennessee. The year: 1960.

*   *   *

Nashville has been in world headlines since 1957. Many people wonder why this relatively moderate border community, not typical of the American South, has been catapulted into such prominence as a center of racial and religious tension. The 375,000 people of Nashville —183,000 Protestants, 14,000 Roman Catholics, and 3,000 Jews, (the balance unaffiliated)—wonder, too. Why Nashville?

More religious literature is printed in Nashville each year than anywhere else in America.

It is a center for popcorn processing and the manufacture of self-rising flour.

It is the home office of the General Shoe Corporation.

It is the Broadway of country music, the home of Grand Ole Opry, the site of a national country music festival each year.

Davidson County, most of which is Nashville, has more than 600 churches.

Nashville boasts many colleges and universities: Vanderbilt, Fisk, Peabody, Tennessee A&I, American Bap-

tist Theological Seminary, Belmont College, David Lips-
comb College, Free Will Baptist Bible College, Madison
College, Trevecca Nazarene College, Scaritt College for
Christian workers. Nashville is a center for both liberal
Protestantism and for Fundamentalism.

Baptists and Methodists have major national institutions in Nashville—the National Association of Free
Will Baptists, the National Baptist Convention of America, the National Baptist Convention, U.S.A., the Southern Baptist Convention, several divisions of the Methodist Church.

The Presbyterian Board of World Missions functions
from Nashville. The Southern Publishing Association of
the Seventh-Day Adventists publishes books and periodi-
cals here which are distributed throughout the world.
The Thomas W. Phillips Memorial Building of the Disciples of Christ has an archives collection which draws
scholars from far and wide.

The Roman Catholic bishop of the diocese of Nashville has his headquarters in the city; the diocese en-
compasses the entire state. In the chancery are the offices
of the diocesan newspaper, the *Tennessee Register,* the
Ladies of Charity, and the Catholic Youth Organization.

The Jewish community of Nashville is regarded as
one of the most active and affluent in the South. There
are three synagogues. The largest and most influential
is the Reform congregation, Ohabei Sholom, with a membership of about 700 families. The Conservative congregation, the West End Synagogue, has a membership of
about 500 families. Sherith Israel, the Orthodox synagogue, has about 125 membership families. There is
some overlapping of memberships.

In addition to its synagogues, the Jewish community of Nashville supports a Community Center and the Woodmont Country Club.

A host of organizations and activities compete for the time, interest, and money of Nashville Jewry. The city has given vigorous leadership to national Jewish organizations. Jews have been most diligent in meeting their obligations to the United Jewish Appeal, the Zionist movement, the B'nai B'rith, and other community relations agencies, to national religious bodies.

These activities and the program of the Jewish Community Center provide unifying processes for the three religious wings, despite the deep differences among them. The center is a typical one—community meetings and interest clubs for young and old meet there; it provides gymnasium and recreational facilities; it sponsors mass educational and cultural activities which, in recent years, the center has tried to make more Jewish and less secular. (There has been tension between the center and the congregations, chiefly in the areas of adult education and youth work. These are abating as synagogue and center leadership become increasingly identified, as rabbis meet regularly with center professionals for advisory and programmatic cooperation, as time and maturity work their magic in the community generally.)

About 300 of the more affluent Jewish families belong to the Woodmont Country Club. Once the almost-exclusive preserve of Reform Jewry, it now represents a fair cross-section of all three groups. There is no perceptible change in its functions, however. It is a Jewish institution only because all its members are Jews (except two Christians married to Jews). Its program is a characteristic country club program, including Christmas observances and evenings devoted to food and decorations of various countries. It exists and flourishes because the socially-elite Belle Meade and Richland Country Clubs exclude Jews altogether.

There is a Jewish Community Relations Council in Nashville, composed of representatives of all organizations in the city. It was not an effective agency until 1958. The Anti-Defamation League of B'nai B'rith traditionally controlled the community relations area, and the JCRC could not challenge its power. But when tension erupted in Nashville, the Jewish Community Relations Council sought to rise to the challenge.

In Nashville, Jews meet, work, and serve with their Christian associates until darkness draws its fine daily line of religious segregation. Only rarely are Jews invited to mingle socially with Christians—primarily in the areas of upper-bracket affluence plus professional social workers and such. A Jewish president of the Nashville Red Cross will be invited to a social gathering at a Christian home following a meeting. Community agency executives often become close friends, along with their wives and children. But such social contacts between Jews and Christians are rare.

Jewish children mix harmoniously with Christian children in school, in school athletics, in school activities. But it is assumed that Jewish children will not be invited to dancing clubs, fraternities, sororities, and "exclusive" social affairs.

The rabbis of the community, especially the Reform and Conservative rabbis, are invited to Protestant churches to address youth groups, ladies' circles, and brotherhoods. Seldom, if ever, is a rabbi invited to occupy the *pulpit* of a Christian church at a worship service. The Temple Brotherhood joins two Christian men's groups at an annual interfaith banquet meeting. The ministers of those churches have occupied the temple pulpit at Sabbath services. No rabbi has ever preached at the churches. This is not too surprising. Since 1950, the by-laws of the National Council of Churches require acceptance of the Trinity as a requirement for occupying a pulpit.

There is usually one Jew on the city school board and one on the county school board. Most civic clubs have a percentage quota on Jews, and one luncheon club excludes them altogether.

Nashville's Jews experience little employment discrimination (most are self-employed). But housing discrimination is still wide-spread even though many wealthy Jewish families have now penetrated into fashionable Belle Meade and other suburbs formerly closed to them. Occasionally, a wealthy Jewish family has moved into a previously-restricted area, accepting a "gentleman's agreement" that they will not encourage other Jews to seek the same "privilege."

As is true in most of the South, rabbis, Roman Catholic priests, and Unitarian ministers are not eligible to join the Ministers' Association, though they are invited from time to time to attend special meetings. The constitution of the Association requires a belief in the divinity of Jesus and adherence to the gospel of Christ. Many Protestant denominations do not participate in the Association, either, including the most populous—the Southern Baptists. There is not sufficient sentiment as yet that the community requires a broader clergy group on a more representative basis.

But the Ministers' Association is now interracial, and in 1959 it elected a Negro preacher as its president. This was not too hard, but as one Methodist minister put it, "All hell would break loose if we elected a rabbi or priest to membership."

It is fundamentally erroneous to speak of a Protestant community, though we shall be doing so. There are many Protestant communities in Nashville, divided not only denominationally and racially, but also, and perhaps most important, in terms of social and economic classes. The social elite of Nashville—the "cream of Belle Meade"—are Episcopalians, Congregationalists, with a very small sprinkling of Presbyterians. To belong to small but swanky St. John's Episcopal Chapel is to wear the badge of high society.

At the other end of the Protestant spectrum are the Negro gospel churches, numerous, noisy, and impecunious. Educated Negro clergymen fight hard against the tendency toward fragmentation of Negro churches.

In between these two polar groups which never meet, let alone speak, lies the broad range of American Protestantism, from Unitarian to Four Square Gospel, from intellectualized near-humanism to deeply-emotional fundamentalism.

In general, the Roman Catholic community is isolated in Nashville. Most forms of interreligious activity are discouraged by Bishop William L. Adrian, though he himself has participated in one of the two city-wide interfaith meetings organized in the community to plan for school desegregation. From time to time, a priest will agree to speak at a forum on church-state relations or in connection with interracial problems.

The local round table of the National Conference of Christians and Jews comes to life once a year during Brotherhood Week, when a perfunctory observance takes place. No one appears to care much; even the Jewish community, which was once enthusiastic in its support, is generally passive about this annual exercise. No attempt is made to organize any kind of interreligious youth activity, either under NCCJ auspices or by cooperative action on the part of synagogues and churches.

The mood of interfaith relationships in Nashville is polite, with occasional friendships and cordiality, but mostly it consists of surface graciousness in business relationships, in civic activity, in anything that happens before the 5:00 o'clock shadow sets in. Then Nashville's citizenry goes its four separate ways—Jews, Protestants, Roman Catholics, and Negroes.

NEGRO RIGHTS

The focus of attention currently, the area of swirling community movement, is and will continue to be Negro action and the community's response to it.

There are approximately 70,000 Negroes in Davidson County. The city and county are completely segregated in housing patterns except for a small area immediately around the campus of Fisk University, a distinguished Negro university. Employment discrimination against Negroes is almost universal. Though employment in manufacturing has increased 20 per cent since 1950, Negroes occupy only 5 per cent of those jobs. But 80 per cent of all unskilled labor in Nashville is performed by Negroes. Of 13,700 public utility employees in the city, less than 1 per cent are Negroes—all of them porters, janitors, maids. Some 2,724 persons were employed in telecommunications at the end of 1960; less than one-half of 1 per cent were Negroes—virtually all of them porters, janitors, maids, plus a few messengers.

In the religious publishing houses of which Nashville is so proud, the ratio of white to Negro workers is 35 to 1; all the colored workers are unskilled.

Negroes do not attend white theaters in Nashville, nor are they welcome in most restaurants or any downtown hotels. White liberals eat with Negroes at meetings of the Council of Community Agencies; Negroes are welcome to use the cafeteria of the Methodist Board of Education, and the (Baptist) Sunday School Board. Negroes attend dinner meetings at the Jewish Community Center, at churches and synagogues. But there are no Negro undergraduates at Vanderbilt University. And, as we shall see, the determination of the Negro community to eat at lunch counters in downtown stores brought on rioting and community tension in 1960 and 1961.

Rays of light appear from time to time. Since 1948, there have been Negro policemen on the force. One was promoted to the rank of detective in 1960. Of course, all Negro policemen work in all-Negro housing areas.

Two members of Nashville's City Council are Negroes, and others have been appointed to the Board of Education, the transit authority, and the hospital authority. There is a clear increase in the availability of Negro community leadership—and in the willingness of the white community to work with them. There has been a pronounced increase in the leadership role of Negro churches and their ministers, with enhancement of the status of the church in the community. This has been evidenced by increased church membership and more activity on the part of Negro intelligentsia—university professors and other professional people.

This, then, is Nashville, a southern community which is not typical of the Deep South at all. It doesn't sound like a keg of dynamite. But dynamite exploded in this, the Athens of the South. Why Nashville?

The extremist segregationists of Nashville, unlike those of the Deep South, are not community leaders, respectable politicians, the "cream of society." They are "poor whites," the occupational and educational failures, the loafers—that peripheral segment of society which could be influenced by John Kasper and his ilk. Kasper came to Nashville—on invitation—because segregationist leaders apparently believed that enough trouble could be fomented to prevent the integration of Nashville's schools. If this border city, cultural leader, progressive star of the South, could be terrorized into resisting the integration decisions of the U.S. Supreme Court, what southern city or state would dare to admit a Negro child to an integrated school?

But by dynamiting the Hattie Cotton School and the Jewish Community Center, the rabid segregationists miscalculated badly.

*   *   *

Less than a year after the 1954 integration decisions of the U.S. Supreme Court, the Nashville Community Relations Conference was formed (not to be confused with the Jewish Community Relations Council). Its founders were individual Protestants and Jews, though religious, civic, and other organizations have since joined, along with individuals of all faiths. (At the end of 1961, the president was a Roman Catholic layman.) Unfortunately, though many good people have been involved in the NCRC, the most powerful men of Nashville, especially those with financial power, have been conspicuously absent. Its first major action was to organize a two-day institute of several hundred persons, on an interracial basis, to discuss school desegregation. The institute was held at the Jewish Community Center. A year later, a second such two-day institute was held at a Methodist church.

These institutes aroused some tension in the community, and leaflets began to appear threatening violent response to any desegregation attempt. But no violence developed. Kasper was needed for this, and Kasper was sent for.

The Nashville Community Relations Conference did not stand alone. On November 26, 1956, the General Assembly of the Tennessee Council of Churches passed a strong resolution urging the governor, the state board of education, and local school boards to begin work immediately to desegregate the schools of Nashville. The State Council of Churches itself had been desegregated long before. In April, 1957, the same body sponsored a Conference on Christian Faith and Human Relations for white and Negro leaders from all over the South. Some 300 of them attended, views were exchanged in depth and in detail, and wide-spread publicity was given the sessions.

In September, 1957, the Nashville Board of Education

opened desegregated classes in the first grade. The immediate result: the bombing of the Hattie Cotton School. But the board persisted and, in March, 1958, announced grade-a-year desegregation plans. The superintendent of schools spoke to P.T.A.'s, to church and civic groups, urging compliance. The Community Relations Conference continued its work. Individual clergymen and community leaders worked and planned. The segregationists expressed themselves primarily through a Parents Preference Committee, which urged a plan giving parents the choice of desegregated or segregated schools for their children. Federal Judge Miller refused their petition. The JCC was dynamited on March 16. Desegregation continued.

During 1957's campaign to persuade the Board of Education to take a positive stand on desegregation, among the organizations which supported desegregation publicly before the board were: B'nai B'rith, Fellowship of Southern Churchmen, Nashville Association of Churches, Nashville Ministers' Association, United Church Women, and the YMCA. Two community organizations officially joined the segregationists: Kiwanis and the men's club of the Monroe Street Methodist church.

The Association of Churches urged ministers to appeal to their members to accept desegregation the Sunday before the opening of school in 1957. Some preached; most were silent.

During those tense weeks, the segregationist campaign took on an ever-more vicious anti-Semitic tone. Anti-Semitic literature poured into the community, ranging from *Common Sense* to copies of the *Protocols of the Elders of Zion,* that hoary and oft-disproved phony document. A group styling itself "Christ's Crusaders" "intercepted" a document allegedly distributed by the "Central Conference of Rabbis." The fraudulent notice began:

> We are about to reach our goal. World Wars I and II furthered our plans greatly. We succeeded in having many millions of Christians kill each other and returning other millions in such condition they can do us no harm. There remains little to be done to complete our control of the stupid Christians.

Missionary tracts addressed to Jews for conversion purposes took on a political emphasis and became virulent in approach. The Jew is the Antichrist, who seeks to destroy Christianity by mixing the races. Jews are susceptible to Communism and "nigger-loving" precisely because they refused to accept Jesus as Messiah!

This crude anti-Semitic literature may have influenced a few relatively uneducated individuals in Nashville. Christian-Jewish relations among most of the people remained virtually what they had been before the desegregation battle began: friendly and superficial to the extent that relationships existed at all. The Ministers' Association continued to be preoccupied with its campaign to close grocery stores on Sunday. Next on the agenda—drug stores.

* * *

How did Nashville react to the bombing of the Jewish Community Center? Was there any difference now in the feelings of Jews who had urged silence upon their leaders? In the feelings of Christian ministers and laymen?

The reactions of the Jewish community can be divided into three main conflicting points of view. One group, minuscule in number, insisted that the bombing was to be expected, that Nashville was rampant with anti-Semitism as was every city in America and Jews should plan immediately to leave for Israel. To the best of our knowledge no one left, but the viewpoint was heard in a few parlors.

A second group, and perhaps the largest, was annoyed and angered at the bombing, but continued to counsel silence. Some said the word "Jewish" never should have been on the building at all, that separate Jewish institutions, except synagogues, shouldn't exist on the American scene. They urged the rabbis and Jewish civic leaders to avoid the subject of desegregation at all times.

Finally, there was a group whose views were expressed by a resolution of the Board of Trustees of The Temple: "We will not be intimidated by fear. As Jews and as Americans we shall continue to speak and act for social justice for all men."

Within hours after the smoke and dust of the blast had cleared at the Jewish Community Center, the executive committee of the Jewish Community Council met. A six-point program of action was determined upon: immediate repair of the building; maintenance of program; continuation of the center's policy of permitting interracial meetings and meals; the sending of a letter to the entire Jewish community urging calm and confidence in the position of the Council; statements of position were

NASHVILLE 153

drafted for the newspaper, radio, and TV; a request was sent to local editors that all releases from national agencies be discussed with the CRC before publication, to avoid confusion.

Regardless of viewpoint, there was little panic in the Jewish community and the Community Council's desires were, for the most part, followed.

Protestant ministers denounced the criminals from their pulpits and demanded law and order. Many of those who had maintained silence on the problem of desegregation now excoriated the fanatics for their violence and wanton acts of hatred. The dynamiting of the Hattie Cotton School and the Jewish Community Center gave many clergymen the opportunity to decry violence without committing themselves irreparably to desegregation. Laymen expected their ministers to protest against violence, even though many would continue to denounce and to threaten to fire those ministers who took a bold stand in favor of racial equality and desegregation.

The Roman Catholic response was quieter. Catholic parochial schools were already integrated, and the segregationists, amazingly enough, did not pay any particular attention to that fact. A few Roman Catholics continued to work in the Community Relations Council; most Catholics continued to stay off by themselves and keep their own counsel.

* * *

At the end of 1961, five grades of Nashville's public schools were integrated. Cub Scouts and Brownie Girl Scouts were beginning to function in the schools on an integrated basis beginning with the third grade. Roman Catholic schools maintained full integration, including social activities. Not all citizens of Nashville were happy with the situation, but violence had ceased and tensions were almost non-existent. In reality, however, the war was not over. The battlefield had changed . . . from schools to lunch counters.

The decision to make downtown lunch counters the next order of business in the desegregation battle appears to have been taken by the Southern Christian Leadership Conference, headed by the Rev. Dr. Martin Luther King of Atlanta, formerly of Montgomery, Alabama. Nashville has a branch of this Conference, organized in 1957. Until that time, the Negro community's organization was fragmentary and weak. The churches and Negro professional leaders pooled their energies in the Nashville Christian Leadership Conference, and it has become their most important unifying group.

The decision to organize sit-ins in Nashville's downtown lunch counters was taken by this representative group, and the sit-ins began in the spring of 1960. The project chairman was the Rev. James M. Lawson, a graduate student at Vanderbilt Divinity School, a Negro. Enormous community tensions were generated by the sit-in movement; the religious leadership of Nashville could not sit idly by. Father Morgan of the diocesan Chancelry met periodically with Rabbi William Silverman and the Rev. William Campbell, local representative of the National Council of Churches. This pioneering venture was a useful one. Many clergymen in the community took a more responsible and constructive attitude toward the sit-ins as a result.

The sit-ins evolved into a boycott of those downtown businesses which refused to integrate their lunch counters. Business was deeply affected; estimates range from a 25 per cent to 35 per cent drop-off. The entire matter was carried on with the religious approach characteristic of Dr. King's movement. The Rev. Kelly M. Smith, chairman of the Nashville group, characterized it this way:

> If you are fighting for a moral issue, you have to stay on firm moral grounds. Our ground for the boycott was simply that it is morally indefensible for Negroes to cooperate with a system we consider evil and which we are trying to change.

A group of Jewish merchants, apparently acting as individuals, sat at five and ten cent store counters next to Negroes during the sit-ins, trying to assure them of their friendship. The move boomeranged. This action was stereotyped by Negroes as an attempt to get business, not friendship at all. "There go the damned Jews, out to make a buck." Fortunately, however, the Negro leadership did not attempt to circulate this story widely, and it had no adverse ultimate effect on community relationships.

The organized Jewish community, like the organized Protestant community and the Roman Catholic diocese, did not respond formally to the sit-ins. It was discussed in the Jewish Community Relations Committee, but no consensus could be reached. Some individual whites were involved in the movement.

When the downtown boycott got serious, the Nashville

Community Relations Conference recommended that the mayor appoint a biracial committee to deal with the matter. The suggestion was accepted, and the committee performed useful service.

Negotiations to end the boycott and settle the problem of sit-ins were made almost impossible for a time by the bombing of the home of City Councilman Z. A. Looby, a Negro, on April 20, 1960. The Negro community march on City Hall gave new impetus and strength to the sit-in movement.

In general, the sit-ins were successful. A large number of lunch counters were integrated. In November, 1960, a group of students tried to extend the integrated area with a new series of sit-ins. The Christian Leadership Conference was not involved at first, and confusion attended the effort.

One nasty incident resulted from the 1960 sit-ins. The Rev. James Lawson, chairman of the committee, was expelled from Vanderbilt Divinity School by Chancelor Harvie Branscomb. Divinity School faculty members protested, then resigned when their protests were rejected. Dean Robert Nelson of the Divinity School resigned, too. After long and complicated negotiations, the faculty members agreed to return to their posts, and an invitation was issued to Mr. Lawson to return. He did not accept because, as was known to the chancelor, he had already matriculated in a northern university. Dean Nelson did not return, and the whole matter remained somewhat ambiguous morally. But for the academic year 1960-61, seven Negro students were accepted in the Vanderbilt Divinity School.

Nashville is gradually breaking down its remaining

racial barriers. In 1961, the Nashville Symphony Orchestra decided to desegregate its concert audiences. Similarly, a chain of movie houses accepted integration after helpful conferences with the Christian Leadership Conference to prepare the ground for change. Programs are now under way to strengthen equal employment opportunities for Negroes.

POLITICS

The national elections of 1960 brought new expressions of interreligious tension to the Athens of the South. The election was taken seriously in Nashville. Toward the end of the campaign, in fact, it was virtually impossible to hold general community meetings; everyone was too busy with politics! But, as has been indicated, the primary irritant in the campaign was not an issue of principle, not a question of domestic or foreign policy—it was religion. Even though local newspapers deliberately played down the question of John F. Kennedy's faith, it was the major topic of conversation, concern, and controversy.

There were perceptible manifestations of anti-Catholic feeling among Jews, including leaders of the community. But it was relatively quiet and appeared to taper off as November 8th approached. Reliable sources indicate that most Jews voted along traditional Democratic lines, although wealthier Jews tended to vote Republican.

As happened all over the United States, the Roman Catholic group was officially quiet. No official election statements emanated from diocesan headquarters or from individual parish priests. Even though Protestants and

Other Americans United for the Separation of Church and State had a Nashville chapter at work, and even though some of their statements were openly hostile to Mr. Kennedy's faith, the Roman Catholic community did not get embroiled in the controversy.

Led by some Southern Baptists, some Protestant groups began to go down the bigotry road, but few public steps were taken in Nashville. Several factors militated against wide-spread open bigotry: the presence of national religious boards was one. The Methodists, in fact, not only kept their community in equilibrium, they made it openly clear that some of their leaders were pro-Kennedy.

The fact that Nashville is the state capital was an even more important factor in minimizing public expressions of bigotry. Many leading Democratic politicians are Protestants and their interests were vitally at stake.

Kennedy's loss of Tennessee was attributable, in large part, to the heavy anti-Catholic vote in the Bible Belt. Shortly after the final tally was in—showing that Nixon carried the state by some 65,000 votes—Protestant and Jewish leaders acknowledged that the religious issue had been decisive there. "It is very obvious that the religious issue did influence the thinking of Tennessee voters and that it was the determining factor in Senator Kennedy's defeat," said Rev. C. Tom Baker, executive secretary of the Tennessee Council of Churches. Rabbi Randall M. Falk, spiritual leader of The Temple in Nashville, lamented the "breach" which had opened among the faiths during the campaign and he urged that it be repaired speedily. Davidson County (Nashville) itself went Democratic but only by 7,000 votes. Adlai Stevenson, in 1956, had carried the county with a plurality of almost 20,000. Senator Kefauver carried the county by more than 2 to 1 in 1960.

CHURCH-STATE RELATIONS

No discussion of interreligious relationships in any community could conceivably be complete without a look at that community's response to problems raised by the separation of religion and the state. Where does Nashville, the Athens of the South, stand with regard to this problem?

In preparation for the White House Conference on Children and Youth, held in 1959, the Tennessee State Committee prepared a preliminary report. Its statements on religion in education are a good place to begin:

> Many of the county reports indicate a strong conviction regarding moral and spiritual values, and their place in Tennessee life. Frequent expressions are found indicating concern by groups for advancing the general spirituality of the citizens of Tennessee. Illustrative of this approach is the report submitted by the Dyer County White House Planning Committee. This report emphasizes that the most valuable of all values are the spiritual ones—especially those associated with love. Love, in the words of the committee, encompasses the following: (1) love for country; (2) love for self; (3) love for home; and (4) love for God.
>
> Fostering moral and spiritual guides for conduct is best expressed in the deeply ingrained recognition of the family unit in Tennessee as

the institution for the nurture and upbringing of the youth—as the shelter for their protection as they grow into adult life. Strengthening family life is cited as a need in most of the county reports, and many cross-references indicate this concern.

A spokesman writing for the Catholic school system in Tennessee states:

> Since education (formal) consists essentially in preparing man for what he *must be* and for what he *must do* here below in order to attain the sublime end for which he was created, it is clear that there can be no true education which is not directed wholly to man's last end. From this fact flows the supreme importance of Christian education, not merely for each individual, but for families and for the whole of human society whose perfection comes from the perfection of its elements.

In addition, in its recommendations the State Committee recommended that parents should help set desirable standards of conduct for their children by: "Attending church regularly and showing toleration for differing religions and creeds while staunchly defending their own beliefs" (p. 52).

The practice of sectarian religious ceremonies and the teaching of sectarian religious ideas, the reading of the Bible, required prayer by students—all these violations of the separation of religion and the state are standard practices in the public schools of Nashville.

Pressure is mounting in Nashville for more sectarian

religion in the public schools. Christian athletes speak to high school students and exhort them to be saved through Christ. Ministers are frequent assembly speakers. In many schools, devotionals, mainly Christological, are conducted as the school day begins. A (county) high school principal stated, "Nashville is a Christian city and my school is a Christian school."

The Ministers' Association strongly affirms the principle of separation of church and state but it also insists upon bringing Protestant religion and Christ into public schools. The ministers apparently see no inconsistency in simultaneously supporting the principle of church-state separation and Bible readings, devotionals, Christmas and Easter celebrations in the public schools.

Religion is deeply implanted in Nashville public education. Some principals refer to their schools as "Christian," although as many as 100 Jewish students attend their schools. The Gideon Society used to distribute its Bibles and texts at assemblies and in classrooms. As a great "improvement" the schools now only announce the availability of the Bibles. The Bible is read at the beginning of each school day. State law requires that no more than ten and no fewer than two verses be recited daily, but no comment is to be made. The latter injunction is frequently ignored. Although the state law does not specify which Testament should be used, the New Testament is commonly utilized. A Jewish parent recently asked a teacher why she never read from the Old Testament, which is accepted by both Christians and Jews. "Too Jewish," she replied. "This is a Christian school and we read from the New Testament."

Each year, outstanding athletes are invited to the

schools to "speak for Christianity." One year, the athlete invited was Herbert Rich, a former Vanderbilt great who had just been released by the Los Angeles Rams. Rich was asked to speak for the "Christian way of life." "I will be glad to speak," said Rich, "but I will speak for the Jewish way of life. Didn't you know I was Jewish?" They didn't. Alas, poor Rich did not speak.

Evangelism is omnipresent in public education in Nashville and is seldom challenged. A Unitarian mother once asked one of the rabbis to protect her child's rights. She reported that her child's teacher had carried on an evangelistic session in class and had announced that anyone who did not accept Jesus was damned forever and would burn in hell. The child ran home, hysterical, shrieking, "I'm going to hell! I'm going to hell!" The rabbi spoke to the principal who elicited a promise from the teacher not to do it again.

In 1959 a rabbi addressed a seminar at Peabody College Graduate School on "Religion in the Public Schools." He urged the elimination of sectarian religion from public education. The principal of a fashionable high school rose and interjected: "The only religion that I will permit in my high school is my religion. I'm not a Jew or a Catholic so you know what religion that will be!"

RELIGION IN SCHOOLS

So heavy is the Protestant coloration of the community's education that Jewish parents and community groups shrink from opposition in any public way. The suggestion of legal action to challenge practices of almost certain illegality is anathema to the Jewish community and to other dissenting groups. "Why should we bloody our heads in a hopeless battle?" said one Jewish leader. "Let well enough alone." A Unitarian, Philip Carders, had brought suit with the help of the ACLU challenging Bible reading. The State Supreme Court ruled against him in 1956.

The subtle and sometimes blatant pressures on Jewish children express themselves in many ways. One result is that many Jewish children hesitate to ask permission to be excused for some Jewish holidays. While the Jewish Community Relations Council believes that no religious practices belong in the schools, many Jewish children and parents have indicated a wish that Chanuko and other Jewish holidays might be celebrated in public schools alongside of Christian celebrations. Increasingly, Nashville schools are including some expressions of Chanuko, particularly in schools with sizable numbers of Jewish youngsters. Said an eleven-year-old Jewish boy, "Before we had Chanuko in our school, I used to feel like an outsider at the Christmas season. Now I sing Christmas carols, because I know that my Jewish songs are being sung, too."

Christmas is observed in the public schools of Nashville with strong Christological emphasis: carols, Nativity scenes, pageants, the exchange of gifts. In one school, there was a large sign: "Put Christ Back into Christmas." No official protests were made by any Jewish organization. But the JCRC is gradually developing relationships within the schools designed to decrease such occurrences.

Some Nashvillians believe that the most controversial problem is still the Negro question. The angry conflict over Negro lunch counter rights in 1960 gave testimony that Nashville had a long way to go in meeting its responsibilities to all its citizens. Other Nashville observers insist that the question of religion in the public schools is equally combustible.

Said Rev. Will Campbell, "To me this is a serious problem. In my school, morning devotions are held by the teacher daily and the assumption seems to be that not only are all the children Christians, but all are 'baptized by immersion' Christians."

A Jewish leader claims: "This is potentially the most controversial issue in our community. The reason that the problem of religion in the public schools doesn't seem to be too acute here is because the Jews of Nashville regard it as too dangerous to touch and thus take no forthright action. I am of the conviction that should the rabbi bring this matter out into public focus, the entire community would be thrown into an uproar, the Jews would be bitterly condemned, and the rabbi would be compelled to leave his pulpit within a week. This issue has the seeds of even more bitterness than the problem of integration."

*   *   *

This, then, is Nashville. Publicity given its problems has tended to highlight the negative in community relationships. But those who are quietly working for justice, for harmonious race and religious relationships, for community progress, and for brotherhood in action—they should not be forgotten. For they are at work, they are making progress—agonizingly slow progress it sometimes appears, but progress nonetheless—and they are forging the Nashville and, hopefully, the South of tomorrow.

NEW YORK CITY
The Falling Star

"NOW WE COME TO NEW YORK CITY," WROTE JOHN Gunther in his encyclopedic *Inside U.S.A.*, "the incomparable, the brilliant star city of cities . . . the supreme expression of both the miseries and the splendors of contemporary civilization . . . the publishing center of the nation . . . the art, theater, musical, ballet, operatic center . . . the opinion center . . . the style center." A "star city" it is, but its star is neither high nor bright in the interreligious firmament.

Doubtless the attributes described by Gunther present a rather awesome and forbidding spectacle to its half-million daily visitors, many of whom remain forever certain that New York is the place they want most to visit but not to live in. But for those who make it their home, New York has at least one additional but indefinable characteristic, never noted in the guide books, and difficult fully to appreciate save by actual experience. The city is a haven in which one may live in more or less complete religious anonymity if one chooses. This comforting state is traceable to New York's vast heterogeneity, to the unique interreligious relationships of its eight million inhabitants, and to its laissez-faire traditions. Thus one will find that most New Yorkers would not worry about the religion, if any, of their neighbors, even if they knew who they were. And New Yorkers are most unlikely to equate sound Americanism with church affiliation, a not uncommon trait in our national life today.

Here we have the ingredients for a deceptively tranquil picture of religious harmony. Immediately beneath the surface, however, smolder a host of unresolved dissensions on issues of vast social significance. Yet the anticipated religious discord never quite erupts into actual conflict, so that New Yorkers live in a never-never land of seemingly perpetual suspension. Nor is the prognosis a happy one, for the religious scene is all but void of meaningful communication between the Catholic hierarchy and the organized Protestant and Jewish communities.

CITY OF CITIES

In the context of this discussion it is necesary to think of New York City as a sprawling political entity embracing a host of rather distinctive communities, some of which are as populous as many of our well-known cities. There is, for example, the apartment house development known as Parkchester which, though covering but a few acres in the Bronx, houses over 12,000 families, probably close to 50,000 people.

The years have wrought noticeable changes in the neighborhood patterns with which the city has so long been associated. The Lower East Side is still identifiably Jewish, but no longer as distinctively so as in the immediate past. So, too, with the formerly Irish Catholic Chelsea section, the area familiarly known as Little Italy, and German Yorkville. These and other pockets of ancestral association are slowly undergoing a transformation, in part the result of the exodus to the suburbs, and in part because of strenuous efforts by Negroes and Puerto Ricans to break out of their tight ghettos.

Typical are the dizzying changes which have engulfed the section of Manhattan from 72nd Street north to 96th Street on the West Side, from Central Park West to Riverside Drive. The old town houses, which in the thirties were occupied by many Jewish families to the manor born, have now been converted into rooming houses packed to bursting with hard-pressed Puerto Ricans, ostracized by "better neighborhoods." Their presence, in turn, opened the way to Negro occupancy which, however, is still minimal. As a result, most Jews withdrew from the side streets and those whose incomes permitted, relocated on the East Side. Those who, from preference, convenience, or necessity, remained true to the West Side are now self-confined to the broad and "still nice" thoroughfares of 72nd, 81st, 86th, and 96th Streets.

The City of New York has now embarked on a tremendous rehabilitation program for precisely this area, beginning with the Lincoln Center for the Performing Arts and including enormous middle-income and upper-income housing developments. Once again, the faces walking the streets of Manhattan's West Side will change!

Chelsea, the famous neighborhood redolent with the peppery aromas of Hell's Kitchen, has simmered down to an old age of genteel decay and decorous behavior. The "fighting Irish" who once gave color to this community are no longer numerically dominant. They have been largely displaced by an increasing Jewish population as well as Puerto Ricans and Negroes. Elliott House, a low-income, subsidized project is open to all who qualify financially. Though tenanted also by many Negroes and Puerto Ricans, Jews have a slight numerical edge. The new cooperative development being constructed by the ILGWU is expected to have as high as 85 per cent Jewish tenancy.

Religion and religious institutions are rarely the subject of direct or overt public criticism or attack in New York City. The mass media, particularly, are models of good behavior in this respect. The church itself or the failings of institutional religion rarely result in ridicule or censure or even mild criticism. The churches exercise a decorous restraint toward one another, too. Unlike the days of Puritan New England, attacks from the pulpit on the shortcomings of a sister institution are rare. In a word, the city is probably a poor barometer of the deep theological and communication gulfs that separate Protestant from Catholic and Christian from Jew.

Certainly, the religious climate in New York makes it unthinkable for a member of its official family to indulge in such indiscretions as the one made by Governor Orval Faubus of Arkansas in charging that a group of Protestant ministers who had disagreed with his views on the closing of the schools in Little Rock, Arkansas, in 1958, had been brainwashed by left-wingers and Communists. With such an unfortunate pronouncement a foolhardy official in New York would have written his political death warrant.

It is true that the city has witnessed religiously-based disputes from time to time, yet it, like most other cities, has seldom been gripped by any really serious religious battles. This rests on the fact that its religious communions have confined their clashes to social issues. Many of these, to be sure, have their genesis in dogma. But the results, apparently, are not nearly so shattering when people differ in matters of education, family life, and social welfare, as they could be if they were to come to grips publicly over, let us say, the dogma of the Bodily Assumption of Mary or the doctrine of Salvation, as has tended to happen in Europe.

A second reason may possibly be found in the apparent reluctance of the New York public to get emotionally involved in issues that have created havoc elsewhere. In Ardsley, New York (20 miles from Manhattan), some 1,300 adults—very nearly the whole population—petitioned their Board of Education to set aside a policy statement on "moral and spiritual values" because, they claimed, it failed to reflect their theological views. Thereafter, more than 500 of them crowded into a school board meeting to force a revision of policy. But, in a conflict in New York City regarding the very same problem, fewer than 100 organizational representatives appeared at a school board meeting to express a viewpoint. Apparently, the great mass of city residents are content to have organizational spokesmen represent them on even such far-reaching issues as the character education of their children. Most of the time they do not even appear to know that they are being represented!

It is interesting to reflect on the striking difference in attitude between the citizens of Ardsley and New York City on the same problem. One suspects that, while such battles rage on institutional levels and in the mass media, the plain people in the teeming tenements of New York prefer to remain personally aloof from the conflict. Perhaps they rarely talk to one another about these awkward matters—or anything else! It may well be that "brotherhood" represents little more than an absence of communication, or a colossal detachment from vital social issues on the part of the great mass of the city's residents.

VANISHING PROTESTANTS

New York has long-since lost its original deep Protestant coloration. A little over a century ago a Roman Catholic bishop bitterly assailed the public schools of the city because of their overwhelming Protestant emphasis. He said, probably with much justification, that Catholic children could not in conscience attend them. No such concern need be felt today.

Early in 1959, the Protestant Council of the City of New York made public the results of a survey which statistically underscores this dramatic change. It disclosed fewer than 1,000,000 Protestant inhabitants, more than half of whom are non-white. Of the 68 per cent of the population who were reported as church-affiliated, only 12.5 per cent were Protestant, while each of the Catholic and Jewish communities is recorded as having somewhat over two million adherents, the former 27.1 per cent of the population, and the latter 26.5 per cent (*New York Herald Tribune,* January 5, 1959). To accelerate the drastic decline in Protestant numerical strength, there occurred, beginning about 1940, the rapid rise of a traditionally Catholic Puerto Rican population, reaching close to 600,000 by 1961.

These factual data should neither astonish nor perplex. Putting his finger on the explanation, noted Protestant leader Truman B. Douglass, in a frank appraisal of American Protestants' role in the big cities, finds that: "In almost direct proportion to the increasing importance

of the city in American culture has been the withdrawal
—both physical and spiritual—of the Protestant church.
The statistics of one denomination's history in New York
City shows that during the past century in Manhattan and
the Bronx it has dissolved fifty-four churches and merged
forty-two with other congregations" (*Harper's,* Nov., '58).

The diminution of Protestant numbers is emphatically
reflected in the official life of the city. "Protestants are in
a disproportionate minority in city government," protested Dr. Dan M. Potter, executive director of the Protestant Council of the City of New York. "Of thirty-four
persons in leadership positions in city departments, only
three are Protestants," he said, adding that of 208 judges,
only eleven are Protestant, and of twenty-two executives
in the Department of Public Welfare, only one is a Protestant (Religious News Service, April 27, 1959). Dr.
Potter might also have noted that there was not then a
single judge of the Protestant faith on the State Supreme
Court bench in the Second Judicial District which includes
an area covering the boroughs of Brooklyn and Rich-
mond (Staten Island).

A political scientist, Dr. Ralph A. Straetz, noted (*New
York Times,* May 24, 1961) that in recent years four of
the five borough presidents have been Roman Catholic;
the other turned out to be Episcopalian (John Cashmore,
late Borough President of Brooklyn), "but most people
thought he was Catholic." Of 25 members of the New
York City Council in 1961, 12 were Roman Catholic, 11
Jewish, and 2 Protestant (both Negroes).

The controlling positions in the machinery of the Democratic party, which dominates the political life of the
city, have long been held by Roman Catholics. Indeed,

for many years—except during the interim of the administration of Fiorello H. LaGuardia, who won the mayoralty after a bitterly fought campaign in which he exposed and excoriated wide-spread graft and corruption in the city government—top places on Democratic tickets went to Catholic candidates. Other important posts are then assigned in something like an equitable division. Traditionally—and significantly—certain strategic posts have been reserved for Catholics, such as the office of the Corporation Counsel, the Commissioner of Licenses, and with rare exceptions that most desirable judicial plum, the Surrogate's bench, which handles the crucial matter of child adoption.

One of the most striking concomitants of this arrangement, though one that could hardly be deemed remarkable by any practical politician or sophisticated student of American urban politics, is the fidelity with which most Democratic party officials and city office-holders, regardless of their personal religious identification, adhere to Roman Catholic doctrines and positions on public issues. Although on many of these the views of the Chancery of the Archdiocese of New York are in conflict with the policies of major Jewish and Protestant organizations in the city, including the rabbinic and synagogual bodies and the Protestant Council, it is the voice of the Chancery that almost always sounds most persuasive to the politician and to the elected or appointed official, whatever his faith.

A striking illustration was the testimony which Mr. Charles Silver, then chairman of the New York City Board of Education, presented at a congressional hearing in Washington on federal aid to education in April, 1961.

Identifying himself as president of a Conservative synagogue and active in other Jewish and communal causes, the chairman of the Board of Education of the largest public school system in the world made an eloquent plea for federal aid to parochial as well as public education. For this he was severely reprimanded by the press and by several civic bodies in the community which insisted that Silver had far exceeded his authority.

Notwithstanding the greater combined voting strength of Protestants and Jews, and the absence of Catholic ownership or control of any of the city's leading newspapers,* Roman Catholic interests dominate and control even aspects of law enforcement, by holding over law enforcement officers the power of reward or punishment according to their show of regard for the sensitivities and wishes of the Catholic church.

The case of Deputy Chief Inspector Louis Goldberg is instructive on this score. In 1954, Inspector Goldberg, a policeman for thirty-six years, was head of the Brooklyn Morals Squad, charged with cracking down on all forms of gambling, which he did with great skill and devotion. To Inspector Goldberg, gambling was gambling—including bingo (then not legal). But bingo, vigorously defended by the Roman Catholic churches, which are its chief beneficiaries, had been tacitly countenanced for years by the city's officialdom. When the inspector turned

---

* An editor of *America* once made a study of the obituary columns in the New York evening papers. The obits in the *World-Telegram* were overwhelmingly Protestant, the *Journal American* mostly Catholic, and the *Post* nearly all Jewish. He concluded that each religious group had its own evening paper. A New York rabbi commented: "Yes, but they all die for the *New York Times*."

his attention to bingo he ran into a stone wall, high and impregnable. First he was reprimanded, then demoted to captain. At that point he resigned. The then Police Commissioner Adams fatuously insisted that "bingo in this case is irrelevant." But the commissioner's disclaimer failed to impress the newspapers, which pointed to Goldberg's fine record as a police officer, and hinted broadly at "political pressure." The Protestant Council also came to Goldberg's defense, saying, "It is an amazing spectacle when a conscientious police officer is taken to task for performing his duty of enforcing the law. Whether one is in favor of or opposed to bingo for charitable purposes is irrelevant. Law enforcement is the issue . . . ." (*Newsweek,* September 20, 1954). Bingo is now legal in New York by virtue of a state law enacted in 1959.

BIRTH CONTROL

The controversy over birth control therapy in municipal hospitals is another example of official sensitivity in deference to Roman Catholic views. For many years the municipal hospitals had abided by an unwritten law which made such therapy taboo, though the ban was never officially acknowledged. The hand of Dr. Morris A. Jacobs, the Commissioner of Hospitals, was forced when, early in 1958, the director of obstetrics at Kings County Hospital tested official policy in a carefully selected case, that of a Protestant woman seriously ill with diabetes who would be in danger of death in the event of a pregnancy. Accordingly, the woman was ordered fitted with a contraceptive device, but Dr. Jacobs (a career civil servant) refused to allow the prescription to be filled.

The Protestant Council at once leaped into the fray, as did other groups, including the New York Board of Rabbis, the American Jewish Congress, and the United Lutheran Church, demanding a reversal of his action. A statement by the Chancery office of the New York Archdiocese quoted Pope Pius XII as authority for the principle that any attempt, through contraception, to hinder the natural results of the conjugal act was immoral.

The Board of Hospitals eventually reversed Dr. Jacobs' ban on contraceptive therapy, ruling that such measures are proper medical practice when a patient's health or life may be otherwise jeopardized; that municipal hospitals should provide such therapy where warranted in a physician's judgment and acceptable to the patient; but that hospital personnel who have religious or moral objections should be excused from participation in contraceptive procedures.

Resourceful Dr. Jacobs was equal to the task of placating the aroused Roman Catholic Church to the extent that it was possible to do so in the circumstances. In translating the hospital board's decision into departmental policy he added a number of embellishments: "The patient shall be advised to consult with her spiritual adviser as well as with members of the family." (In respect to this rule the *New York World-Telegram and Sun,* September 24, 1958, asked editorially, "By what authority does Dr. Jacobs assume this pious posture?") The written consent of the patient must be obtained before the recommended contraceptive services may be performed; and the written consent of the spouse of the patient should also be obtained, if possible. As one medical critic of these obviously hamstringing rules observed, Dr. Jacobs' regulations "will create in the minds of decent and well-meaning patients the thought that they are doing something wrong if they accept contraception."

In actual effect, the result of the controversy was little more than a stand-off. The directives of the hospital board reversed the unofficial ban on contraceptive therapy, but Dr. Jacobs' restrictions so diluted the board's policy pronouncement that its practical application became extremely difficult.

CHILD ADOPTION

Religion also plays a crucial part in child adoption in New York State. Indeed, a childless couple must affirm a religious faith if they hope to adopt a baby in the state, according to a study made by the *New York Times*. Atheists and agnostics are wasting their time; their applications are likely to be turned down, whether the application is made to an adoptive agency or to a court. The reason is that the couple is expected to raise the adoptive child within a specific religion. Moreover, said the *Times*, members of the Ethical Culture Society cannot qualify; they are not accepted as a religion but only as a "religious fellowship."

New York State's adoption law provides that, when practicable, a child must be placed only with persons of the religious faith of its natural parents, or, if the child is born out of wedlock, the faith of its natural mother. Roman Catholic welfare leaders strongly defend the present requirement and the rigid interpretation of it. Said Msgr. Michael F. Dwyer, director of the Catholic Charities department of child care, in an interview with the *New York Times:* "Roman Catholicism is the only true religion as revealed by the Son of God. It is the greatest heritage which a child can be given—the truth by which we live. There are laws protecting the material heritage of our children, and it is right that they should. It would be the height of illogic that we should not protect the spiritual heritage of the child, which far exceeds the material heritage."

Jewish and Protestant welfare leaders have argued that "a loving home" should take precedence over purely sectarian requirements. Some have condemned the New York law as an unconstitutional infringement of religious liberty. Domestic Relations Court Justice Justine Wise Polier has posed the issue in this way: "Any attempt by the state, through over-zealous employees in the courts, public departments, or hospitals, to infringe on the parent's religious freedom, or right to choose adherence or non-adherence to any faith, violates the Constitution and its guarantee of freedom of conscience and religion."

This issue is filled with potentialities for interreligious conflict on an emotional level. Other states have provisions similar to New York's. It may remain for the courts, ultimately, to determine whether the state has the right to impose such religious requirements in the adoption of children. In the meantime, religious tension will continue and, occasionally, will break through the surface to mock New York's pretensions of harmonious group relations.

The selection of probation officers for the Children's Court Division of the New York City Domestic Relations Court is another case in point. In a complaint to the State Commission Against Discrimination, filed in January, 1955, the American Jewish Congress charged that a system of religious quotas was used to satisfy the requirement in the law that "when practicable" the court shall assign a probation officer of the same religious faith as the child or family he will serve. The complaint touched off a bitter dispute which found the then-presiding officer of the Children's Court, John Warren Hill, and Roman Catholic circles arrayed against Jewish groups, the Protestant Episcopal Diocese of New York, and most of the professional social workers.

Justice Hill interpreted the "when practicable" provision in the law to mean that an applicant for a probation officer's job with the Domestic Relations Court could be asked his religion on the theory that the court was justified in making appointments to match the religious composition of its case load. Jewish children comprised only about 5 per cent of the total number coming before the court and the American Jewish Congress charged that the quota system militated unfairly against Jewish applicants. Justice Hill's answer to this was that religious quotas were used only in assignments to the Children's Court Division, rather than to the Domestic Relations Court.

But, said the American Jewish Congress, with the system of assigning probation officers on the basis of religious faith, a preponderance of the Jewish officers has been assigned to the Family Court where their work has been largely that of "alimony collectors." For this reason many skilled, eligible people have declined to apply. The controversial practice of inquiring about the religion of probation officer applicants with the Domestic Relations Court was finally abandoned when Commissioner J. Edward Conway of the State Commission Against Discrimination initiated the customary conciliation proceeding. However, in the view of the American Jewish Congress, Justice Hill's agreement to cease requesting the Civil Service Commission to certify applicants on the basis of their religion by no means resolved the matter, for the Justice was still determined to follow the policy of appointing officers to the Children's Court Division according to creed. Commissioner Conway was of the opinion that this phase of the controversy could only be resolved by legislative action (*New York Times,* July 10, 1956).

The demonstrated Catholic power, tantamount to a veto on some issues, is by no means confined to the governmental realm. New Yorkers have seen evidence of this great influence in other areas. The anguished history of the New York Health and Welfare Council provides one illustration. The council performed invaluable service as a planning and coordinating agency. It provided basic information to help improve health and welfare services; it was a force in assisting organizations to join in seeking solutions to their problems; and it acted as a clearing-house for information about persons receiving assistance from welfare agencies, thus avoiding duplication of services.

Today, this very useful organization is no more because a majority of the council admitted the Planned Parenthood Federation as a member. With this decision, all Catholic health and welfare agencies quit. Without this considerable number of organizations, the council could no longer operate as a coordinating agency. Replacing the council is the Community Council of Greater New York in which, by the way, the Planned Parenthood Federation functions. But, unlike the old council, the new structure is a non-membership organization, so that the city is without a democratic voice in the health and welfare field.

There is a widely-held assumption that complete Catholic uniformity of mind exists on all matters, whereas a like solidity is lacking in the Protestant and Jewish communities. Yet, it is undoubtedly true that there is often a considerable difference of opinion within Catholic ranks even on issues as basic as birth control and censorship. But the crucial point is that, regardless of existing differences within Catholic lay, and in some cases even clerical, circles, once the hierarchy has spoken, the great mass of Roman Catholics in the city closes ranks. The problem of the state's divorce law offers an example. The law is a mockery. The only legal ground for divorce is adultery. As a result, there has arisen a collusive racket to provide "evidence" of adultery for couples who wish to be divorced. In addition, many New Yorkers utilize the divorce mills of Nevada and Mexico with legal impunity. Numerous efforts have been made to change the statute but they have failed in every instance because city representatives in the state legislature believe that, whatever may be the private views of their Roman Catholic constituents, it is reasonably certain that a vote to ease the stringency of these laws is political suicide.

Moreover, the New York public has learned that the economic boycott is a weapon Roman Catholic leadership is capable of using. Still fresh in mind is the fiery denunciation of the picture *Baby Doll* by Francis Cardinal Spellman and his open appeal to Catholics to boycott the film. In a similar vein was the effort of the Anchor Club, which is composed of members of the Knights of Columbus, to enforce a more reverent observance of Good Friday. Shortly before the holiday in 1952, Jewish merchants in the Highbridge section of the Bronx were visited by representatives of the organization and requested to close their stores for three hours on Good Friday. The merchants who consented were rewarded with a printed card for window display, which said: "We will close from 12 noon to 3:00 P.M., April 11, 1952, in observance of the death of Christ."

Storekeepers who demurred were none-too-subtly threatened with a loss of Catholic trade. In the newspaper reports of the period, only one of the shopowners would permit the use of her name; all the others were fearful of retribution. This story, however, had a moderately happy ending. After representations were made by Jewish groups, the Chancery office issued a statement in which it said that it did not approve the campaign to persuade Jewish merchants to post the placards and to close their stores on Good Friday, adding that if approval had been sought it would not have been granted (*New York Times*, April 8, 1952).

One of the compelling factors in the New York picture is the absence of authoritative spokesmen for either the

Protestant or Jewish community on these important social issues. This is in no sense intended as a critical observation. Indeed, many Protestants and Jews insist that it be just that way—no central power or authority in a position to commit them on these questions, even though they would readily acknowledge that the current situation presents something of a handicap. Of course, the Protestant Council of the City of New York and the New York Board of Rabbis are influential and eloquent spokesmen on moral and political issues, but they do not speak for all the Protestants or all the Jews. For example, such organizations as the American Jewish Committee, the Anti-Defamation League, the American Jewish Congress, and the National Council of Jewish Women, to name but a few, are not at all bound by the decisions and pronouncements of the Board of Rabbis. And on many issues Orthodox Jews do not agree with Jewish welfare leaders. Moreover, there are occasions when the Protestant and Jewish communities are so torn internally on important issues that it is impossible for them to speak for their constituents with one voice. And in New York, more so than in any other city, a large percentage of the Protestants and Jews belong to no religious constituency at all.

A case in point is the problem of the Sunday closing laws, in respect to which there is considerable disagreement within Protestant ranks. Because of that division, the Protestant Council took no position in 1958 on the Asch-Rosenblatt bill, a home rule measure designed to exempt those New York City merchants who observe a day other than Sunday as their Sabbath from the penal provisions of the closing laws. But these Protestant differences were not reflected in the New York City Council. There the vote on the home rule request to the state legislature went strictly along religious lines, 14-7, the eleven Jewish and three Protestant councilmen voting for the measure. The seven negative votes were cast by Roman Catholics. Observers of the political scene discounted the significance of this alignment of Jews and Protestants on the grounds that the decision was foredoomed in Albany, where the opposition of the Roman Catholic Church and many upstate Protestant leaders made defeat of the Asch-Rosenblatt measure certain.

It might be fruitful to compare these results with the momentary difference of opinion which appeared to develop among Catholic leadership on the very same issue, a difference that quickly disappeared from view once Cardinal Spellman's office firmly reiterated official policy. The influential Jesuit magazine, *America* (March 8, 1958), had suggested: "Perhaps New York City might try a one-year experiment with Sunday openings in a limited section where there is a heavy concentration of Jewish merchants and predominantly Jewish population. If during the period it is established that Jewish shops are actually closed on Saturdays, relaxation of the Sunday closing laws would seem to be in order in their cases. . . ." No more was heard from *America* on this specific proposal after the Cardinal flatly reaffirmed his opposition to any relaxation of the closing laws.

The New York Board of Rabbis was quite as embarrassed by Congressman W. R. Poage's "humane slaughter" bill, subsequently enacted by the U. S. Congress, as was the Protestant Council by the Sunday closing measure in the state legislature. Because of the temporary disagreement between the Orthodox Jewish group, on the one hand, and the Conservative and Reform groups on the other, it became impossible for the Board to achieve an official position on legislation to assure humane slaughter of animals. Doubtless, the Board would find much the same difficulty if it undertook to develop policy on such controversial subjects as censorship and the religious factor in child adoption. It already faces such a cleavage on federal aid to parochial schools.

Even the comforts of large numbers and of commensurate political power do not guarantee that any one of the three faith groups will respond to an attack upon itself with calm dignity and security. Several incidents arose in 1960 which proved this fact anew.

The arrival in New York City of George Lincoln Rockwell, self-proclaimed Führer and leader of the American Nazi party, stirred hysteria within the Jewish community which, most authorities believed, was far out of proportion to the threat posed by Rockwell. It is true that the nerves of New York Jewry had been rubbed raw by a wave of swastika incidents and the vivid memories of Nazism reawakened in the hearts of Jews everywhere by the capture of Adolf Eichmann in Argentina. It is also true that Rockwell advertised a psychopathic platform which urged nothing less than genocide for American Jewry. But Rockwell was clearly a small potato with virtually no following whatever. Giving him a public forum would be a threat largely to himself, not to New York Jewry. Yet several Jewish organizations strongly pressed Mayor Wagner to deny Rockwell the right to speak, and they prevailed. The traditional civil libertarian position of the Jewish community broke on the rock of an inflamed public opinion; and it remained for the American Civil Liberties Union and the courts to assert the right of free speech, however noxious the advocate. If this was a triumph for New York Jewry, it was a triumph only for their sense of insecurity and fear.

Jewish emotions were fired again in September, 1960, when, on the eve of the historic session of the U.N. General Assembly which featured Khrushchev, Castro, Nasser, and Kadar, New York City's then Police Commissioner Stephen Kennedy announced his refusal to allow Jewish policemen to be relieved from duty for the Jewish High Holy Days. He coupled this announcement with a gratuitous and insulting comment on the religious sincerity of the Jewish policemen. Understandably irked, Jewish leaders sought a public apology from Kennedy as well as a revision of his order regarding Jewish policemen. Neither was forthcoming. In the gathering storm, former Governor Lehman pleaded with Jewish leadership not to lose perspective and not to blow up the incident out of all proportion. The pressures which stemmed from the unprecedented U.N. session and the good record of the commissioner as a foe of racism and bigotry— these seemed to be swept aside in the heat of conflict.

Despite the deep-seated differences that exist among the major religious groups on moral issues, they manage somehow to avoid a showdown in most cases. With commendable ingenuity they resolve their basic differences so that life goes on in what amounts to a state of suspension between the extremes of viewpoints.

In connection with the Sunday closing laws, for example, the police almost certainly have instructions to exercise a benign indifference to the beehive of activity on the Lower East Side on Sunday. To be sure, there are token efforts at enforcement, from time to time, but there is an obvious recognition that a strict enforcement would create a most embarrassing religious conflict.

SCHOOLS

The sagacity, if not necessarily the courage, with which a "guiding statement" on moral and spiritual values was laid to rest by the then Board of Education of New York City, under conflicting pressures from the religious community, is another apt example. The document, which had been adopted by the Board of Superintendents in June, 1955, encountered opposition from the Protestant Council and every segment of the Jewish community, rabbinical and lay. Urging that the statement be revised to "take proper account of the rights of those teachers, parents, and others . . . who take a non-theistic position with respect to ethical and moral values," the Protestant Council noted that the public schools "are for the children of all Americans, regardless of their creedal beliefs," and added that "we are not disposed, as great as is our concern that education should meet the needs of the whole child, to advocate measures which a minority of our fellow citizens regard as an infringement upon their freedom" (from statement dated January 20, 1956).

The New York Board of Rabbis objected to the "guiding statement" because, among other things, it charged the public school teacher with the responsibility of predisposing public school children to the faith of their parents and assigns to the school the task of helping to strengthen belief in God. The Board of Rabbis asserted that such a course would "catapult the public schools into an area where they do not belong," charging that the intrusion of the state in the religious education and training of the child is "clearly neither desirable nor welcome" (from statement dated November 10, 1955).

The Archdiocesan office of education of the Roman Catholic Church on November 23, 1955, applauded the "noble purposes" of the "guiding statement," urging its adoption because "we are convinced that moral and spiritual values have their ultimate source in God and are meaningless without God. We are anxious to see God given due recognition in our public schools."

It would seem altogether impossible to reconcile these completely diverse points of view. But the Board of Education accomplished the impossible. The "guiding statement" was rewritten in such deft terms that virtually every organization—Protestant, Catholic, Jewish, educational, and civic—found language in it that supported its position. As the Protestant Council said in a statement dated September 17, 1956, "While there has been some expression of concern that this (revised) statement is not as strong as some might wish, it is felt that it will prove generally acceptable to the diverse elements of our religious communities." And the Board of Rabbis was satisfied that New York's public school teachers no longer would be charged with the responsibility of "predisposing our children to the faith of their parents" and "helping to strengthen belief in God." The archdiocese was equally satisfied that moral and spiritual values would be taught in terms of religious sanctions since they have "their ultimate source in God." How the school system's already harried teachers are bearing up under these colliding interpretations is anybody's guess!

The Board of Education was equally skilful in dealing

with the controversy created by a recommendation for daily prayer in the schools, made by the State Board of Regents in 1951. The New York City Board of Education sat on the proposal for many months, recognizing that it must find a way of satisfying the conflicting views in the religious community. The board brought representatives of the three faiths together for meetings which stretched over a year—without result. Finally, it developed an amazing "compromise." It required the daily recitation of the fourth stanza of "America." Catholics welcomed this additional symbolic recognition of religion within the classroom because, said they, the fourth stanza (which begins "Our Fathers' God to Thee") is a prayer. Those who opposed the regents' recommendation because they consider prayer an act of worship, were fairly well handcuffed by the school board's maneuver. Who could possibly object to the recitation of *any* stanza of "America"? Now, every day of their school lives, New York children dutifully engage in the rote recitation of these beautiful and stirring lines (to the point where the words have probably become virtually meaningless to them), because the board felt impelled to find a formula for a prayer that would not be recognized as one.

There is, however, one issue of such extraordinary difficulty that even the vaunted skills and ingenuity of the Board of Education failed to measure up to its formidable challenge—the observance of the Christmas holiday in the public schools. The problem presents the classic case of the irresistible force meeting the immovable object: Christmas commemorates the birth of the Christian savior, and is, therefore, an event of profound religious significance. Nevertheless, Christians insist that the schools devote weeks of their crowded curriculum to a celebration of the holiday. Most Jewish organizations, on the other hand, insist that sectarian programs, whether Christian or Jewish, have no place in a public school setting. Still others, including some Jews and Christians, urge a school program at Christmastime which will stress the universal appeal of the holiday and omit its sectarian emphases. To this comes the answer that a watering-down of the religious implications of the event would be an affront to Christians. Obviously, one side or the other must give ground or a solution becomes impossible.

In the winter of 1947, the Board of Education fumbled an opportunity to play a constructive role in the resolution of this problem. Early in December of that year, Dr. Isaac Bildersee, assistant superintendent in charge of the Brownsville, Canarsie, and East Flatbush sections of Brooklyn, whose schools included large numbers of Jewish children, directed the principals in his jurisdiction to avoid religious expressions in the celebration of the Christmas holiday. He said later that his order was given "in the spirit of seeing to it that what is done does not offend the sensibilities of even one child." Accordingly, he suggested the use of Santa Claus, holly, mistletoe, and such songs as "Jingle Bells"—anything that was not specifically religious. Overnight, a wave of protest developed against Bildersee's "exclusion" of religion from the schools. The Knights of Columbus termed the order an insult to Christianity. Dr. Norman Vincent Peale referred to the directive as "a very serious error." Even Kate Smith got into the act, denouncing the order on her nation-wide radio broadcast. "Never in my memory," said she, "have the approximately 135 million Christians of this country been so insulted. . . ."

Finally, Superintendent of Schools William Jansen issued his yearly Christmas greeting—a little earlier than usual—and seized the occasion to calm the troubled waters. He ruled that the school programs will be such as are "in the good judgment of the principal, teachers, and the participants, suited" (*Herald Tribune,* December 6, 1947). Asked if his statement meant that he was revoking Dr. Bildersee's order, the superintendent is quoted as saying, "If you want to put it that way you can, but I don't know whether it is or not" (*New York Times,* December 7, 1947).

This unfortunate episode should not be concluded without a reference to the action taken by Father Vincent O. Genova of the Holy Family Church in Canarsie, the district most affected by the disputed order. After the thunderous denunciation had subsided, he issued a quiet statement in which he expressed his respect for Dr. Bildersee and included a comment he had solicited from the harried assistant superintendent, all of which he asked the *Brooklyn Eagle* to print in fairness to all concerned. In his statement to Father Genova, Dr. Bildersee said, in part, ". . . I should be the last one to ask that the Christmas spirit of good will be in the least abated or that . . . its essential spiritual meaning should be denied to children of those faiths who accept it as such. I had hoped to avoid the hurt to children's feelings that I know has ensued in some instances because they were required to join in the singing of songs that were directly contradictory of their own established faiths. I do not believe that any of us would seek to hurt 'even the least of these.' "

New York City's mushrooming parochial school system is making strong inroads into the public schools. In

January, 1961, the enrollment in Roman Catholic parochial schools was 37 per cent that of the public schools of the city. But in the fall of 1961 there were indications that Catholic schools would enroll four times as many new pupils as would the public schools. The growth indicates the desire of many Catholic parents to give their children a parochial school education; undoubtedly, it also reflects some dissatisfaction with the bad conditions of the New York City public school system.

The road to religious peace and tranquillity taken in New York is suggested by the fiction of statistical equality maintained by New York's Board of Education until the entire board was dismissed in the wake of school scandals in 1961. By unwritten law the nine-member appointed board always consisted of an equal number of Catholics, Jews, and Protestants. In recent years one of the latter three has invariably been a Negro. The custom of appointing members of the board according to religious affiliation was once condemned by the New York Board of Rabbis as a thoroughly pernicious practice. Similar censure from the Protestant and Catholic communities has not been heard. But Charles F. Preusse, then city administrator, was quoted by Terry Ferrer, education editor of the *Herald Tribune* (March 12, 1959), condemning appointments based on religious representation as a "perversion of principle."

Following disclosures of wide-spread irregularities and inefficiency in the operation of the city's schools, the state legislature, in 1961, voted the existing board of education out of office. The mayor retained the right to appoint the new board, but was required to make his selections from a list of at least nineteen names to be submitted by a panel named by the state. (The panel actually submitted a list of twenty-six candidates.) After all the agitation and public upheaval resulting from public dissatisfaction with the schools, in September, 1961, Mayor Robert Wagner proceeded to the naming of a new board, consisting of— three Catholics, three Jews, and three Protestants, one of whom was a Negro! In the interest of strict reporting, it must be noted that one of the non-Jewish, non-Catholic board members is rumored to be religiously unaffiliated.

The system of religious balance also embraced the influential Board of Superintendents which is now modeled after the Board of Education. The equilibrium trembled after the retirement of associate superintendent Regina Burke. Next in line to fill the vacated post, in fact recommended for the promotion by Dr. Burke herself, was Florence Beaumont. But Miss Burke was Catholic, and Miss Beaumont—Protestant. This difficulty was not too much for the resourceful Board of Education to hurdle. It solved the problem by holding up the Beaumont appointment for a year or more until it succeeded in inducing the state legislature to enlarge the Board of Superintendents from eight to nine, thus making possible a tri-faith balance. Only then did the Board of Education simultaneously appoint Miss Beaumont and a Roman Catholic to the Board of Superintendents!

Not long after that, the president of the Catholic Teachers' Association of Brooklyn, Dr. James V. Cunningham, was emboldened to suggest that the Board of Examiners, civil service employees of the school system, ought also be "representative of all religious faiths." At that time the eight-man Board of Examiners had six Jewish members, with two vacancies to be filled. The

Civil Service Commission was then preparing a new list from which appointments to the Board of Examiners would be made. Of course, the list would be compiled from applicants who had taken open, competitive examinations. Dr. Cunningham was altogether frank in giving his reasons for scrapping the merit system in this respect: ". . . in its efforts to improve the moral and spiritual values in the children through their teachers, the Board of Education might well consider how we can provide the Board of Examiners with men of religious faith who will be capable of selecting the best teachers for developing the whole child" (*World-Telegram and Sun,* March 16, 1954). In the same newspaper the Board of Rabbis emphatically opposed the suggestion: "Character, competence, and experience are now the sole criteria for such appointments. This is precisely as it should be."

CENSORSHIP

The delicacy of religious issues in the Big City was strikingly revealed in 1949 when the then New York City School Superintendent William Jansen banned the *Nation* magazine from public school libraries. This unusual action was prompted by publication in the *Nation* of a series of articles on Catholicism by Paul Blanshard. These articles were denounced by Catholic spokesmen as "bigoted" and demands were made that public school children not be exposed to such "anti-Catholic" material. Mr. Jansen's ban on the *Nation* was upheld by the city Board of Education. Upon appeal, the state education commissioner ruled that the case was not within his jurisdiction. The suppression of the *Nation* was protested by the American Civil Liberties Union as "against the interests of our society, which depends for its democratic survival and continuation upon citizens capable of critical judgments on controversial issues and subjects, and which is hurt by restrictions upon intellectual freedom." At the end of 1961, the *Nation* was still not being read in the libraries of New York's high schools.

Catholics are far from being united in support of censorship drives conducted under church auspices. A poignant episode in this regard unfolded in New York City in May, 1960, when a Decency Committee of the Roman Catholic Church of the Good Shepherd set out to banish "obscene" materials from news-stands in upper Manhattan. All but three of the thirty-two news-dealers who were approached yielded to the committee's obscenity list, banned the "objectionable" material (including *Tortilla Flat, Room at the Top, Look Back in Anger, On the Road*), and in return received a colored "purity" sticker for window display. Three dealers refused to be intimidated. Denied a sticker, they faced the stark threat of boycott. One of the resistant dealers was Fred Werner, who was both Catholic and blind. He survived the boycott of his news-stand, thanks in large part to the outpouring of new customers, Catholics and non-Catholics, who read about his fight in the newspapers and came from all parts of the city to sustain him.

"It's not easy to fight your own church," Werner told the *New York Post*. "But it's not right to dictate to all people what they can and can't read. I think the list of books should be published for members of the parish and let it be up to each individual's conscience whether they want to read a book or not."

How to meet the post-World War II threat of Communism, external and internal, has also pointed up sharp and bitter differences among the faith groups. Because New York City is the communications center of America, these differences have emerged with special sharpness there. The period of McCarthyism was a marked example. A Gallup poll in March, 1954, at the height of McCarthy's popularity, showed that 56 per cent of the Catholics, 45 per cent of the Protestants, and only 13 per cent of the Jews approved of McCarthy. These differences were both deep and emotionally charged. While many Protestant and Jewish organizations condemned McCarthyism and urged the Congress to adopt a code of proper standards for investigating committees and fairer procedures for security programs, the Catholic position was much more ambiguous. Because Francis Cardinal Spellman and other prelates defended Senator McCarthy, many Americans mistakenly concluded that the Roman Catholic Church as such supported the Senator's views. Actually, there was no united Catholic position, and the anti-McCarthy views of Bishop Bernard Sheil and of such Catholic publications as *America* and *Commonweal* were aired alongside the wildly hysterical rantings of arch-conservative Catholic publications such as the Brooklyn *Tablet*. (The *Tablet,* which characterized the anti-McCarthyites as "anti-anti-Communists" guilty of "Lehmanism," has been a perfervid influence for decades in New York's interreligious affairs.)

Senator McCarthy is now dead, and the legacy of McCarthyism has passed to such extremists as the Birch Society. Differing assessments of the danger of Communism—and how to meet that danger—continue to exacerbate interreligious relations in New York City.

Illustrations are legion, but one may suffice. When Nikita Khrushchev first came to New York City, upon the invitation of President Eisenhower, Catholic reaction ranged from hostile to cool. Jewish and Protestant reaction from mild acceptance of reality to enthusiastic hope that the exchanges represented a new initiative in breaking the grip of the cold war. Cardinal Spellman, on the eve of Khrushchev's arrival, issued a special prayer from St. Patrick's Cathedral, warning against a new Pearl Harbor and a new appeasement of the forces of evil. Jewish and Protestant leaders sent separate messages of congratulations to President Eisenhower on his "courageous initiative."

While these and other issues divide the faiths, religious institutions are a source of strength to New York. *Fortune* magazine, in a special issue on New York City,* described New York City's religions as the cement which holds the vast city together:

> So what gives New York its coherence? No city could exist for three hundred and thirty-odd years in incoherence. For one thing, surprisingly enough, it hangs together on the cord of its religions.
>
> . . . From its religions the city derives much strength and character. Protestantism's vigorous social ethic, with which the city began, is still a force in New York as throughout the nation. Probably a majority of the city's most influential civic leaders are of the Protestant faith, no less than eighteen of the great Protestant organizations have national headquarters in New York. Quite apart from the fact that Jewish intellectu-

---

* February, 1960.

ality and artistic appreciation give the city a special elan, Jewish philanthropy, with its deep religious base, lifts the level of the whole community. The emergence of Catholics to higher levels in the city's social structure, symbolized by the civic prominence of Francis Cardinal Spellman, brings to New York's amalgam the ancient firmness and cultural richness of that church. For all their differences, these three faiths are united in the conviction that the community exists to serve man. New York, for all its reckless air, is a stronghold of Western morality.

All things considered, this seems to be a rather rosy estimate of the New York scene for it fails to take note of the uneasy peace which prevails among the religious leaders, because of the sharp and apparently irreconcilable differences among them.

UNQUIET NEIGHBORHOOD

The occasionally dangerous potentialities of New York City's interreligious picture are most evident in the neighborhoods, many of which are taut and restive under the lightning bolts of racial and ethnic change. An example is the Chelsea area of New York City which runs from 34th Street south to 14th Street and from the Avenue of the Americas to the Hudson River. It was described thus by the Christian *Century:* "Once a quiet residential area it is now given over to business and small industry and to tenement and apartment dwellings. On the west it is fringed by some of the busiest docks in the port of New York. Today the neighborhood suffers from deterioration, disorganization, and decay. Its 61,000 residents, almost half of them Puerto Ricans, are constantly on the move. For the most part they live in squalor, enduring delinquency, crime, social conflict, anxiety, and fear. The area has a small middle-class Protestant population and a larger Jewish group of the same class. Most of the rest of the people are Roman Catholic."

In 1954 the New York Foundation invited Mr. Saul Alinsky, founder and guiding spirit of Chicago's Back of the Yards Council, to apply his social theories to selected New York communities, of which Chelsea was one. The New York Foundation provided $120,000 and the Emil Schwarzhaupt Foundation the other $60,000 to launch the Chelsea Citizen Participation Project. Mr. Alinsky served as its consultant; Mr. H. Daniel Carpenter, headworker of the Hudson Guild Neighborhood House and a long-recognized leader of the area, was asked to serve on a part-time basis as director.

Included among the eighty-three community organizations at the inception were the Hudson Guild and a dozen of its affiliated but autonomous bodies; the parent-teacher associations of Chelsea's three schools; the Democratic, Republican, and Liberal party organizations; veterans groups; General Theological Seminary; two YMCA's; nationality societies; locals of the International Longshoremen's Association and the Bartenders' Union; B'nai B'rith; four Protestant churches; two synagogues; and the four Roman Catholic churches which claimed to represent 30,000 of the community's residents. Father Dunn, assistant pastor of St. Columba Church, after receiving approval from his immediate superior and the New York archdiocese, accepted the presidency.

He was empowered to appoint the members, chairmen, and vice-chairmen of all committees except the

Nominating Committee. Six of the seven officers were Catholics, the seventh a Jew. Father Dunn also drew into the membership minor subgroups of the Roman Catholic Church, declaring they were valid community organizations and, once in, these small groups exerted an influence equal to the parent organizations under the unit rule vote.

According to his critics, Mr. Alinsky's philosophy of "power-to-the-most-powerful" prevailed. They charged that the voice of the council was, in reality, the voice of the Roman Catholic Church. The non-Catholic and non-sectarian organizations felt themselves a minority without representation on the policy-making level. They rebelled. Charges and counter-charges became more bitter and more frequent. When Father Dunn dismissed two Jewish committee members because he found them obstreperous and hard to work with, he was mistakenly charged with anti-Semitism and the situation worsened. The climax came over the issue of a city-financed housing project, the Penn Station South, for middle-income groups. All member organizations of the council except the Roman Catholic factions favored the project and urged the council to support it. The council refused on the grounds that it would displace a large portion of the residents— mostly the poorer families, largely Roman Catholic— without providing alternative housing.

The opposing philosophies of community organizations and representation were now irreconcilable. Mr. Carpenter led forty-seven organizations out of the council, including all the Protestant groups, most of the Jewish, the P.T.A.'s, the Liberal Party, one Democratic club, neighborhood groups, and at least one union local.

Mr. Carpenter regards this as a "most unhappy chapter

in my career," and attributes the failure primarily to the views of Mr. Alinsky which are, he says, "the antithesis of the ways that we would work."

Father Dunn, whose deep love for the neighborhood is questioned by none, blames the debacle primarily on Mr. Carpenter, but has suggested that he might try a new organization with "maybe block representatives to get more Protestants and Jews into the council—make it more democratic." Catholic leaders have acknowledged privately that the bitter Chelsea experience has further soured Catholic groups in New York City on interfaith cooperation on civic projects.

BRIDGES AND WALLS

Efforts to build interfaith bridges are made by the New York chapter of the National Conference of Christians and Jews, which was among the first NCCJ groups to abandon the concept of "brotherhood for the sake of brotherhood." It has been turning its attention increasingly to community relations and functional projects of value. Its program includes a concern for public schools, for problems of religion in the schools, for the status and well-being of the Puerto Rican minority, for better housing, for the problems of censorship in TV and other media. It performed a useful service with a series of Career Train projects, the result of which was to broaden the vocational horizons of hundreds of New York junior high school pupils, especially in areas heavily populated by Puerto Rican and Negro families.

But there is still lacking, on even the most rudimentary scale, the day-to-day conversation between Roman Catholic and non-Catholic leadership that might hold the promise of understanding, if not full agreement, on some of the major issues that divide New Yorkers. Catholic officialdom frequently maintains an arms-length policy of no contact with other religious groups, even extending this frozen attitude to the point of refusing to join Episcopal Bishop Horace W. B. Donegan in 1953, in an interfaith rally "in the interests of civic righteousness," because participation "would constitute an official act of the church" and "would be construed as having partisan political implications that might be unfortunate" (*New York Times*, May 13, 1953).

Rigid aloofness in matters theological is thoroughly understandable—even defensible. It reflects the hard fact of implacable religious difference. Why gather around the conference table if there is no possibility of a meeting of minds in the area of faith? But when eight million souls live in close proximity, it would appear that responsible religious leaders have an obligation to join hands in seeking solutions to social problems that affect the temporal peace and happiness of all.

Harmonious group living in these unsettled and anxious days is at best a haphazard enterprise. As Henry James observed in a different context, "It is a complex fate to be an American." Nor is the task made easier in the absence of accepted rules of community conduct which could help to create an atmosphere of reason in which religiously-related issues can be decided on their merits, or at least without destructive conflict. In time we might all agree on one simple prescription—fairly regular discourse on community problems, a course of conduct already followed with gratifying regularity by the Protestant Council and the Board of Rabbis. In the absence of such a cooperative spirit among all of the major religious communions, one can only hope that the New York public will survive recurring religious clashes without serious injury to existing neighborly relations. The hope may well be a reality, for there is virtually indigenous in the New York climate an impulse to live and let live, an atmosphere that can best be described as deeply democratic. Under the pervasive influence of this beneficent tradition, New Yorkers may somehow manage to create real and lasting interreligious cooperation and amity worthy of the greatest city in the world.

Perhaps the gravest charge against the religious communities of New York City is a failure of social energy and creative imagination. Although New York City is notably cosmopolitan, the religious groups are surprisingly ingrown. Rare are the prophetic voices, demanding action against the conditions in which some 2,000,000 New Yorkers live in 7,000 acres of fetid slums; and against the daily corruptions which corrode the spirit of a great city. Mostly, the churches and synagogues have accommodated themselves to what is. There is more than an element of truth in the indictment levelled by the Rev. Dr. C. Kilmer Myers, a Protestant Episcopal priest of Manhattan's Chapel of the Intercession, that the churches of New York have fallen victim to the "system that condones immorality in business and politics." Characterizing the voice of religion in New York as a "mere squeak," the cleric accused the Protestant and Catholic churches (he might have added synagogues, as well) of "chirping away" on such trivialities as bingo and *Baby Doll,* while the city's moral and social conditions cry out for bold action. In New York's religious life, as in its political, it is largely true that "the bland lead the bland." And the magical star continues to fall.

PHILADELPHIA
City of Brotherly Love

And thou Philadelphia, the virgin settlement of this province named before thou wert born, what love, what care, what service and what travail has there been to bring thee forth and preserve thee from such as would abuse and defile thee. Oh, that thou mayest be kept from evil that would overwhelm thee, that faithful to the God of thy mercies, in the life of righteousness, thou mayest be served to the end. My soul prays to God for thee that thou mayest stand in the day of trial, that thy children may be blessed of the Lord, and thy people saved by His Power.—WILLIAM PENN'S Prayer for Philadelphia. Written in 1684 and inscribed on a bronze plaque in City Hall courtyard.

BEFORE HE LEFT ENGLAND, WILLIAM PENN, FOUNDER of Pennsylvania, prepared the Great Law, the frame of government for his colony, which declared: "All persons living in this Province . . . shall in no way be molested or prejudiced in their religious persuasion or practice in matter of faith or worship."

This was enacted into the first laws of the Province at Chester, Pa., on December 10, 1682, two months after Penn's arrival. And so was set the climate for a pluralistic society in Pennsylvania and in Philadelphia, its principal city.

Making the long trek to Pennsylvania to escape Europe's religious wars were hardy souls who became known as the Pennsylvania Deutsch (casually Americanized to Dutch). By 1776 the Deutsch represented about one-half the population of Pennsylvania. Many of these people had indentured themselves—sold themselves into voluntary slavery—in order to pay their passage to a colony that promised religious and civic freedom.

Launched on a tide of idealism, Philadelphia has become a majestic center of American freedom, symbolized by Independence Hall where the Declaration of Independence was born, and the Liberty Bell, "proclaiming liberty throughout the land." Philadelphia is deeply conscious of its noble traditions. Moreover, to a large measure, the city has been faithful to its heritage of tolerance. But there have been lapses, some of them serious, which served to shock Philadelphians into the realization that a heritage, however prized, must be renewed in every generation.

On May 12, 1844, Francis Patrick Kenrick, bishop of Philadelphia, published the following notice to the Catholics of the city and county of Philadelphia:

> Beloved Children—in the critical circumstances in which you are placed, I feel it my duty to suspend the exercises of public worship in the Catholic churches, which still remain, until it can be resumed with safety, and we can enjoy our constitutional rights to worship God according to the dictates of our conscience. . . .

Mobs and 5,000 troops roamed the streets in a warlike atmosphere. Two Roman Catholic churches were burned down, and volunteer firemen were afraid to extinguish the blaze of the smoldering churches and of Irish homes in the neighborhood. Local authorities, incapable of coping with the violent passions which swirled through the bloody streets, called upon the militia. Fourteen persons were killed and some fifty wounded. Forty dwellings and their contents were destroyed. Two rectories and several convents lay in ruins. Hundreds of Irish Catholics, homeless and hunted like animals by boisterous mobs, sought refuge, many in the homes of anguished Protestants. The Bishop himself was welcomed into the home of a Protestant minister. The mayor of Philadelphia, trying desperately to calm the rioters assembled before St. Augustine's Church, was felled by a brick. Death, arson, and hatred presided over the birthplace of American liberty, spilling over into many other American communities.

What had evoked such a frightful nightmare in the City of Brotherly Love? Bishop Kenrick had protested that the religious conscience of Roman Catholics was violated in the public schools by the singing of hymns, by the recitation of prayers, and by the use of the King James version of the Bible instead of the Douay (Catholic) Bible. The Board of School Controllers responded with a ruling that no children whose parents are conscientiously opposed could be required to attend, or join in, the reading of the Bible; and that any particular version of the Bible might be furnished children without comment.

The hatred and violence which swirled through the streets of Philadelphia in that wild episode left a scar on the city's consciousness.

Religious tension flared in Philadelphia again in the 1930's. Nazi propaganda, exported from Hitler Germany, found an echo in Philadelphia, as in many other cities throughout the United States. The anti-Semitic poison which Father Charles Coughlin transmitted via his radio program found a ready reception among the many extremist groups then flourishing in Philadelphia. The city was the headquarters for the national hate sheet of the German-American Bund.

A minimum of 9,000 Philadelphians, some of them men of influence, were members of the Ku Klux Klan. Some thirty fascist, anti-Semitic "hate" groups operated out of Philadelphia. Vandalism was a daily occurrence. The climate was harshly uncongenial to Jews, liberals, and men and women of good will.

Eventually, Philadelphia rose to the challenge and asserted its traditions of brotherhood. On October 11, 1941, twelve people, representing four organizations, met and created the Philadelphia Fellowship Commission to pool their strength in building a better climate for group relations. Their goal: "intergroup understanding and equal treatment and opportunity for all racial, religious, and nationality groups." Their budget was precisely nothing, their staff consisted of three professionals on part-time loan from constituent organizations, and they seemed to be fighting a losing battle. The community at large considered problems of discrimination to be problems of concern only to the victims—Jews, Catholics, Negroes—and not to the total community.

From tiny beginnings, the commission became a powerful conscience of the city, an extraordinary vehicle of intergroup understanding, at least among community leaders. The commission established the closest of relationships with the school system, sponsoring a program of "intercultural education" which blazed trails in human relations. It sponsored distinguished radio programs, exposing bigotry. It drafted statutes and guided them to passage—a city FEPC, a requirement of non-discrimination in public housing. A Code of Fair Housing Practices was developed, followed by a Fair Election Practices Code to eliminate unwarranted racial and religious issues from election campaigns. The climactic achievement of the commission, however, was the drafting of the human rights sections written into the new Philadelphia Charter. Philadelphia was the first city in the country to include such protections and a provision for a Commission on Human Relations in its charter.

Today the Fellowship Commission has nine constituent agencies: American Civil Liberties Union of Greater Philadelphia; Council for Equal Job Opportunity; Fellowship House; International Institute of Philadelphia; Jewish Community Relations Council of Greater Philadelphia; National Association for the Advancement of Colored People—Philadelphia Branch; Greater Philadelphia Council of Churches—Community Services Department; Friends Committee on Race Relations; National Conference of Christians and Jews—Philadelphia Area Office. More than 5,000 individuals are members, and 500 cooperating organizations assist in the work.

The Fellowship Commission is now self-sufficient. It is to the credit of the Philadelphia Jewish community that for nineteen years (until 1960) it made available to the Fellowship Commission at no charge the services of Maurice Fagan, then executive director of the Jewish

Community Relations Council. In 1960, Mr. Fagan became the full-time director of the Fellowship Commission and Jules Cohen, an outstanding Jewish community relations worker on the national scene, became the director of the Philadelphia Jewish Community Relations Council.

The Fellowship Commission had helped to make the community aware of its responsibilities for human relations. But, despite tremendous gains, Philadelphia still faces immense problems, problems of a new dimension arising out of a rapidly shifting population and changing relations among religious and racial groups. The city has a population of about 1,200,000. The ratio has been changing quickly in the past ten years so that today there is almost an equal division of 32 per cent white Protestants, 32 per cent white Catholics, about 22 per cent Negro Christians (mostly Protestants), and 14 per cent Jews. In addition, Protestants and Jews show a much higher rate of movement to the suburbs than do either Catholics or Negroes. Thus, Philadelphia is well on its way to becoming a Roman Catholic city with a heavy Negro minority.

Much of the story of Philadelphia today lies in these statistics. The Protestant community, which always maintained a proprietary attitude because the city was in their hands, has gradually developed a nervous minority response. Protestants feel edgy, picked on, elbowed out. Not effectively united, with continuing tensions among competing denominations, Protestants feel resentful at the steady loss of their power to the Catholic community. Protestants view, with mixed envy and fear, the apparent tightly-knit unity of the Roman Catholic Church. The Roman Catholic community, on the other hand, is riding a crest of self-confidence. Conscious of growing strength, of the vitality of Catholic schools and institutions, the Church appears untroubled by occasional anti-Catholic utterances or discrimination. Indeed, evidences of anti-Catholicism in the general community seem merely to reinforce the main drive of the Roman Catholic Church: to build a total Catholic enclave in Philadelphia—parochial schools, Catholic colleges, and social agencies.

The status of the Jewish community in Philadelphia can be described as secure. Jews are prominent in the political, business, and philanthropic life of Philadelphia. The anti-Semitic atmosphere of the 1930's has been almost totally erased. Between 1939 and 1949 there were hundreds of acts of vandalism against Jewish institutions and property; in the next ten years very few—until the swastikas of 1959.

AGAIN THE SWASTIKA

The wave of swastika daubings and other anti-religious acts of vandalism and defacement which swept across the United States following the first act of depredation in Cologne, Germany, on December 24, 1959, did not bypass Philadelphia. From January 4, 1960, when the first incident took place, to the end of February, approximately sixty-five such acts of vandalism were reported to the police and to the Jewish Community Relations Council of Greater Philadelphia. The rash covered every part of Philadelphia with no discernible pattern. Swastikas were daubed on some Christian churches and buildings, although most were directed against Jewish religious and community institutions. They occurred in all parts of the city and on every day of the week during the seven-week fever period. There was no evidence that this series of anti-religious acts in Philadelphia was the result of an organized conspiracy.

The rash of swastika daubings drew immediate and strong statements of condemnation from all responsible elements in the Greater Philadelphia community in a striking illustration of the effectiveness of the previous twenty years of intergroup education activities. The serious attention which had been given by the city fathers to the elimination of group bigotry, with the resultant constructive changes in the city charter and the creation of the Philadelphia Commission on Human Relations, paid off handsomely in the swastika situation.

Even before the first incident took place on January 4, the police placed every church and synagogue and other religious institution under twenty-four-hour surveillance. Detectives and other police officers were assigned especially to investigate and try to apprehend those guilty of the acts of depredation. The city council early in January adopted a resolution of strong condemnation. Similar action was taken by all other major religious and civic community organizations. To the accompaniment of wide publicity, unequivocal statements of abhorrence were issued by the Jewish Community Relations Council, Catholic Archdiocese, the Protestant Council of Churches, Board of Rabbis, Mayor Richardson Dilworth, Commission on Human Relations, the Philadelphia office of the National Conference of Christians and Jews, the NAACP, the American Legion, the AFL-CIO, and numerous other religious and civic organizations.

Beyond this, the Commission on Human Relations

convened a "Public Inquiry" with the approval and complete cooperation of Mayor Dilworth. Its purpose was "to help place this current outbreak of anti-religious acts in its proper perspective and to allay anxieties by demonstrating to the public that the city is sensitive to and prepared to cope with such outbreaks."

At this "inquiry," a panel of community leaders, made up of members of the Commission on Human Relations and the heads of private intergroup agencies, heard some fourteen "witnesses" from various city departments and community organizations offer specific recommendations for action programs intended to minimize or eliminate the possibility of a recurrence of similar incidents. It was again made abundantly clear at the "inquiry" that all responsible elements in the Greater Philadelphia community looked with passionate disfavor upon this situation and recognized it as a community problem and not a Jewish problem because, in this instance, the acts of vandalism were directed mostly against Jewish institutions. Instead, this was recognized as harmful to the total community just as acts of racism, directed against Negroes, are recognized as being detrimental to the community welfare.

The series of swastika incidents and other anti-religious acts which took place in Philadelphia proved that the virus of group hatred, in this instance anti-Semitism, still existed and required the continuing and ongoing attention of all forces. At the same time, it also proved the value of positive and preventive intergroup education programming and, as regards intergroup relations, that leaders of the city of Philadelphia are determined to repel the virus of bigotry.

With the growth of human rights legislation and the changing atmosphere of the city, discrimination has declined sharply. Jews, like all minority groups, have gained access to once-closed doors of employment, education, and housing in the city. In employment, opportunities are open to Jews in virtually every field, except perhaps some of the bond and brokerage houses and a few of the top law firms in town. (The recurrent charge is that no Jew, Italian, or Pole is employed in any of the top ten law firms in Philadelphia.)

But forward strides are being registered even in the "executive suites" of Philadelphia. The American Jewish Committee conducted a study of Jews in banking, notoriously and traditionally closed to Jews. The study found that the door is slowly opening and that, in addition to the remaining attitudes of prejudice against Jews, a significant problem is "overcoming among Jews their own stereotypes of banking and sensitivities resulting from centuries of persecution and cultural conditioning." The yeast of change is working in the city's elite law firms, too. A striking demonstration was the merger, in 1961, of two of the top law firms in Philadelphia. One firm was originally MacBride, Von Moschzisker, Bradley, and Carroll. The other was Wolf, Block, Shore, and Solis-Cohen. Many of the partners in this merger have worked together in intergroup relations and political endeavors. No doubt, this widely-publicized merger will give impetus to the employment of Jews (and probably Negroes, too) in non-Jewish law firms.

Housing barriers against Jews, once notorious in sections of Philadelphia, have crumbled rapidly. Finding a good apartment or a house to live in is no real problem for Jewish citizens; at worst, there may be minor irritations or inconveniences. The hard core of the problem is housing discrimination against non-whites. For Jews, only a few of the posh apartment houses in the city and some sections of exurbia out on the Main Line are still verboten. Occasionally, an ad like this will appear in one of the papers: "If you enjoy living in a street where every house is lighted at Christmas, come to —." But Philadelphia, like most cities, has experienced kaleidoscopic changes of population during the last decade of extreme mobility. Some of the sections from which Jews were once rigorously excluded are now heavily, perhaps even predominantly, Jewish. Such rapid changes in the religious character of the community do create problems of adjustment and accommodation for all groups, particularly in relation to the schools.

Leaders of the Jewish community feel concern about discrimination in higher education. Recently, the Philadelphia Fellowship Commission and the Jewish Community Relations Council jointly undertook a study of the admission policies of the various medical schools located in the city. This was followed by a comprehensive five-year study of the experiences of pre-medical students graduated from the University of Pennsylvania and the School of Liberal Arts at Temple University in seeking admission into medical schools elsewhere. The study turned up a wealth of fascinating material, including the following excerpts:*

---

* A five-year study of the selection of medical students by the Philadelphia Fellowship Commission and the J.C.R.C., December, 1957.

The applicant's religious background . . . bears clear relationship to acceptance for medical training. Religion cuts across every other factor, including scholastic grades, extracurricular participation, and even father's occupation. Although there were variations and anomalies in the data, it is evident that Protestants fared best, Catholics next, and Jews least well.

When students of the same scholastic level but of different religions are compared, Protestant applicants are accepted more frequently than Catholic or Jewish in every grade category. The only "A" students who were rejected were Catholic and Jewish. A higher percentage of Protestant "B" students was accepted than of Jewish "B+" students. Whereas no Protestant "A" and "B+" student was rejected, 12 per cent of both Jewish and Catholic "A" students were rejected, and 20 per cent of Catholic "B+" and 37 per cent of Jewish "B+" students were rejected. In the "B" grade category 32 per cent Protestant, 76 per cent Catholic, and 70 per cent Jewish students were rejected.

When students of different religions are compared on both scholastic grades and participation in extracurricular activities, it is found that (despite some variations) Jews generally fare worse than Protestants regardless of average grade or category of extracurricular participation. Catholics also seem to suffer a disadvantage, but it is not as marked. For Jews, participation in athletics and/or other activities appeared to have little systematic effect on acceptance, regardless of grades. Yet athletic participation did appear to aid the chances of Protestants with grades below "B+," and Catholics with grades below "A."

Even sons of physicians do not fare as well if their fathers happen also to be Catholic or Jewish. While *every* Protestant applicant with a physician father was accepted, only about three-quarters of Catholic and Jewish students whose fathers practiced medicine gained acceptance.

Among accepted students of all scholastic levels, 78 per cent of Protestants and Catholics, but only 63 per cent of Jews, were able to enter the medical school of their first choice. None of the accepted Protestants, regardless of grade, was obliged to train in schools which he ranked below his third choice; yet 3 per cent of the Catholic and 11 per cent of the Jewish students were obliged to enroll at schools below their third choice.

NATIONAL ORIGIN AS A FACTOR

Medical school applicants whose parents are United States-born have considerably better chances of acceptance than students of foreign-born parentage. This difference may be closely related to the religious factor.

These statistics describe a serious situation. But we must look at them in the perspective of rapid improvement, particularly since the end of World War II.

If Philadelphia is moving toward *racial* equality and better relations between the *races,* experts disagree as to whether the city is making comparable improvement in the relations among the religious *faiths*. One sign is clear and hopeful. Prickly religious issues—which once would have been swept under the rug—are now being discussed with increasing candor and regularity in Philadelphia. But, except for such promising contacts among a handful of leaders at the "summit," there does not appear to be wide-spread progress toward interreligious understanding and cooperation in the community at large.

In Philadelphia, as in most large metropolitan centers in the north, there are four perceptible, legally equal, but psychologically separate communities to reckon with—Catholic, Protestant, Jewish, and Negro. Despite the effectiveness of the Fellowship Commission and other agencies cutting across faith lines, these generally involve only the top leaders. And even these top leaders, working together on civil rights and community problems, spend their social evenings, by and large, with members of their own group. The most active Jewish community workers acknowledge that their own social mingling with non-Jews is not frequent. Jewish groups have been particularly sensitive to the problem of Jewish-Negro relationships. The Jewish Community Relations Committee has set up a committee on Negro-Jewish relationships to overcome unfriendly attitudes and stereotypes in each group about the other and to build upon the positive potentials in each group for good relationships. The program involves stimulating face-to-face social contacts through meetings between Jews and Negroes on a peer-to-peer basis: for example, rabbis and ministers, teachers to teachers, trade unionists to trade unionists. The well-known interreligious "dialogue" is being tried in the interracial area, as well, in Philadelphia.

Few cities in America have waged more diligent war against segregation and discrimination. Yet Philadelphia, too, is still pocketed with racial and religious ghettos. Private housing patterns result in one-group, one-race, one-class neighborhoods. In nineteen public schools, every teacher and every child is Negro. In forty schools, 50 to 90 per cent of the children are Negro. About fifty schools are completely white. In six schools, 90 per cent of the children are Jewish. It is patent that the goal of democratic living is violated when one religious grouping predominates so heavily; or when a colored child can go through his entire public school education and never have a white classmate; or when white children have no healthy relationships with non-white youngsters, except perhaps an occasional (and generally unhelpful) contact with the maid's child. The richness and vitality of democratic living are denied when neighborhoods are thus segregated, whether voluntarily or involuntarily. "How can I teach my kid about other religious and racial groups when we live in a gilded ghetto like this?" is a frequent complaint of sensitive, social-minded parents. Philadelphia has not yet come up with a satisfactory answer.

Protestants and Jews—in the city as in the suburbs—usually get along better together than either group does with Roman Catholics. In part, this is due to the self-induced isolation of the Catholic community, as such, from the mainstream of Philadelphia's cultural and communal life. In addition, Catholic social doctrine not infrequently collides with the prevailing social principles of Protestant and Jewish groups. This is especially true in such issues as censorship, federal aid to parochial schools, and birth control. But frequently, these differences spill over into exasperation on the part of non-Catholics which borders on bigotry in tone.

A leader of Philadelphia Protestants, chatting pleasantly about local issues with a friend and co-worker in the community, suddenly balls his hand into a fist and sputters, "Every time I think of the Catholics——." A well-known rabbi in the community, addressing a forum attended by members of his synagogue, declares, "You just can't trust them." The public image which the non-Catholic has of the Roman Catholic Church in Philadelphia is one of a militant, conservative, aggressive, monolithic institution, preoccupied with its own internal goals, largely isolated from the general community. This image is clearly distorted but the Church shows little interest in correcting it. It is, perhaps, revealing that a Catholic dignitary, with whom an interview was sought for this chapter, refused on the grounds that a frank report of interreligious relationships would only "help the Communists."

Protestant and Jewish leaders agree that the Roman Catholic community is isolated from the rest of the community. Catholic groups do not participate in the Fellowship Commission, in the United Fund, or in the joint program for securing chaplaincy service for city institutions.

"The Catholic community," says the Rev. William D. Powell, executive secretary of the Greater Philadelphia Council of Churches, "appears to try to isolate itself from the rest of the community. It does this in business, industry, social groups, schools, fraternal orders, and even civic bodies. If the Catholic community's goal is to isolate itself, it is succeeding in Philadelphia."

Echoing this view, Mr. Maurice Fagan, director of the

Fellowship Commission, made this distinction in 1959: "The Catholic clergyman is almost completely isolated. But the layman is not. For example, Thomas D. McBride, president of the Fellowship Commission, is a Roman Catholic. Many of the most prominent civic workers in the community are Catholics. But the Church, as such, is withdrawn and aloof from general community affairs."

Roman Catholic leaders defend the Catholic role by pointing out that the Catholic community is actually performing a tremendous service to the general community by financing their own schools, welfare agencies, hospitals, and other institutions. Moreover, Catholic laymen indicate privately that the nature of participation of the Church in the general community depends more on the personality and outlook of the particular archbishop heading the diocese than on abstractions of Catholic doctrine. Some Catholic officials believe that the separatism of the Church has actually contributed to public harmony by not bringing such controversial matters as birth control, divorce, child adoption, and censorship into sharp interreligious collision. They point, for example, to the lack of serious tension between the parochial schools and the public schools. Philadelphia is favorably contrasted with some other large cities where a constant tug-of-war is maintained to keep the balance of power on the school board either Catholic or Protestant.

In 1960 an interreligious squabble in Philadelphia cast its shadow over the national political campaign. To memorialize the four chaplains who had died heroically on the "U.S.S. Dorchester" in World War II, a special Chapel of the Four Chaplains had been created in Philadelphia. Moving spirit behind the Chapel of the Four

Chaplains was Rev. Daniel Poling, editor of the *Christian Herald* and colorful Protestant leader in the community. Dr. Poling's son had been one of the four chaplains. Controversy boiled up when the Chapel of the Four Chaplains was installed in the Baptist church on the campus of Temple University. Although there was a separate entrance from the street to the chapel, Catholic spokesmen excoriated the placement of the chapel in a Protestant church and no member of the clergy attended the dedication exercises or any subsequent event there, in accordance with Catholic dogma. In 1960 Dr. Poling stirred the political winds by charging that John F. Kennedy, a few years earlier, had agreed to participate in a ceremony at the chapel but had canceled out at the urgings of the late Dennis Cardinal Dougherty. The Senator explained that he had accepted the engagement as a Congressman, not as a "representative" of the Roman Catholic Church, and that he declined when his appearance was advertised by the sponsors as official Roman Catholic participation.

In 1960, also, the Chapel of the Four Chaplains named Rabbi Maurice N. Eisendrath, president of the Union of American Hebrew Congregations, as recipient of its Spiritual Freedom citation. Dr. Eisendrath was eager to close any rift which might mar the memory of the four chaplains and their self-sacrifice which, he felt, deserved the fullest recognition from all three religious faiths. He sought to enlist Roman Catholic participation in the ceremony on February 7, 1960, at which he was to receive the citation. After great difficulty and frustration, the appearance of interfaith amity was achieved. While no Roman Catholic clergyman would enter the Baptist church, Dr. Shane MacCarthy, a Catholic layman and executive director of the President's Council on Youth Fitness, finally agreed to address the occasion. Even this fragile compromise was almost upset at the last moment when the program was opened with a religious service. No Roman Catholic could conscientiously participate, in view of canon law, so Dr. MacCarthy felt constrained to absent himself from the religious service, entering later for his stint in the program.

Notwithstanding difficulties like these, Philadelphia survived the 1960 election with relatively little fuss and overt religious tension. Anxiety about a Roman Catholic candidate was not much of a public issue. The question was largely limited to the parlor and the closed meeting. At one such meeting, a proposal was made for the issuance of a three-faith statement against bigotry. The Protestant Council of Churches, an uneasy coalition with many diverse views, chose not to join. Similarly, Protestant leaders at an interfaith seminar preferred not to schedule a discussion of religion in the election. Roman Catholics present were most understanding of the Protestant hesitation. The election brought forth little bitterness. Pronouncedly Democratic Philadelphia gave Kennedy a large 300,000 majority, giving him substantial help in capturing the pivotal state and the nation.

RELIGION AND THE PUBLIC SCHOOLS

Perhaps the most tender problem in the area of interreligious relations has to do with separation of church and state, and specifically the question of religion in the public schools. In this matter, it is the Jewish community which feels the deepest sense of anxiety. The usual Protestant-Jewish cooperation breaks down, Protestant and Catholic groups find themselves supporting the same general thesis, and the Jewish community is isolated except for a small group of humanists, secularists, and liberal Protestants.

What is the issue? The Jewish community believes that religion belongs in the church, the synagogue, and the home—and not in the public schools. It believes in a strict interpretation of the principle of separation of church and state, holding that the government must not aid any or all religions. It believes that bringing religion into public education is divisive, creates ill will and religious conflict, reflects a failure of the churches to reach and teach their children in church schools, and imposes religion unfairly upon a captive audience.

Philadelphia Protestants, as represented by the Council of Churches, recently drew up a statement on this subject which declared that the public schools "may not teach about religion or its values in such a way as to serve the sectarian needs of any ecclesiastical institution individually or collectively." Protestants believe, however, that a good education cannot ignore religion, and that the unstable times in which we live require our children to have a rooting in the Judeo-Christian heritage.

Roman Catholics, once ardent foes of religion in public education, now are among the most vigorous advocates of "recognizing God" in the public schools throughout the United States. This, too, is without doubt a reflection of the rising confidence of the Catholic community; there is now little fear that the religious practices introduced into public education will offend Catholic sensibilities. Many Catholic leaders appear to regard religious practices in the public schools as necessary antidotes to Communism, juvenile delinquency, and other social evils.

These divergent views make some conflict inevitable in Philadelphia. The conflicts take many forms. A teacher seeking to balance the Christmas emphasis in the classroom with some material on Chanuko, calls upon a rabbi for literature and advice. The rabbi declines, pointing out that the Jewish community objects to all religion—Christian or Jewish—in the public schools. A Catholic mother, exasperated by the opposition of Jewish organizations to Christological carols in the schools, drops in at the office of the Philadelphia Fellowship Commission to complain. A Protestant staff member calms her down by asking, "Look, you are a Catholic, I am a Protestant. Would you allow our children to sing 'Jesus is *not* the Son of God'? Well, that is the dilemma of the Jewish mother when we sing carols in the public schools that say 'Jesus *is* the Son of God.' "

Despite such irritations and the annual general rise in temperature, just before Christmas, particularly in the Jewish community, the public schools in Philadelphia proper avoid the extreme kinds of religious programs which have stirred communities elsewhere. The Nativity play, for example, is not part of the usual Christmas celebration. Strong doctrinal programs are discouraged. Teachers are cautioned not to inject sectarian comment. Generally, the less Christological carols are sung. Uniformly, there is full recognition of the right of a child of any faith—or of no faith—not to participate in any such exercise which might offend his conscience. In the suburbs, where the community has not yet come to terms with the sudden influx of non-Christian residents, no such sensitivity is evident. Religious holiday programs, prayers, major events on Friday evenings, unwarranted comments by teachers on a child's absence for religious holidays—all these are sources of annoyance which jolt the quiet of suburbia. Mostly, they appear to arise from an unfamiliarity with Jews and insensitivity to minority problems, rather than out of malice.

Philadelphia has one unusual population characteristic. Many of its suburbs are within the city limits. Suburban character predominates there, however; the city's boundary lines are secondary in significance. Wherever the suburb, its old residents resent newcomers and resist them. Wherever the suburb, problems of interreligious relationships center about the public schools, about sectarian symbols on public property, about an almost-universal absence of real social and personal relationships among suburbanites of differing religious persuasions, even as increasing numbers of these suburbanites affiliate with religious institutions. Political activity is complicated by interreligious tensions, in both major parties. And if a suburb happens to border on a Negro ghetto or that rare suburban phenomenon, an integrated neighborhood, the racial factor looms large in all relationships.

Bible reading in the public schools has been required by law in Pennsylvania. Readings from the Old Testament, and recitation of the Lord's Prayer, occurred daily in schools throughout the state. In 1959, however, a Unitarian family in Abington, a suburb outside the city limits, brought suit challenging the constitutionality of these practices, denying the right of school authorities to compel their children to attend such religious exercises. The total Jewish community was in deep conflict as to whether to join in this action. Undoubtedly, virtually all Jewish groups sympathized with the plaintiffs and wished them well in their action. But the Jewish Community Relations Council, representing the organized Jewish community, decided not to enter the case, fearing harmful interreligious effects. The American Jewish Congress, dissenting from the JCRC view, did join as *amicus curiæ*. In going into the case, the American Jewish Congress irritated many Jewish leaders who felt that Bible reading was not a top priority in the scale of church-state problems for the Jewish community. In addition, there is an unspoken tradition in Philadelphia which lays great stress on "working things out," on reasonable accommodation, and a legal fight seemed out of keeping to many Philadelphians.

A three-judge federal court handed down a far-reaching decision, striking down compulsory Bible reading and the Lord's Prayer as contrary to both state and Federal constitutions. The case has been appealed to the U.S. Supreme Court. In the meantime, the Pennsylvania State Legislature complicated the situation by amending the statute to make attendance at compulsory Bible reading voluntary. This too was struck down by the court.

In 1961, the Philadelphia Jewish Community Relations Council, reversing its earlier position, filed a brief *amicus* in the Schempp case. Interestingly, the decision was made unanimously by the many groups which comprise the J.C.R.C. Of equal significance, the J.C.R.C. action was accepted with equanimity by the non-Jewish, as well as the Jewish, community, evoking few of the bitter letters to the editor, hostile phone calls, and similar expressions which often follow in the wake of church-state controversies in many communities.

In November, 1959, when the nation was watching a controversy resulting from the Roman Catholic bishops' attack upon a proposal for birth control information as part of the American foreign aid programs, the late Cardinal O'Hara published a pastoral letter to his flock, denouncing those who urge birth control as the answer to the population explosion. His statement was hailed by other Catholic spokesmen as an authoritative and significant expression of Catholic thought. It said, in part: ". . . If they do any research at all, they must know that in this country only Catholics and Negroes show any extraordinary increase in the births—the latter about 60 per cent and the former 100 per cent over the totals of, say, fifteen years ago. Are those who want to supplant divine wisdom by their own planning disturbed by this? Let them leave us to God. We ask no sympathy."

BETTER UNDERSTANDING

Maurice Fagan has pioneered in the creation of a Seminar on interreligious understanding, held under the auspices of the Fellowship Commission, which he directs. The seminar meets four or five times a year, bringing together some thirty representatives of the Protestant, Roman Catholic, and Jewish groups for frank discussions of interreligious issues. They speak as individuals, and they speak openly. Through the seminar, a dialogue has been created which makes it possible for a few leaders to ventilate their fears and concerns, to exchange their honest views, and to develop some mutual understanding.

The Jewish Community Relations Council, under the spirited leadership of Jules Cohen, has sparked a series of interreligious conversations between Protestant and Jewish leaders. The Protestant Council of Churches has demonstrated its deep interest by making available the top clerical and lay religious leaders of Protestant denominations. Candid and friendly discussion has ranged over such touchy and important topics as "the chosen people," Sunday laws, Bible reading, Israel, the crucifixion story, and Zionism. The hope is that this new process of communication can be brought down to the neighborhood level throughout the city.

But Mr. Fagan feels the problem of interreligious relationships is not being met adequately in Philadelphia. "There is nothing in the press, radio, or television that shows any real promise of developing interreligious leadership. There is nothing that I can see in the seminaries —Christian and Jewish—which holds any real hope of promoting interreligious understanding. Somehow, somewhere, we will have to find ways to get our religious forces to teach respect for each other's faith and, also, to work together—all of them—more effectively for common community goals."

But if any city can be looked to for leadership and creativity in coping with the new dimensions of human relations, it is Philadelphia. The will is there, the tradition is there, and the resources are there. The Commission on Human Relations, the Fellowship Commission, the Friends—these, and many more, are struggling to preserve the vision of William Penn.

One of the most interesting and hopeful of such agencies is Fellowship House (associated with the Fellowship Commission). Fellowship House is a beacon that shines above the miasma of misunderstanding. Its founder, Miss Marjorie Penney, was honored, along with Maurice Fagan, with the Philadelphia Award (a gold medal and $10,000) for outstanding service to the city. Its objective is "to help build communities where prejudice and discrimination give way to opportunity and equal rights for all."

At Fellowship House, people of varied backgrounds learn to understand others and themselves. Twelve other cities have Fellowship Houses, all patterned after Philadelphia's.

Fellowship House has offered the city's only opportunity for people of all faiths and races to meet their common Father together. Services are held the third Sunday of each month with distinguished preachers of various denominations. These services are held at a time when they will not interfere with the regularly scheduled services of the churches.

At the Christmas-Chanuko season, Jews and Christians break bread together and learn that there is nothing to fear from religions which teach brotherhood and peace, a heritage to all. Likewise, they learn that Chanuko marks the first struggle for religious liberty, also a heritage to all men without regard to creed or color or nationality.

"How do we operate?" The quiet-mannered, yet dynamic, Miss Penney repeated a question often asked her. "We ask God and tell people. From the beginning we were church people. I see things that deal with human relations start and stop or get so organized that all the life is choked out of them. We got practically nothing from the churches when we started, but our convictions were strong. We started in an abandoned firehouse in 1941.

"When the Philadelphia Award was made in 1948 we got our first sizable recognition. We had Catholics, Protestants, and Jews, non-Christians, Buddhists, Moslems —many different kinds of people, but their roots had to be religious. The Jews and the Christians would pray together. We have Jews who come to us who are better Jews when they leave us; Christians are better Christians and Moslems are better Moslems, too. Fellowship House does not tear you from your roots but sends you back more useful, more clear.

"Fellowship House bakes a hundred loaves of bread at a time, each with three marks on it. One indicates that every living man needs bread. Another indicates that every living person in the world needs education for his mind and opportunities for his hands. And the third means that every person needs affection and understanding for his heart."

Philadelphia, like every other city, has its problems of race, religion, and group relations. But unlike many another American city, the resources of social creativity and civic imagination are being brought to bear in their solution in Philadelphia.

PLAINVIEW
From Potatoes to Rhubarb

A DECADE AGO, WHAT IS NOW PLAINVIEW WAS A SERIES OF Long Island potato farms about forty miles from New York City. Today, it is a typical, thriving suburban community with a population of over 30,000 men, women, and children—mostly children. The well-kept ranch and split-level houses were built at prices ranging from $13,000 to $30,000 and most of them have FHA or GI mortgages. The tax situation is serious, ranging from $500 to $900 per family, mostly for schools.

The community practically exploded into being. From a small, two-classroom schoolhouse ample for a farm community, Plainview has expanded to nine elementary schools, a junior high school, and a spanking new high school, which boasts a swimming pool, tennis courts, and an auditorium that many a commercial theater would envy. Yet more facilities are acutely needed.

Plainview was once solidly Christian. Today, it is a religiously heterogeneous community. Racially, it is still homogeneous. No Negroes own homes in Plainview as of 1961. Just under 50 per cent of the community is Roman Catholic; 35 per cent Jewish; 15 per cent Protestant. While there is little formal contact among the churches and synagogues, Jews and Christians as individuals work well together. Four Jews were elected in 1957 to the recently-centralized seven-man school board. Two Catholics and one Protestant made up the rest of the board.* In general, newcomers were accepted without animosity of any consequence. That is, until the "incident"—the issue of religious holiday observances in the public schools—broke in town.

What follows is a study in depth of this incident as it unfolded in a rather typical American suburban community. The study is, consequently, different in two ways from the other parts of this book. It is narrower in scope. It makes no attempt to depict or analyze interreligious relationships in Plainview beyond one incident. And, second, it concludes with recommendations, from the expert who prepared it, to both Christians and Jews in every community who inevitably face incidents like the one which follows.

In December, 1956, the clergymen in Plainview received a policy statement worked out by the public school administrators on moral and spiritual values and on the observance of Christmas and other national holidays. The district principal had received some calls from Christian parents who had heard rumors that carols might be eliminated. He suggested a meeting with the clergymen to discuss the statement. The statement itself urged that moral and spiritual values be taught in the schools, called for a "non-sectarian" prayer to begin the school day, and declared that Christmas parties, music, art, stories, poems, and such have the same place in the public school program as any other curriculum materials, provided they are presented so as not to influence the religious convictions of anyone. The statement implied

---

* In 1961, it was three Catholics, two Protestants, and two Jews.

that the singing of Christmas carols and religious songs should not be restricted, although the needs of the children and community should be considered in the selection of material.

One of the rabbis in the community replied. Citing the stands of national Jewish organizations, he declared that religion does not belong in the public schools. Religious teaching, he said, is the task of the church, the synagogue, and the home—not the public schools. He predicted the policy statement would stir interreligious discord. With regard to "non-sectarian" prayers, he expressed fear that such prayer would be synthetic and meaningless. He felt that neither Christmas nor Chanuko, nor any religious holiday, should be celebrated in the public schools.

Deeply concerned about the statement, the rabbi met with a group of Jewish leaders to discuss the question. They approved the rabbi's letter and agreed that it would be unwise to create a public issue. Instead, an effort should be made to work the problem out by informal discussions with the school administration and the Board of Education.

What follows are entries in the diary of one of the Plainview Jewish leaders as this community drama unfolded.

MARCH, 1957

I called the district principal and he graciously offered to drop in at my home to discuss the problem "for a few minutes." It took three hours. He said that the statement had been drawn up in order to avoid the kinds of rumors which swept the community during recent Christmas seasons—that carols were banned, for example—and to give guidance to school personnel. He didn't know much about the general question of separation of church and state, and made it clear that he had confidently expected the statement to be applauded by Jews as well as by Protestants and Catholics. I filled him in on the views of the Jewish community, gave him some literature, and made it quite clear we were not asking for Chanuko to be included. He thanked me for my frankness and said he would now sound out some of the Christian leaders.

OCTOBER, 1957

At the suggestion of our informal committee of Jewish leaders, I talked with the president of the school board and, as a result of that conversation, I was asked to meet with the entire board and the district principal. We again covered the entire subject, as I did with the district principal last spring. At the end of the meeting, the board announced it would now write its own policy statement and would solicit the views of all the clergymen. They stated their unanimous view that "sectarian and religious practices" do not belong in the public schools. I went home happy, confident that things were working out.

LATER IN OCTOBER, 1957

Well, the board did as it promised. They called together all the clergymen to discuss this whole thing. The two rabbis in town submitted their views in writing. They said religion in public education violates the principle of separation of church and state, but they recognized that Christmas has taken on aspects of a national celebration and that its observance in the public schools is of long standing. They urged that, at the least, a distinction be drawn between the deeply religious or doctrinal aspects of Christmas observances and such practices as gift-giving, Christmas trees, and harmless songs. The meeting was friendly. The Christian ministers disagreed with the rabbis in some matters, but the board felt it could now draw up a statement to the total community.

We shall see.

THE STORM BREAKS

NOVEMBER 27, 1957

All hell has broken loose in Plainview! Last night, we had the kind of Board of Education meeting about which I've read but never really believed possible. The gym was filled and then some. The meeting was turbulent, to say the least, with clear anti-Semitic overtones.

Ten days ago, every resident received a copy of the guide for the observance of holiday seasons in our schools, written by the Board of Education following their meetings with me and the clergymen. That statement didn't satisfy the Jewish leaders, but we could live with it, since it recognized both the realistic impossibility of removing all celebrations connected with religious holidays from the schools and at the same time cautions against sectarian observances and doctrinal activity or discussion.

Our informal Jewish committee met and agreed that this was a vast improvement over the district principal's previous statement, even though we still had many reservations. On behalf of all of us, the rabbis replied in writing to the guide.

Over the week-end, it became clear that there was much concern in the Christian community over the guide. There was a flurry of telephoning. It was mentioned in sermons, and everyone in town soon knew that last night's board meeting would be the occasion for the generation of much more heat.

What a night! For four hours, over 500 people, mostly non-Jews, heatedly discussed this problem. The rabbi represented all Jewish organizations, and he stated his views to the accompaniment of heckling, boos, and even some openly anti-Semitic remarks. At one point a heckler asked him if he had been born in America!

The board stuck to its position. The guide was not changed, though the board did agree to write a supplementary statement as preamble, incorporating a recognition of religious values and beliefs.

Until now, the informal Jewish committee had felt it unwise to communicate to the total Jewish community either the nature of the problem or our activities in handling it. Now that the fight is in the open, we've agreed to send one letter in the name of all five Jewish organizations telling the community exactly what has happened and why.

DECEMBER 20, 1957

What a month this has been! The Board of Education policy respecting religious holiday programs is darned near the only subject of conversation in Plainview. It's difficult to assess the general climate but, in general, the Jewish community appears to support the stand of our committee, even though an occasional, "Why did you start this fracas?" or "I sang Christmas carols and it never hurt me," or even "you weren't speaking for me" reached us in the innumerable telephone calls we have received. Among Christians, there's no question about it: they don't want any "tampering with Christmas programs" and they're out to change the policy of the board.

At the board's weekly business meeting, so many people turned up that a second meeting of the board was convened. They finished their regular business meeting in the board offices, then moved to a school. The telephones were really working overtime, because by 9:30 more than 250 people were at the school. The non-Jews held a caucus and chose a committee of six to represent them before the board. I presented the views of the Jewish organizations.

I had to remind everyone that all Jewish organizations continue to believe that no religious observances, songs, decorations, or symbols belong in public schools, then added that we were not asking for the elimination of all such programs but were urging some consideration toward keeping them on a non-doctrinal basis, at least. They weren't buying any generalizations. I had to be specific about crosses, Nativity scenes, trees, "Silent Night," and angels.

The board decided to meet privately with a committee of Christians and Jews, and we got together on Sunday. What a difference! No acrimony, no heckling—though the conflicts were just as deep. We finally reached a compromise which both sides were willing to accept. So I don't forget the details myself, I'd better record them:

1. Introductory paragraph acknowledging importance of belief in God and religion.

2. Christmas programs would continue in the schools,

but all personnel were to be guided by "non-doctrinal" considerations. (This was a compromise; I wanted "non-theological" and the Christians didn't like the idea altogether.)

3. "Customary" songs could be sung. (This was our concession. They wanted "traditional" songs; we wanted carols excluded completely.)

4. Teachers were to consult with the district principal (who'd consult with the board) if they were in doubt.

DECEMBER 22, 1957

Well, the board distributed their new guide tonight. What a shocker! This statement says, in effect:

1. There's general acknowledgment of the importance of belief in God in American society. The responsibility for religious training, though, belongs in church, synagogue, and home, not public schools. So far, so good.

2. Holidays like Christmas and Chanuko have a proper place in the schools. Exchange of gifts, trees, singing of customary songs and carols are all permitted. The understanding about "non-doctrinal" programs doesn't appear. Carols are specifically mentioned, and, of all things, Chanuko is dragged in and OK'd, despite our understanding to the contrary.

We raised Cain with the president of the Board of Education, and the rabbis are writing him for the Jewish community. But we're not going to press for cancellation of this year's Chanuko programs, since they're already in rehearsal and we don't want the kids to bear the burden in this controversy.

The newspapers are having a field day with this fight, especially in the "Letters to the Editor." Although many of the letters were moderate and intelligent, in some letters Jews have been called atheists and no-good Communists. We've answered only one, both because it was decent and because it named me specifically. I emphasized separation of church and state and urged more and more religious observances, more and more recognition of Jesus' birthday in all its religious significance—but outside the public schools. I responded to a reference to business and financial profits by decrying the over-commercialization of Christmas and suggesting that this is a Christian problem; they've created this emphasis on gift-giving and parties at Christmas time.

The Jewish organizations' committee is definite about not dropping this matter. We'll wait to see how the board answers our letter.

JANUARY, 1958

The Board of Education answered our letter after Christmas, and now we're more confused than ever. They wrote that Chanuko programs are optional, not required, and they assume that they were historical and cultural in nature, not religious. Then they said that their second policy statement, the stinger, did not replace the first, but is merely an amplification of it. This just isn't so. The new statement does not refer in any way to the earlier statement which clearly is now a dead letter. Fortunately, they wound up their letter with an offer to meet with us. The session is scheduled early next month.

FEBRUARY, 1958

It was a sour meeting. The board made it clear to the Jewish delegation that they have no intentions of changing their policy statement on holiday observance. They did agree to make public our letter and their reply of December 26, which indicated that the first statement was not rescinded by the second. We got nowhere on Chanuko; they won't eliminate the programs, though we hit hardest at that.

MAY, 1958

The darndest things happen in Plainview! A gang of us were sitting at a Little League baseball game the other week and Mac brought up the whole Christmas-school controversy. At the Little League board meeting a couple of days later, a group of us talked about the problem. What came out of that discussion was a meeting of fourteen of us—Protestants, Catholics, and Jews. I could almost hear the tension when we sat down to talk, but it disappeared quickly. The whole story came out, all sides and all attitudes. We were pleased at the number of things we agreed on:

We can live with Christmas programs which include a few customary songs; Chanuko doesn't belong in the schools as long as the Jewish groups don't want it; Nativity scenes and crèches and such don't belong, either; and we don't think of this as the opening wedge in a campaign to drive Christmas programs out of school altogether. We decided we would convene additional meetings like this and expand the number of people. Each of the fourteen promised to invite two others.

JULY, 1958

Plainview is an OK community. I'm proud of it. Three larger meetings have taken place since May. Thirty-five persons attended a meeting in June at the temple—pretty equally divided among the faiths. Some sixty-five came to the second June meeting at the Methodist church. Forty-five showed up at the July meeting, including most of the members of the Board of Education. At each of the meetings, the chairman of the original group gave the entire story. Tom Dailey is Roman Catholic, a wonderful guy, very active in the community, and most fair-minded. At each meeting, he set forth the "understandings" which became better crystallized each time. At early meetings, there was plenty of suspicion and some fears, but as the meetings progressed, there was much less of that and much more mutual respect.

Among other agreements reached at these get-togethers, it was decided to stimulate discussions of this subject at organization meetings and parlor meetings, preferably on an interreligious basis. As a result, P.T.A.'s, civic organizations, and service clubs have talked this matter over intelligently. The Citizens Advisory Committee to the Public School is planning a community forum. While they have not yet discussed the issue, the rabbis and Protestant clergymen have had good, frank meetings, and they are even planning a joint religious census in the community.

JANUARY, 1959

Well, Christmas and Chanuko have come and gone and all is quiet on the public school front. The interreligious "Continuations Committee" has really brought light where there was too much heat. And, you know, for all the endless meetings, boiling tempers, and excitement, I can't help thinking that Plainview is a better town for having gone through the "issue." Maybe an incident like that forces a community to discover itself and to think through where it stands.

SEPTEMBER, 1959

All of a sudden I'm a prophet with honor in my own community. The Plainview hassle appeared in the local newspapers and all kinds of people have written me about it. One of the national Jewish organizations asked me to put down on paper such lessons as can be learned from the Christmas-Chanuko issue in our town. This has been a great experience. So I finally wrote down the following "helpful hints" and words of caution which might be borne in mind by the school system, the Jewish group, and the Christian community in situations similar to ours.

GUIDE LINES

School people can help to keep to a minimum and perhaps avoid community controversy and divisiveness along religious lines entirely if they would keep the following in mind:

1. Members of boards of education, superintendents of schools, principals, and teachers should be knowledgeable about the general subject of church-state relationships in the United States and especially regarding the area of religion and public education.

It is not for me to say how this should be done, but it strikes me, since school people are bound to be confronted with religion and public school problems, they should be given a course or at least some lectures on the subject in the teacher-training colleges which they attend.

National, state, and local associations of administrators, school boards, and teacher associations can do a better job with school personnel.

2. School personnel, particularly administrators, should realize that the subject of religious holiday programs in the schools cannot be treated casually in a heterogeneous community. There should be intensive discussion within the school system, at all levels, before formal action is taken. In our case, it came as a shock to learn the district principal's statement had not even been checked with the Board of Education before it was put into effect.

3. This may come as a radical thought, but school administrators may be better advised not to attempt to put a policy into writing. I know this makes it a little tougher on the building principals and the teachers, but it sure can save the community a severe interreligious headache. With no written policy, Jews and Christians are less likely to make an issue of the school programs which may not be to their liking. On the other hand, a formal written policy forces a crystallization and a defense of particular viewpoints. The respective adherents to particular positions are constrained to react to a written policy lest their silence be construed as approval or acceptance.

4. There is no room for heroics by anyone. Christian school personnel should not take positions as defenders of the faith. By the same token, school people who may be agnostics or civil libertarians should not ignore the existence of religious groups and the deep feelings of citizens who are religiously committed. The district principal's 1956 statement is a good example of the first extreme. The first statement of the Board of Education, which made no mention of Christmas or Christians, but

instead referred vaguely to the winter season, good will, and differing cultures, is an illustration of the other extreme. Neither will be acceptable and either kind will cause a blow-up in the community.

5. Assuming the decision has been made to write a policy statement, some important "do's" and "don'ts" seem to be:

a. Plan carefully. The Christmas season has been and will continue to be with us for a long time. The world won't come to an end if the statement isn't published *this* year. Thoughtful planning can make even the controversial issue of religious holiday programs in the schools a medium for education in the community, for better schools and a better community. No planning, hasty or poor planning, may embroil the schools and the community in interreligious controversy.

b. Careful planning means an advance process of discussion and self-education in the school community— for as long a period as necessary and concurrently with:

c. Consultation with all the clergymen and the leaders of the religious and civic groups in the community, followed by discussions in the respective religious institutions and organizations and in the community-at-large. I am convinced it is far better to have differences of views aired in the calm context of discussing a community problem in preparation for a statement of policy rather than have them injected into an emergency situation in what can become a religious war.

6. Lastly, it would be wonderful if school administrators would stand up for the public schools and not run for cover and rush to comply with the wishes of a particular religious pressure group—Christian or Jewish. School people know that the school is not "Godless" and

that they do a pretty good job of teaching moral and ethical values. Let them say so and they may be pleasantly surprised to learn there is a large body of citizen opinion which will support their position and respect them all the more for their courage and devotion to the public school system.

Jews can learn much from an experience such as the one in our town. Let me list some lessons for the Jewish community:

1. As a Jew, I am satisfied that the position taken by our Jewish organizations on this issue is a sound one. It is best for the democratic ideal, for public education, and the religious freedom of all faiths to keep religion out of the schools. The pressures against our position are great and I know how difficult it is to withstand them, but I would urge against any change. Our position on principle is good. The problems arise in connection with their application in specific situations as in our case.

2. My deep involvement in the situation in our town forced me to do a lot of thinking and a great deal of studying of the subject of church-state relations and the relationship of religion to public education. We were lucky in our situation in that the two rabbis of our town were knowledgeable on the subject, but I have talked with rabbis from neighboring communities who were referred to me by our rabbi and I was appalled at their lack of information. So much depends on what the rabbi knows, not only about the subject but, more important, how to deal with concrete situations. If it isn't being done, students for the rabbinate should be given a thorough grounding in the subject before they leave the theological seminaries.

3. In this connection, I would respectfully advance

another thought for the rabbis. They ought not try to handle matters such as this on their own. We were wise in having the issue discussed in the congregation and its Social Action Committee before any contact was made with the school system. I say without hesitation that had our rabbi written his first letter to the District Principal or otherwise taken action without the understanding support of the lay leaders of the congregation, he would have been in serious trouble.

4. We were also lucky in the decision we made in our Social Action Committee to bring the issue to the attention of the other Jewish organizations in our town. We felt the lack of a Jewish community council or a community relations committee, and I would heartily recommend the establishment of such a central community channel where none exists. But, failing such a permanent set-up, I commend creating at the outset of a specific situation an informal committee of leaders of Jewish organizations such as we have. It made for better understanding in the Jewish community and greater respect from the Christian community.

5. There is no such thing as a private, informal approach to the school system or off-the-record negotiations with the school administration or the Christian community. In fact, such attempts lead only to charges of conspiracy and deviousness. Moreover, they are ineffective. In retrospect, I realize now, we made a mistake in this regard. It is much healthier to deal with the matter on the basis of open covenants openly arrived at. Attempts at private talks and negotiations with the school administration lends credence to the mistaken impression that this issue is one between Jews and Christians only and

not a community problem. Dealing with it openly and publicly may not avert community dissension but it will avoid the added complication of suspicion of motive and methods.

6. We also learned that it is essential to carry on an educational program within the Jewish community. But it sure is a rough row to hoe. One meeting or distributing the printed materials from the national Jewish agencies doesn't begin to do the job. Not enough members of a given organization attend the particular meeting; most do not read what they receive in the mail and even if they do, reading a few printed items is only the beginning.

7. Jewish leaders with responsibility for dealing with these matters must be prepared to take abuse. From Jews as well as from Christians! Then there were the many telephone calls at odd hours with the caller hanging up when I answered the telephone. But these irritations are minor compared to the calls from uninformed or scared Jews, usually not identified with any synagogue or other Jewish organization, who complained bitterly about our "antagonizing" the Christians and how else will Christians know about Judaism and Jews if there are no Chanuko programs in the schools? I spent hours on the telephone —literally—in an effort to interpret the whys and wherefores of the issue, our position, and our actions to a number of such individuals. One of the satisfactions in our situation was the way in which the leaders of our Jewish organizations stuck to their guns. But it isn't easy and requires an assertion of leadership and steadfastness to positions of principle.

8. In a concrete local situation, we learned you have to spell out to the last jot and tittle just what you will accept

and what you cannot live with. A position must be taken on each specific aspect of a school Christmas program: the tree, decorations, parties, exchanges of gifts, and carols. Especially carols. Will you accept the inclusion of any carols? If so, how many? Which of the carols? At this point, there is the danger of appearing to ask for the opportunity of screening or censoring carols. In our case, we said that as Jews we would never place ourselves in the position of censors and I think we were right. In any event, generalities won't do and the Jewish group in a community situation must be prepared to say where it stands in the most specific and detailed terms.

9. I know we made a number of mistakes in our case, but the one which stands out most is our failure to take the matter to the Christian community either before or concurrent with our approach to the school system. Where Christian contacts exist, so much the better. Where they don't, they can be found. In our town, Little League relationships between Christians and Jews provided the channel of communication. In other places, other inter-sectarian and civic activities can serve the same purpose. But, however it is done, the importance of frank and open discussion with Christians cannot be overempha-sized. It's still the best way of allaying suspicions, pre-venting distortions, scotching rumors, and fostering un-derstanding, if not complete agreement.

10. Jews must recognize that Christians, by and large, are bewildered by the charge that it is wrong to celebrate Christmas in the schools. To them, Christmas is a symbol of good will, brotherhood, and friendliness. How can any-one object unless as part of a conspiracy to take God out of the schools? Or out of antichristian or antireligious

motives? This means we must patiently explain the issue and our position. That this should be done by Jews identified with the religious community goes without saying. Otherwise, we lend substance to the charge of irreligious motivation. We must also be alert to the Christian view that observance of Christmas in the schools is a matter of right and any attempt to take away any part or eliminate entirely what many Christians consider rightfully belongs to them, will be bitterly resented. We learned that much of the anti-Jewish reaction of Christians stems from a fear that Jews are trying to take something away from them. The violent reaction is defensive in the sense that these Christians are trying to safeguard what they believe is properly theirs by every moral right.

11. To the extent possible in a given situation, the views of the Jewish group should be put in writing. Rumors are rampant when the explosion comes, and distortions fill the air. The safest bet is to write it down so there can be no misunderstandings. Oral statements lend themselves to misinterpretations; so do written statements, but not to the same extent.

12. Finally, I would point out the extreme difficulty, if not the impossibility, of sticking strictly to principle and acting accordingly. In principle, we should oppose any and all Christmas programs no matter what their content. As a practical matter, this cannot be done. For one thing, the price of such an effort must be continuing interreligious dissension from year to year. Secondly, the Jewish community will rebel and disavow its rabbis and lay leaders if they were to suggest taking so pristine a position. I am convinced that few, if any, Jews will support a campaign looking toward the elimination of all

recognition of Christmas in the schools. I would caution local communities against taking this logical but unrealistic position.

The Christian community also can learn some lessons from the experiences in our town:

1. Christians must take into account the religious composition of the community. Where the community is religiously mixed, they should take into consideration the sensitivities of their Jewish friends and neighbors and realize that Christmas programs in the schools cannot take the form of church or home celebrations.

2. They should recognize the fear in the Jewish community that, if left unopposed, new religious content may be added to the Christmas programs. The song, "Go Tell It on the Mountain," which is not a Christmas carol but was sung in our schools, is evidence that there is justification for this fear.

3. Christians, too, should become informed on the subject of church-state relations in the United States and especially about problems in the area of religion and public education. They should apply Christian principles of fair play and understanding by recognizing the community nature of such problems and avoid leveling charges against Jews and others who disagree with them.

4. They should be willing to discuss the matter with Jewish representatives, without giving up any of the principles in which they believe but also without acrimony. Such discussions can be held in a spirit of seeking a workable compromise solution to an explosive and delicate community problem. In this respect, we were most fortunate in Plainview. I am convinced that the same understanding and cooperation can be found in the Christian community of every other city.

5. Lay Christian leaders must not assume their ministers and priests are necessarily well-informed on the subject. They may be, but then again, perhaps not. A Christian clergyman who is not knowledgeable on the issue of church-state relations is likely to take an extreme position in defense of the faith, as he sees it. This only adds fuel to the fire and hinders finding a solution. Where necessary and, of course, by going through proper channels, consultation should be had with national Christian religious bodies such as the National Catholic Welfare Conference, the National Council of Churches of Christ in the U.S.A., or individual national Protestant denominational groups.

6. As in the case of the Jewish group, the Christians must decide for themselves where they are willing specifically to draw the line between what should be included in school Christmas programs and what should be left out. This means a lot of thinking about and discussion of the issue, some soul-searching plus a weighing of the values of good community interreligious relationships on the one hand and, on the other, fighting for Christmas programs in the schools which are not much different from church services. In our town, responsible Christian leadership said immediately that such markedly devotional practices as processionals, Nativity scenes, and Nativity plays do not belong in the schools, but in the churches and in the home.

7. Again, as in our own situation within the Jewish community, Christian leaders who work out a compromise yet acceptable formula with their Jewish neighbors must anticipate that they will be attacked by extremists in the Christian community who will contend they have sold out to the Jews in going along with the compromise

solution. The essential point is that steadfastness to any agreement which is worked out by the responsible leadership and moderates on both sides, is essential.

SUBURBIA

Plainview is a typical eastern suburban community; it may well be roughly typical of much of American suburbia. The problem which arose in Plainview has been popping up all over the United States; rare indeed is the suburban town which has not been plagued by a variation of this theme.

But Plainview's *response* to the shock of population change was not typical. Just a few miles away, for example, in one of the Levittown, L. I., school districts, the issue of religion in public education has triggered off an acrimonious and seemingly interminable wrangle. It has had the effect of weakening the school system. It has evoked furious campaigns for school board positions. It has caused interreligious divisions to spread even to votes on annual school board budgets.

Too few suburban communities handle their growing pains with the statesmanship of Plainview's leaders. Too few suburban dwellers are as well informed as many Plainviewers have become. It is to be hoped that more and more suburban communities will be able to use inevitable interreligious differences as an opportunity for increased communications among citizens of all faiths, for an increased sense of community, and for increased opportunities to solve community problems amicably and creatively.

ST. PAUL AND MINNEAPOLIS
Unlike Twins

A FEW DAYS BEFORE THE ELECTION OF 1960, A MINNE-sota Jewish leader was summoned out of a meeting by an urgent telephone call from Senator Hubert Humphrey. The Senator, running for reelection, confessed that he was "scared to death" that he—as well as Senator Kennedy and Governor Orville Freeman—would be "clobbered" by heavy anti-Catholic sentiment evident in many parts of the state. Public opinion polls at that time indicated that Humphrey had good reason to fear. In the end, of course, the popular Senator came through with a margin of 200,000 but Kennedy carried the state by only a hairline. And Governor Freeman, who had placed Kennedy in nomination at the Democratic convention, was toppled in his quest for reelection (and had to accept the dubious consolation prize of the Agriculture Department hot seat).

Ironically, only a few months later, the other Minnesota Senator, Roman Catholic Eugene McCarthy, was anxiously telephoning Monsignor Frederick G. Hochwalt, chief of the National Catholic Welfare Conference education department, about the strong assault of the Catholic bishops upon President Kennedy's federal aid-to-education bill. "What are you trying to do to us down there?" asked McCarthy. "Senator," the Monsignor is reported by *Look* to have replied, "this is a political fight. You know what that is."

Politics in Minnesota frequently express themselves in religious and ethnic terms. This make-up of the state's population provides the ingredients for a potent interreligious brew, which can be stirred to a boil by political controversy: 21 per cent Roman Catholic, 41 per cent Lutheran, 27 per cent other Protestant denominations, and 4 per cent Jewish, and others. The religious factors are anything but predictable in unpredictable Minnesota. In 1958, for example, Eugene J. McCarthy, Democratic-Farmer Laborite and Roman Catholic, swamped Edward T. Thye, Republican and Lutheran, in a campaign in which religion tended to yield to party loyalties.

The 1960 campaign, however, was another story. With a Catholic vying for the White House, religion played a strong, and frequently bitter, part in the Minnesota struggle. In Minneapolis, Osterhus Publishing Company turned out millions of copies of inflammably anti-Catholic tracts, flooding the state (and the nation) with suspicion. Fundamentalist Protestant ministers throughout the state waved the bloody shirt of "Vatican Power" from their pulpits. So violent were these appeals to religious prejudices that a strong counter-appeal was launched by 250 non-fundamentalist Protestant clergymen, together with all Minnesota rabbis, who joined in a public statement against bigotry. All of the clergymen made financial contributions to get their statement published as an ad in the Minnesota newspapers on the Sunday before the election. The Roman Catholic archbishop and the Catholic clergy maintained silence throughout the campaign, despite all provocations.

Immediately after the election, Archbishop Brady (who met with Minnesota rabbis during the heat of the campaign for the first time in his four years in St. Paul) expressed gratitude to those who had fought against religious bigotry. Obviously reacting to the orgy of hostility which had marred the campaign, the Archbishop said, "We should begin a program of understanding soon."*

To any close observer of interreligious relations in Minnesota, it could not be too soon. Such a program is already long overdue and seriously needed. For, although the Twin Cities earned major league status in the baseball world in 1960, the level and character of interfaith cooperation in the area are still decidedly minor league. Religion has deep roots in Minnesota; but too often religion has been the source of community conflict and unworthy squabbles.

THE PAST

Minnesota is a land of churches. Catholics, Protestants, and Jews came to the state in quest of religious freedom and economic betterment. Radisson and Groseiliers, French explorers and fur traders, were the first to arrive in the land of the Sioux and the Chippewa Indians to challenge the Manitou, mighty god of the red men. In 1648 these Frenchmen came down from Montreal by canoe, through Lake Michigan and across Wisconsin's rivers, then up the mighty Mississippi, the glistening

---

* Archbishop Brady died in 1961.

"Father of Waters." They came from Catholic France and when they settled, they immediately built a chapel and began to teach their faith to the Indians. Father Louis Hennepin, a Franciscan priest, arrived by the same route late in the 1600's and was captured by the Sioux who, it is said, robbed him of his chalice and vestments. It is recorded that Father Hennepin baptized a dying child, giving Minnesota its first Christian convert.

In the early 1800's, men of all faiths found their way to the territory of Minnesota. Up the Mississippi they came—bright-robed Catholic priests, Presbyterians and Methodists and Swiss Protestants. A Slovenian priest, the Rev. Francis Xavier Pierz, dedicated a cedar bark-deerskin chapel at Grand Portage and opened a mission school, the first in the new land. Later Father Pierz wrote: "Since I wish to train these poor savages to become not only good Christians but also industrious laborers and good men, I also lead them from temporary misery to befitting prosperity. . . ."

Soon thereafter, the missionaries, both Catholic and Protestant, made their way to the area where the Twin Cities—St. Paul and Minneapolis—are now located and which later became the center of civilization in Minnesota. They faced back-breaking obstacles. William Watts Folwell has written: "The first group of missionaries in the state were most disappointed in the impact which they had upon the heathen and the savages. The new religion had to supplant an old one, ardently believed and interwoven with the traditions of the ages. . . ."

An early missionary describes the following scene: "Ah, good morning, Great Chief. May the blessings of Our Savior, Jesus Christ, be upon you this day." The Indian replies, "Hm! White Father talks much of Jesus.

Other white men not so good, they talk of Jesus, too. Is it the same Jesus they call to when they are drunk or angry?" The missionary replies, "No, O Chief, it is not the same Jesus. Some white men are good. Some Indians are bad." To this the Indian replies, "O White Father, you have spoken strong words against firewater and impurity. White Father, my friend, these are words you should carry to your white brothers who bring us the firewater and who do evil to us. They are the sinners."

A new strain of immigrants began to stream into Minnesota in the 1850's, mostly Irish and German Catholics. By 1850, the Catholic population had grown so large that St. Paul was made the seat of a diocese, and remains so today. The crude log church built by Father Galtier was replaced by a cathedral. This later was rebuilt and made a most imposing cathedral which still stands on the same spot today. It is known as "The Hill" in St. Paul. The Protestant ranks swelled also, and the roar of the revival meeting was heard throughout the state.

Jewish merchants and traders, among the very first settlers, organized themselves into congregations although they were still only a small religious minority. The first synagogue in Minnesota was Mt. Zion Temple in St. Paul, founded in 1856. Rabbi Leopold Wintner was its first full-time rabbi and was the first Jewish spiritual leader in the state. Under subsequent rabbinic and lay leadership, the Neighborhood House was established in 1897. It remains today as one of St. Paul's great social welfare institutions, catering to all people without regard to race, creed, or national origin.

When East Europe's Jews flocked to the United States between 1890 and 1914, another Minnesotan, Rabbi Judah Wechsler, broadcast his urgings to them to settle in the western farm lands which he described as a true land of religious freedom and civic and economic opportunity.

In 1870 there were 877 churches in Minnesota; by 1900 the number had skyrocketed to 4,000. Thousands of Protestant immigrants from Norway, Sweden, Denmark, Finland, and Germany swelled the Lutheran churches in Minnesota, making Lutheranism the largest denomination in the state. By 1914, the Scandinavians forged a strong alliance with the Republican party, in fierce opposition to the Democratic party which held the allegiance of most of the Irish Catholics. Religious antagonisms were powerful. The American Protective Association, a nativist movement founded in Iowa in 1887, charged that Catholics were manipulating political affairs in America for the benefit of their church. Their bigoted outcries took quick root in Minnesota's fertile soil. Anti-Catholic hatred swept the state. Duluth became a hotbed of APA-ism, and the movement actually gained control of city offices and the public schools in 1893 and 1894. Exposed by influential newspapers in St. Paul and elsewhere, the APA quickly declined in status and number. By 1896 it was no longer worth talking about. But the religious tensions and enmities upon which the APA fed persisted.

Religious leadership has made itself felt in social causes in Minnesota. A Congregationalist minister, Hastings Hornell Hart, led strong crusades against industrial exploitation, the low-pay scale of farm hands, and the horrible conditions in the mental hospitals of the state. He also surveyed the jails of Minnesota and found deplorable conditions. His leadership bore fruit.

But religious leaders also led reactionary crusades. One such exacerbated the state in the 1920's. Rev. Wm. B. Riley, First Baptist Church of Minneapolis, was the leader of the anti-evolution forces in the state. The battleground was, naturally, the University of Minnesota and other institutions of higher education. The campaign reached its climax in 1927, when Dr. Riley presented a bill in the State Legislature outlawing the teaching of evolution in all tax-supported institutions. The legislative committee hearings were wild, with both Dr. Riley and his opponents shouting their views, allegations, counter-allegations, and determinations. The State Senate finally defeated the anti-evolution bill, 55 to 7, and the House allowed it to die quietly in committee.

In later years, the same Dr. Riley was responsible for spreading anti-Semitism throughout the state. His pulpit was occupied from time to time by various hate-mongers.

Opportunities for joint religious endeavor between Catholics, Protestants, and Jews in the early days were few. Rabbi W. Gunther Plaut, in his book, *The Jews in Minnesota,* reports that on certain communal occasions, like the public mourning for the victims of the battleship "Maine," Jews participated with services of their own; there were no common services in those days. Rabbi Plaut also indicates that Christian interest in Jews at that time was motivated by missionary hopes. There was a "society for the propagation of the gospel among the Jews in the city of St. Paul." It was doubtlessly encouraged by the knowledge that Samuel Freuder, once a rabbi at Temple Mt. Zion, had become a Christian convert. This group felt that if a rabbi could turn to Christianity, there must surely be laymen to take the step. But the success of this society was negligible, despite its long name and imposing letterhead.

Jews in the early days of Minnesota gave freely to Christian causes: William H. Elsinger left $25,000 for an institution to be built by the Salvation Army, and Joseph Elsinger donated a large tract of land to an Episcopal Home for Aged Women.

In the early days, when it came to defending their faith in public, Jews were forthright enough. Yet the developing relationship between Jews and Christians demanded courtesy on both sides and left little room for the unrestrained pronouncements of earlier days, when such considerations weighed less heavily. In the 1890's, Rabbi Emanuel Hess had simply and strongly affirmed the superiority of Judaism over Christianity. He approvingly quoted a contemporary historian and said, " 'Christianity falls far below the best morality of the ancients, his ideal is negative rather than positive, passive rather than active.' This must be modified," said Hess. His essay left little doubt about his comparative evaluation of Judaism and Christianity. Even when he wrote for a sectarian Christian publication on the subject of anti-Semitism, he did not hesitate to put the blame for this prejudice at the door of Christianity.

A decade later, Jews probably cherished the same ideas, but they were no longer likely to express them as bluntly before other than private audiences. There was more sensitivity now to "public relations" as it was called; and with this greater sensitivity came also a keener awareness of the deeper problems which undergirded dogmatic differences among American denominations.

Some instances of church-state disagreements sprang up as early as the 1870's when Bible reading in the public schools of Minnesota became a matter of controversy. In 1911, it is reported that one Rypins lectured before a university group on the subject, "Shall Religion Be Taught in Public Institutions?" A few years later, the forces favoring a breach in the wall of separation between church and state were found to be in the ascendency and Jews were beginning to feel that this matter affected their vital interests.

Ultimately, some Jews brought suit against the school board of Virginia, Minnesota, which had adopted a resolution of the Ministerial Association requesting that a Bible be placed in every classroom and that passages from the King James version be read daily without note or comment. The Minnesota Supreme Court, in a decision titled, "Kaplan vs. Independent School District of Virginia, Minnesota," decided on April 22, 1927, "that there was nothing wrong with this procedure and that no one's fundamental rights had been injured." Chief Justice Samuel B. Wilson, in a strong dissent, stated, "To require the Jewish child to read the New Testament which extols Christ as the Messiah is to tell them that their religious teachings at home are untrue. There they are taught a denial of Christ, Divinity, and Resurrection. Is it possible that this does not interfere with the rights of conscience of parents and perhaps of the child?"

CURRENT SCENE

By 1960, the total population of Minnesota was 3,350,000. Of this total, 1,100,000 were Protestants,

700,000 Roman Catholics, 38,000 Jews, and 40,000 Greek Orthodox. It is interesting to note that the State Legislature of Minnesota in 1957 passed a bill making the Greek Orthodox Church the fourth major religious faith in the state. There seems to be no record of bills having been passed declaring the other three major faiths officially major faiths in the state of Minnesota. In general, relationships among all the religious groups are superficially calm and friendly. When one probes beneath the surface, however, problems begin to appear on all sides. But far more important than overt interreligious spats is the sporadic nature of relationships among the religious groups in Minnesota. The various religious bodies have been known to cooperate on matters of emergency on an intermittent rather than on a continuing basis. When emergencies arise, the groups usually get together and contrive a solution to the problem. But the cooperation invariably ends there and another emergency must occur before the groups will join again.

Without exception, clergy associations in Minnesota cities and towns are comprised of only one religious group: they are exclusively Protestant, Catholic, or Jewish. There is very little direct clergy cooperation in the round tables of the National Conference of Christians and Jews. There are, however, a number of devoted laymen of the various religious faiths who work with the NCCJ in search of better understanding among the religious groups in the state of Minnesota.

Examples of interreligious cooperation include efforts to better mental health facilities in the state, celebrate World Refugee Year, modify the McCarran-Walter Immigration Law, and support the Community Chest.

Minnesota's interreligious relationships have been plagued by virtually every problem and issue which has arisen anywhere on the American scene. From church-state problems to birth control, from censorship of literature to humane slaughter legislation—Minnesota has lived through them all. What are some of these specific issues? How have the religious leaders of the Land of the Sky Blue Waters tried to meet them? What conflicts have they engendered? How have the conflicts been resolved?

By all odds, the most frequent, the most prevalent, and most complex group of problems which arises to bedevil the interreligious relationships in Minnesota is the thorny problem of church-state relations.

ITEM: A recent session of public school superintendents and principals took note of the deep hostility which exists between Protestants and Catholics in most of the smaller communities. In defiance of the State Fair Employment Practice Laws, some school districts instruct their superintendents and principals not to employ Protestants—or Catholics—as the case may be. Similar prohibitions are wide-spread regarding the employment of Jews, Unitarians, Seventh-Day Adventists, and Christian Scientists.

ITEM: Continual reports of violations of separation of church and state in the public schools come to the attention of various religious groups and especially the Jewish group. Recently, there were tacked up in one of the cafeterias in a public junior high school prayers for grace for the respective faiths. When a local rabbi called this to the principal's attention, he was invited to come to school to discuss this matter with the faculty. He did so, and after the faculty had a better understanding of the entire problem, the prayer signs were removed quietly from the school cafeteria without further protestations from the Jewish community.

ITEM: A rural school board had on its registration blanks for kindergarten children questions about the father's and mother's nationality and church affiliation as well as the child's church affiliation. The statement was made that these blanks, after being filled out, would remain in the child's file through his entire schooling in that particular suburb. Objection was made to the superintendent of these schools, and resulted in the questions being deleted from future registration blanks.

ITEM: Typical complaints are that classes sing Christological songs such as "Jesus Loves Me, This I Know," "I Have Room in My Heart for You, Dear Jesus"; that auditorium programs, requiring compulsory attendance, present Christological plays; that Christmas operettas are performed in which all of the songs are Christological in nature; and that during the week prior to Easter some schools showed crucifixion films which all students were compelled to attend. Representations were made to the principals of some of the schools where the crucifixion films were shown and where attendance was mandatory and, as a result, changes were made so that the student could absent himself from these assembly periods if he so desired. In many cases, the crucifixion films were never again shown in the schools.

ITEM: A Presbyterian minister from one of the smaller communities in the state of Minnesota complained to the American Civil Liberties Union, Minnesota branch, that in his community there were four classes of religious instruction being taught by Mennonites during the released time hour in the public school building instead of in the churches. He charged that these were being taught at the same time that four lower grades of the public school were in session in the same building, although in another wing. This minister asked the opinion of the Minnesota branch of the American Civil Liberties Union as to whether this was legal. The answer was that the Supreme Court decision in the McCollum case (1947) made it illegal to use a public school building for released time. As a result of this particular minister's work in the community, quietly and without fanfare, the majority group in the community decided to remove its released time religious classes from the public school building and to conduct them in the churches or in the homes of that community.

ITEM: Recently, the issue of released time for religious education became a cause of considerable community disturbance in a suburb of Minneapolis known as the Lake Minnetonka area. There the Board of Education voted 4 to 1 to drop released time for religious education for the year 1957-58. Some of the Protestant leaders in that area became incensed and many public hearings were held which drew large audiences on both sides of the issue. A professor of Education at the University of Minnesota, in defending the school board's action, stated: "Right now our people are being plagued by segregation. Seems to me this segregation business is carrying over to areas affecting our children. Sniping at public school time should be studied very, very carefully to prevent further erosion of the school day." Those opposed to the action of the school board made statements similar to this one attributed to a Lutheran minister: "The prime issue, it seems to me, is that many Christians feel the state does not have the right to dictate what hours should be used for secular learning only. We must recognize that religious training is more vital than any one academic subject." In spite of all the public hearings, the board stood on its prior decision against released time for religious education.

ITEM: In September of 1957, the *Minneapolis Sunday Tribune* took a public opinion poll on attitudes toward released time for religious classes and found that 80 per cent of the people of Minnesota polled felt that it was a good program and should be approved. Another interesting question submitted to the Minnesota people by the poll was: "Some people think the public schools should teach the children facts about the different religions—without trying to persuade them that one set of religious beliefs is better than another. Are you in favor of, or against, having facts about religion taught in Minnesota's public schools?" The poll indicated that 37 per cent favored teaching facts about religion and that 57 per cent opposed such instruction.

ITEM: In certain areas of Minnesota, the population is so overwhelmingly Roman Catholic that it is not feasible for the community to build a public school for the non-Catholic children. Arrangements have been made in such cases for the state to rent classroom space in parochial schools. In at least two school districts, controversies have roiled the communities. The state denied school aid to these districts, charging that religious instruction was being permitted in public schools. Crucifixes were hung in the classrooms along with other Christian religious pictures; fonts for holy water were at the entrance to each classroom. The State Commissioner of Education charged further that denominational teaching was conducted daily in the public school classrooms. In February, 1962, all public school instruction was ordered removed from parochial schools and the children incorporated into existing public schools in the area.

ITEM: In 1955 a few Catholic legislators quietly sponsored and put through the State Legislature a bill which provided for tax deductions from state income tax in the sum of $200 per pupil for expenses incurred in connection with parochial school attendance. No protests were made; few even knew about the bill having become law. In fact, very few Catholics took advantage of the provision in their income tax returns for that year. Two years later, however, when an attempt was made to increase the deduction to $400, major Protestant groups and the Minnesota Rabbinical Association opposed the whole idea. Objections were so strenuous that the authors decided quietly to withdraw the new proposal, thus not jeopardizing the original $200 deduction, which is still permitted.

ITEM: Minor religious controversies have arisen over the refusal of children, on religious grounds, to participate in school activities. Some of them are refusal to attend school dances; to change into gym clothes or to take showers on grounds of religiously-required modesty; to salute the flag; to take health examinations, inoculations, or to participate in discussions of disease, anatomy, or sex; to take part in any holiday celebrations; to attend any movies, curricular or otherwise; to participate in band and orchestra or to sing in choruses; and to eat certain foods either on certain days or at all times, due to religious dietary laws.

Depending on "whose ox is gored," reactions by various denominations to these problems range from righteous defense to righteous aggression. In most cases tensions result.

For example, when Rabbi Leon D. Stitskin, chairman of the Social Action Committee of the Rabbinical Council of America, was quoted in the newspaper as urging that all religious holiday celebrations be discontinued in public schools because they constituted a violation of the First Amendment, *The Wanderer,* conservative German-Catholic newspaper in St. Paul, snapped:

> Well, perhaps the rabbi has something there. After all, haven't the Soviet masterminds come to the same conclusion in their Marxist paradise? Didn't they rid the land of any public religious observances? And look how tension and strain have disappeared there—not to mention from the Siberian slave-labor camps!

The same newspaper carried a reprint from the Catholic newspaper *The Advocate of New Jersey* in regard to public schools:

> We believe that the time has come for Christians in the public school system and everywhere else to declare in outright fashion that the United States by culture, tradition, and full right is a Christian country and must not be allowed to change. For that reason Christmas in schools must be kept a distinctly Christian feast with a Christian purpose. . . . No country can be both Christian and non-Christian at the same time, and the only third alternative is irreligion.

Many Minnesota religious leaders, including not a few Catholics, are fearful that the content and tone of such articles make interreligious amity in Minnesota more difficult of achievement.

In 1957 a fascinating issue perplexed the Minnesota community. The subject: baccalaureate sermons. The reason for fascination: roles were reversed, the Roman Catholic Church opposing a religious celebration in the public school system. Archbishop Wm. O. Brady of St. Paul wrote in his official column: "Baccalaureate days and sermons are now so generally a part of even public school graduation plans that few, today, do more than accept them without analysis. It is scarcely remembered that these stem from the times when, in Europe, practically all education was religious and Catholic. In the old-time universities, it was the Catholic church which called together its Catholic students just before the Bachelor's Degrees were awarded to express one last academic affirmation of the interdependence of education, religion, and life."

The Archbishop went on to protest that the public schools had now been "denuded" of religion and that the baccalaureate day should be accepted as purely a social event and not as a religious exercise. He warned that baccalaureate exercises should not be held in churches. "If they are," he said, "our priests will have no part in such matters. . . . Neither will our people attend."

In the baccalaureate controversy, public opinion appeared to oppose the Catholic position. The *Minneapolis Tribune* reported on a public opinion poll which indicated that 83 per cent favored the continuation of such programs; 13 per cent opposed; and 4 per cent had no opinion. Protestant spokesmen were insistent that the exercises should be continued. The Jewish community, ordinarily in the forefront of opposition to religious practices in the public schools, agreed with the Archbishop.

In May, 1955, a similar interfaith problem had hit Minneapolis. Southwest High School held its baccalaureate service; the speaker was a prominent Presbyterian minister who was also, at that time, secretary of the Minneapolis Board of Education. Catholic spokesmen charged that the service brought religion into the public schools and that, moreover, the minister had told the students that Resurrection, Hell, and Judgment are all "legendary myths." Stung, the minister printed his entire baccalaureate address in the *Minneapolis Star* in an effort to refute the charges of religious bias.

Only a few days later, a row broke out in Beardsley,

Minnesota, a rural community in which interreligious bitterness had been simmering for some time. There, the school board canceled plans for a school commencement exercise after it received official notice that Roman Catholics in the parish would be forbidden to attend the exercises if they included prayers. The letter, written by Father Harvey E. Egan, pastor of St. Mary's Church, said, in part:

> Catholics believe that the Catholic Church is the one true church established by Jesus Christ; we believe that all other churches are false. Catholics are not permitted to participate in the religious service of a false church; we may not offer a prayer that contains a sentiment contrary to our belief. An invocation-benediction easily becomes a sermon; occasionally it becomes a religious service. Catholics do not deem it wise to become a captive audience at a program which may go contrary to their religious convictions.

Annually thereafter, the controversy over baccalaureate services and sermons popped up in one place or another. In St. Louis Park, a rabbi offered an invocation and benediction and preached, though he insisted his remarks did not constitute a sermon. A number of high schools in the Twin Cities area and in one suburb voted to drop baccalaureates altogether rather than to have separate denominational services. At these schools, the new services are called "Rededication Services" and stress only moral and ethical values and most often do not have clergymen as their speakers, but judges, lawyers, civic leaders, etc. The Protestant clergy has reacted strongly against this development but there have been isolated incidents of Protestant clergymen speaking out against baccalaureate services.

It was reported in the *Minneapolis Star* on May 21, 1960, that a Methodist minister, Rev. Warren A. Nyberg, advocated that baccalaureate services in public high schools should be abolished wherever there is any controversy about the practice. He went on to say that the rights of religious minorities should be protected. He noted that in Red Wing, Minnesota, which he described as "predominantly Lutheran," baccalaureates are still conducted, but without participation from students of the Missouri Synod and Wisconsin Synod Lutheran churches and the Roman Catholic Church.

He went on to say, "If churches want to recognize the importance of high school graduation, they can do so," he suggested, "either as individual churches or in cooperation with those churches holding each other in mutual esteem." The skirmishes continue and there are indications that more and more communities in Minnesota are going to drop these heat-producing programs.

Though Minnesota can claim no uniqueness in this regard, the state has witnessed a series of incidents involving the placement of religious symbols on public property of various kinds. The Fraternal Order of Eagles undertook a campaign to place Ten Commandments plaques in all schoolrooms, on courthouses, city halls, libraries, and in parks. Each year the Junior Association of Commerce of Minnesota, in cooperation with the Protestant churches in a suburb adjacent to Minneapolis, has sponsored the erection of a crèche on city property. This practice has spread to other suburbs as well. During Holy Week, for a number of years, the St. Paul City Courthouse was lighted up in the form of a cross. Similarly, in one of the public parks in the city of St. Paul, where there is a greenhouse, the floral display was set up in the form of a cross during the same period. Representations were made to the proper authorities in the city of St. Paul and the practice was discontinued in both instances.

The Minnesota Rabbinical Association responded to the growth of this kind of activity by widely distributing a memorandum prepared by the American Jewish Congress "On the Illegality of Display of Religious Symbols on Public Property." Protestant and Catholic reaction was prompt and angry, especially when some public officials accepted the legal arguments of the memorandum!

THE STATE EMBLEM CONTROVERSY

This type of controversy reached its peak in 1957 when planning for the 1958 Minnesota Centennial Celebration was underway. The Centennial Commission adopted an emblem which contained a cross. The conflict had been anticipated on October 12, 1956, when the Jewish Community Relations Council of Minnesota filed a letter of protest with the commission against the proposed inclusion of such a sectarian symbol. Formal hearing was given the protesters in January, 1957; the commission by a 6 to 4 vote refused to remove it. Resolutions by various groups on both sides echoed and reechoed through the state as 1957 proceeded. Opponents of the commission's position were accused of "ritualistic liberalism" as well as agnosticism, unbelief, and pro-Communism. Public opinion polls tended to support the commission. Newspaper space devoted to the fight increased as more and more individuals and groups became involved.

Despite condemnation by the governor's Commission on Human Rights, the governor-appointed State Centennial Commission hewed to its original position, and the centennial seal appeared with the cross throughout the celebration. The Jewish Community Relations Council of Minnesota issued a statement decrying the final decision and indicating that Jews would be forced not to cooperate in certain aspects of the celebration. An editorial in the *American Jewish World,* an Anglo-Jewish publication in Minneapolis, indicated the depth of emotion stirred by the issue:

"The controversial cross on the proposed Minnesota centennial emblem has produced considerable heat. Some relevant light, however, is still missing.

"In urging the cross' retention, Archbishop William O. Brady assumed that the cross was placed on the emblem to mark episodes in the past history of Minnesota. This is not the case. Had the Centennial Commission chosen a replica of the picture in the reception room in the capitol which depicts Father Hennepin presenting the cross to the Indians, or similar incidents in Minnesota's early history, we doubt whether there would have been any opposition.

". . . The cross is a revered symbol of Christianity. It is not the symbol of the non-Christian citizens of the state. Moreover, there are many sincere and devoted Christians who are convinced that a state agency may not impose a denominational symbol upon its citizens, and may not use tax money to disseminate a religious symbol of any particular denomination. We would be false to our citizenship in this country if we failed to protest the commission's adoption of such an emblem.

"We share with Archbishop Brady his concern about the 'disturbing signs of religious discord.' It was not necessary for the Archbishop, however, to remind us that, 'Archbishop Murray publicly defended their (the Jewish) cause in their days of persecution,' and assuring the Jewish community that he, as Archbishop Murray's successor, will continue to offer it a supporting hand.

". . . While Archbishop Brady, in expressing his views on this controversial issue, is anxious to avoid personal tensions in the community, some advocates of the retention of the cross are not so sensitive and understanding. Several members of the Centennial Commission pointedly asked the Jewish representatives whether they were not afraid of the rise of anti-Semitism if they freely expressed their position as citizens on this issue. Dr. C. A. Nelson, chaplain of the State Senate, minced no words. 'For the protection of minorities, this ought not to become an issue at this time,' he said.

"This certainly is a direct threat against citizens who dare to defend their conscience and speak freely in this state.

"Is this the spirit of Minnesota which the Centennial Commission wants to show to the country after a century of the state's progress?

" 'If today's pressure removes the "cross" from the emblem that marks the past,' Archbishop Brady wrote, 'tomorrow's pressure will attempt to tear it from our church and our homes.'

"But, as we pointed out above, the emblem was not designed to represent the past. The issue, therefore, is this:

"If today's pressure forces the cross on a state emblem as the only symbol of the spiritual and religious expression of all citizens of Minnesota, tomorrow's pressure will attempt to force it into our public schools and in other governmental areas. The Archbishop objects—and justly —against the placing of the non-Catholic approved Gideon Bibles in the public schools. He certainly can appreciate the Jew's feeling about the cross on state literature sent to Jewish homes and on state exhibits for which he is taxed. . . ."

But the Jewish community was not alone in its unhappiness with aspects of the Centennial. The Roman Catholic Church later objected to too little religion in the celebration and a tendency to overglorify Scandinavians (mostly Lutherans). Some Protestants agreed with the first of these demurrers. Other Protestants joined Rabbi W. Gunther Plaut in his strong denunciation of all government-sponsored religious celebrations, symbols in public places, and other violations of religious freedom.

The Centennial struggle demonstrated the inflammable nature of interreligious relations in Minnesota. To many persons it demonstrated the touchiness of the Jewish community. It revealed anew the need for better—and continuous—communication among the faith groups. In the bitter Centennial struggle the Jewish community wrote to Archbishop Brady and urged that he meet with representatives of the Minnesota Rabbinical Council. He replied that it would be unwise to meet during the "heat" of the conflict, but that he would meet with representatives of the council sometime in the future. In 1960 he did.

NEVER ON SUNDAY

Sunday Closing Laws have always been a fertile source of interreligious friction in Minnesota. A law was passed in 1894 providing that: "All labor on Sunday is prohibited; excepting the works of necessity or charity." In the years since, the courts have had numerous occasions to decide what is "necessity" and what is "charity." On January 19, 1906, in the *State of Minnesota vs. Weiss,* a devout Orthodox Jew, who regularly attended religious services on Saturday, the Jewish Sabbath, challenged Minnesota's Sunday Closing Laws and suffered a defeat. There has been speculation as to what the Minnesota Supreme Court would do if a similar case reached it now.

In 1957 the Legislature enacted a law preventing the sale of automobiles on Sunday. In 1959 realtors pressed for a similar law outlawing the sale or showing of real estate on Sundays. This latter bill was defeated. These legislative campaigns have focused attention on the basic issues: Are the Sunday laws really religious laws, rather than welfare legislation? Are they discriminatory against non-Christian Sabbath observers? What logic justifies the patchwork which extends permission to one kind of business to keep open on Sundays and denies permission to another?

The Sunday closing issue came to a head in Minnesota in 1961-1962. Following the U.S. Supreme Court decision that Sunday laws are not inherently unconstitutional, a rash of Sunday closing ordinances covered the State. Ordinances enacted in small suburban communities evoked some controversy and occasional legal challenges by discount houses. But the interreligious fur really began to fly when the St. Paul City Council, in January of 1962, adopted a Sunday closing law which had touched off protest and discussion throughout the Twin Cities' political, business, and religious circles. As the bill had originally been introduced months earlier, it had contained a Saturday closing option out of deference to Jews, Seventh-Day Adventists, and other Sabbatarians who keep their shops closed on Saturday. However, at the behest of the city corporation counsel, the option was deleted on the ground that its inclusion might make the ordinance unconstitutional. Thereupon, a chorus of protests by Jewish rabbinic and communal leaders blasted the law as ill-advised, discriminatory, and illogical. The *Minneapolis Star,* in an astringent editorial, characterized the St. Paul no-option ordinance as "the worst kind of Sunday closing legislation." The Minneapolis City Council later enacted a Sunday law which did include a Saturday option.

The ruckus over Sunday closings stirred both inter-religious and *intra-religious* conflict. Rabbi Bernard S. Raskas of the Conservative congregation, Temple of Aaron in St. Paul, coupled his condemnation of the city ordinance with a caustic rebuke against the city's Jewish leaders who had fought for a Saturday option: ". . . I must state emphatically that when the Jewish community asks a special provision because it observes the Sabbath on Saturday, it is a myth. I challenge anyone to find more than two Jewish businesses in St. Paul that are closed on Saturday because of Sabbath tradition outside the kosher butcher shops. I ask simply are we worthy of being defended on this issue? It becomes a source of great embarrassment for me as a rabbi to speak for a Jewish community that does not respect its own traditions and for this reason I have not spoken up in public council. Let us call a spade a spade and a Sabbath a Sabbath."

St. Paul and Minneapolis are twin cities but, like many twins, they do not look very much alike and frequently express considerable hostility to each other. The history of the relationships between the two cities is a colorful story—but beyond the ken of this chapter. Moreover, the passage of time has blurred most of the sharp edges and a common destiny has linked the two cities in growing "togetherness." One of the sharp differences of the past was the contrasting pictures of intergroup relations in the two cities.

St. Paul, the older and more urbane capital city, prided itself on its good interreligious and interracial relationships. Minneapolis, on the other hand, was characterized by Carey McWilliams in 1947 as the "capital of anti-Semitism in the United States." The city was riddled with discriminations against Jews in service clubs, businesses, and public accommodations. Raucous anti-Semitic groups flourished. However, the past decade has brought startling changes to both cities, making them in effect parts of one large metropolitan center. Anti-discrimination legislation in Minneapolis and the state has had salutary effects. Liberal state and city governments have improved the climate still further. Three years after the appearance of the Carey McWilliams article, Minneapolis won an award from the National Conference of Christians and Jews for having made more progress in establishing brotherhood than any other city in the United States. In addition, Minneapolis has become a bustling boom city and, enriched by the great University of Minnesota, has largely overcome the narrowness and bigotry which marred its past. In 1961 the city elected a Jewish mayor and a Jew was elected president of the Chamber of Commerce.

The telephone directories tell much of the story of the Twin Cities' population. The St. Paul book brims with Swedish names—1,660 Andersons (plus perhaps another 100 with mildly bastardized forms of the same name), 2,500 Johnsons, and 1,200 Nelsons. In Minneapolis, the Scandinavian flavor is even more pronounced. More than 4,300 Andersons and 7,000 Carlsons crowd the pages of the directory. The Nilssons, Nelsons, Ericsons, Larsons, Olsons, Petersons, Swensons, and Persons follow apace.

As the directories reveal, the religious composition of Minneapolis is overwhelmingly Protestant (Lutheran) and Scandinavian. Minneapolis usually elects Protestant mayors while, across the Mississippi River in St. Paul, a Protestant would have slim hope of being elected to that office. In 1960 a non-Roman (Greek Orthodox) Catholic became mayor of St. Paul, the first time in twenty-five years that a Roman Catholic did not occupy City Hall. Although Protestants make up a majority in St. Paul also, the Roman Catholics dominate the political life of the community. For example, the St. Paul Municipal Court in 1960 was composed of four Catholic judges and one Jew.

The telephone directories also give a clue to population changes. Twenty years ago, the Jewish names in St. Paul were concentrated in the old Selby Avenue district and in the decaying West Side across the bridge. Today, these neighborhoods are almost empty of Jews, most of whom have moved to the new and fashionable Highland

Park section of the city. There are sections in St. Paul, such as East St. Paul, which have virtually no Jewish inhabitants at all. When a community relations worker addressed a public school in that area, the youngsters asked such questions as: What do Jews look like? What kind of government do they have?

Minneapolis Jewry is in the process of a similar transplantation. The Old North Side, heavily Jewish, is steadily losing many of its Jewish members to the plush suburb, St. Louis Park, and other new sections. Outside the Twin Cities, few communities have enough Jews to maintain their own synagogues.

Minneapolis in some respects is now a more enlightened and liberal community than is her twin sister. A recent example is the birth control issue. Hennepin County, embracing Minneapolis, has long made birth control information available upon request through its Welfare Department. Early in 1959, a similar program was considered by the Ramsey County Welfare Board including plans to establish a birth control clinic at Ancker Hospital in St. Paul, the city-county hospital. Because the capital city is heavily Catholic, St. Paul public officials quickly became apprehensive. It was revealed that Ramsey County Welfare Board employees were under specific instructions from the Welfare Board not to give out birth control information, nor facts about planned parenthood clinics, even if the client requested such information. The Minnesota Chapter of the American Civil Liberties Union and the Planned Parenthood group blasted this suppression as "intolerable limits on public information" and as a serious violation of civil liberties.

TWIN CITIES 281

At the time of this clash, only one non-Catholic served on the Ramsey County Welfare Board. He was a prominent Jewish social welfare leader and he strongly urged the establishment of a birth control center at Ancker Hospital. Two Ramsey County commissioners, both former St. Paul mayors and both Roman Catholics, quickly retorted that there was no money in the county budget for such a program. One of the commissioners, Edward K. Delaney, added, "There was an article in the newspaper recently saying that one of the commissioners wanted to set up a sort of birth control service at Ancker Hospital. If he or any other member of the Welfare Board thinks they have too much money, I'll see that the budget is cut."

No birth control center was established in Ancker. A tortured "compromise," leaving both sides unsatisfied, was announced, which permits welfare department staff and doctors to refer clients requesting birth control information to appropriate private sources. However, the "compromise" requires that any client asking for advice "that may not be in conformity with his or her religious belief should be referred to his or her spiritual adviser."

Because of the demands made by some religious groups for censorship and limitations on civil liberties, the American Civil Liberties Union in the state of Minnesota in 1958 set up a committee of seven on separation of church and state. Membership consisted of a professor of Philosophy of Education from the University of Minnesota; the president of the Augustana Evangelical Lutheran Synod; a bishop from the Seventh-Day Adventist church and moderator of the American Religious Town Hall, Inc., nationally released television programs;

an assistant professor and head of the Department of Psychology from a Catholic college in St. Paul; a Jewish attorney who is the executive director of a community relations agency in the state of Minnesota; a professor of Religion and Philosophy from a Presbyterian college in the city of St. Paul; and a University of Minnesota professor of the Missouri Lutheran faith. It was hoped that, through this committee, infringements on separation of church and state and on civil liberties would be discouraged.

Soon after the creation of this committee, the *Wanderer* on May 9, 1957, attacked it. The article said in part, "Here in Minnesota, too, the State Branch of the American Civil Liberties Union is gunning for Catholic hides. They've formed a committee which will deal—so they say—with 'an interesting number of questions involving separation of church and state in Minnesota.' These questions include such items as a state law banning auto sales on Sunday, release of public school children for religious instruction, the cross—or is it a TV antenna?—appearing on the official Minnesota Centennial emblem, etc."

The *Wanderer* quoted from an article in the Catholic *St. Cloud Sunday Visitor*: "We call this bad news. Not because we are opposed to separation of church and state, but because we are opposed to the naive and ludicrous twists such groups as the American Civil Liberties Union and the POAU give to this American doctrine and practice. We wholeheartedly support a true separation of church and state, but, true to American tradition, we are opposed to separation of religion from government, education, etc. Protestant ministers serving on this committee will find themselves in the embarrassing position of fighting against the very things their vocation as clergymen stands for, namely religion. . . . But whether it be the American Civil Liberties Union's attacks against Catholic censorship, church-state separation, or anything else, we would like to remind the claque that not only American Catholics but the overwhelming millions who recognize this as a Christian nation, are sick of this pettifogging. . . ."

Let no one believe that only church-state problems cause interreligious tensions in the Land of the Sky Blue Waters. Many other issues arise, and each makes its contribution to an atmosphere which continues to be placid on the surface, churning underneath.

Father John J. Cavanaugh, then president of Notre Dame University, lamented the low level of Catholic scholarship a few years ago by citing a survey which demonstrated that, "For every 100,000 Jews in this country, there are 20 listed in *Who's Who;* for every 100,000 Seventh-Day Adventists, 11; but for every 100,000 Roman Catholics, only 7." He noted that 40,000,000 Catholics produce proportionately about one-third as many leaders as do the Jews. "The Jews are an immigrant peoples," he said, "very often from modest homes. They must fight bigotry, but the Jews are producing leaders far out of proportion to their numbers." He warned that, "Catholics must raise the standards of their education." And he added, "Where are the Catholic Salks, Oppenheimers, Einsteins?"

While Father Cavanaugh's statement reverberated through the Catholic press, inspiring searching self-criticism in many publications, it evoked an edgy retort from some Catholic leaders. For example, Archbishop Brady asserted, "No one seems to have thought it worthy to comment that neither do we have any Catholic Hiss or Catholic Rosenberg. Such deficiencies may be wholly irrelevant but no more irrelevant than the rest."

SOCIAL DISCRIMINATION

Religious segregation is strong in Minnesota, even in the large Twin Cities. There is little social intermixing among Jews, Protestants, and Catholics. The proverbial five o'clock shadow prevails. Groups work together and perhaps socialize for lunch but 5:00 P.M., or the end of the working day, marks the real end and the groups go their separate ways and do not fraternize. It isn't possible to determine how much of this isolation is the effect of previous discrimination and how much is the assertion of group identity. The record indicates that Jews have been discriminated against in service groups, golf clubs, the Minneapolis Automobile Association, in summer resorts, and in other social areas for many years. Many of these barriers have been breached but there is still exclusiveness prevalent not only in Minneapolis, but in St. Paul as well.

Recently, strong resistance to such social exclusivity has developed within the Jewish group itself and efforts have been made to open the membership of some Jewish clubs to non-Jews. The Standard Club and the Brookview County Golf Club in the city of Minneapolis have been opened up to non-Jewish members but other country clubs staunchly resist the pressure for an open-door policy. The chief arguments are: "We will be overrun by non-Jews and will cease to be comfortable and relaxed in our places of enjoyment. We opened these institutions in the first place because we were excluded by the non-Jews from their recreation centers." A Minneapolis rabbi helped break down the exclusiveness of the Standard Club by charging that there was nothing "Jewish" about the club anyway, that it did not even have a kosher kitchen, was in no way identified with Judaism, but was really a mere social club.

In tiny rural communities of Minnesota, which are heavily Protestant, a Jew is known as an occasional itinerant salesman. A Jewish family, moving upstate from St. Paul, settled in Swanville, Minnesota, in the 1930's. Swanville was a tiny town of 600 people. The Jewish boys were examined by their schoolmates as if they had fallen from the heavens. One curious boy actually felt the Jewish boy's head for horns. "Are you a Yew (Jew)?" asked a perplexed Scandinavian. In less than a year, however, Swanville had taken the Jewish family to its heart. One of the boys was elected president of his class, another became a star of the school baseball team, and the girl was soon a popular member of the band. When the Jewish family left Swanville some ten years later (partly out of nostalgia for fellow Jews), the community said good-by with genuine emotion and affection.

The year 1962 was ushered into Minneapolis inauspiciously. Five Minneapolis synagogues and the University of Minnesota Hillel Foundation's building were painted with swastikas and anti-Jewish threats. Virulent anti-Semitic mailings, aimed particularly at the Jewish mayor (Arthur Naftalin), added to the tension. Local posts of the Jewish War Veterans reacted to the situation by posting their own all-night patrols around synagogues and other Jewish communal institutions.* The response of responsible community leadership to the swastikas was one of sharp indignation. Many Protestants and Catholics offered to assist in the patrols. City officials, newspapers, religious, labor, and civic groups expressed angry shock and dismay. Said the American Legion: ". . . Many of our comrades gave their lives to destroy what this symbol (swastika) stands for. We feel that the perpetrators of these acts are making a mockery of our comrades' supreme sacrifice. . . ."

While it is true that a number of religious tensions exist in Minnesota, there is a surprising amount of good will and understanding prevalent among the various religious groups that make up the state. It is significant that in the city of St. Paul, a Jew who sits on the municipal court bench, running in a city-wide election, received a greater vote total than the Roman Catholics running for office. In the same election, a Jew topped the ticket of candidates for the city commissioners' positions with the largest vote gathered by any one of the candidates. Recently, a Jewish woman was elected Democratic National Committeewoman from the state of Minnesota. A St. Paul rabbi, W. Gunther Plaut, was the chairman of the Governor's Committee on Ethics in State Government. In August of 1957, when the Lutheran World Federation held their international convention in the city of Minneapolis, the Minnesota Rabbinical Association was the host to prominent Lutheran leaders from

---

* Some Jews chided the J.W.V. for "playing cops."

all over the world for a breakfast meeting. Rabbi Plaut spoke to the group about the problems of the Middle East, especially as they pertained to the State of Israel.

Recently, when a Jewish doctor passed away, after having served in a Catholic community known as Foley, Minnesota, the Roman Catholic church there held only one mass on a Sunday so its members could have time to drive to Minneapolis for the Jewish funeral. One priest, eight nuns, and many Catholic laymen from the community were in the assembly which paid tribute to this doctor who was truly an ambassador of good will in this dominantly Catholic community. They made the following statement with reference to him: "We never before had a doctor like Dr. Fidelman and we don't think we ever will again."

Indeed, in many matters affecting community welfare, interfaith cooperation is excellent. In 1958 leaders of all the major religious groups supported legislation to improve conditions for migrant workers who stream into Minnesota from Texas during the summer months. Similarly, all religious bodies working together succeded in persuading the state legislature in 1961 to adopt open occupancy legislation. Religious forces have helped to achieve substantial progress in civil rights for minority groups. Minnesota has distinguished itself for liberality in this area of concern. Cooperative enterprises have also gained the support of the religious groups in efforts to liberalize American immigration policy, to combat juvenile delinquency, to expand recreational facilities, and in many other worth while areas of concern. These are hopeful signs, but interfaith cooperation in Minnesota is sporadic and spotty in its effectiveness.

Minnesota is the land of 10,000 lakes and a state of breathtaking grandeur. Its Twin Cities now constitute one of the nation's large metropolitan centers, and even support a major league baseball team. The St. Lawrence Seaway has opened its northern port, Duluth, to the sea and the outside world. It remains for Minnesotans to broaden and deepen the channels of interreligious dialogue and cooperation which will permit a greater use of the ample religious resources which lie, not fully tapped, in this rich heartland of America.

OVERVIEW

EVERY CHAPTER OF THIS BOOK SPEAKS FOR ITSELF. THESE studies point up a variety and complexity of communal patterns in rapidly-changing America. They indicate that increasingly urban America, increasingly middle-class America, increasingly fat (and more than a little smug) America, increasingly impersonal America, has been evolving new patterns of thought and action within the ranks of its major religious expressions. They reveal certain trends in interreligious relations which are hopeful and which should be encouraged. They also reveal trends which, in our view, are inimical to the best interests of religion and of the American people. Most importantly, we believe this book indicates clearly that the time has come for Americans to stop beguiling ourselves about the realities of our interfaith relationships and to face our problems candidly in a spirit of free inquiry. Religious conflicts in the political campaign of 1960, and since, underline how far we still have to go as a nation. With dispassion, fairness, and intellectual honesty, we can find solutions to many of the deep-seated difficulties we face in living our diverse religious heritages in a pluralistic society.

There is a tendency among Americans to lump together interracial and interreligious relationships. We tend to assume that these two areas are either identical or so closely related both in causes and in means of resolution that working at one automatically helps with the other. Nothing could be further from the truth.

There already exists an impressive collection of data about American race relations. There has been no comparable body of knowledge about interreligious relations. We do have much well-written, expensively-printed material exhorting Americans of differing faiths to get along well together because "this is the American way." But there are few studies of interreligious realities. Much more research is needed.

In the area of race relations, there is a high degree of agreement among leaders of American opinion regarding the principle of human equality. While there are sharp differences about methods of solution and the timing of action, there is wide agreement on the ultimate goals of racial justice and equality. There is no comparable agreement among religious leaders regarding either goals or methods in achieving interreligious understanding. The three major American religious expressions cannot even agree on definitions of fundamental terms like "establishment of religion" or "freedom thereof" in the First Amendment to the U. S. Constitution!

The floodlights of world attention have been focused on the day-to-day developments in America's racial drama. In the pitiless glare of that light, we have been compelled to look more seriously at the situation and to move, however falteringly and painfully, in the only direction mankind and our own consciences will let us move. The "religious issue" of 1960 briefly provided a comparable spotlight on the rapidly-evolving interreligious area. The ubiquitous interreligious conflict over federal aid to parochial schools indicates the continued need to concern ourselves seriously with interfaith relations.

Our ten studies of American cities demonstrate clearly that religious tensions and conflicts are wide-spread in America today. Students of American history tell us that this is nothing new, that such conflicts have existed since colonial days, though their content and expression have changed from generation to generation. Today, the precise occasions of conflict, the issues around which they revolve, certainly tend to vary from community to community and from month to month, but they are invariably civic and social rather than theological in nature. Sometimes they remain subterranean and chronic for many years—like the sometimes pathological distrust by old-line Protestants of the Roman Catholic Church— and then they burst above the surface, as in 1928 in the Smith campaign and again in the 1960 political campaign. Sometimes they are hardy perennials, like Christmas in the public schools or tax funds for sectarian purposes. Sometimes the explosion never comes, and infection festers underground. The specific issues vary: In Plainview, religion in the public schools; in Muncie, discrimination in housing; in New York City, birth control; in Los Angeles, public education; in Boston, child adoption; in Minnesota, religious symbols on a state-sponsored seal. Just as varied are the responses of religious organizations and the public. From apathy to near-violence they range, but there is one universal fact in today's America: Interreligious tension can no longer be concealed, can no longer be swept under the rug as un-American. Today, more and more newspapers, magazines, even television stations, realize that interreligious conflicts are a part of the American reality—they are news and must be treated as such.

The preceding chapters of this book suggest that there is serious interreligious tension which cannot be explained away only on the basis of increased publicity or greater public awareness. Careful analysis is required of the question: Why in a more mature America are interreligious conflicts apparently sharpening? And is this good or bad?

Religion and religious institutions ocupy a more prominent place in American communities than at any time in more than 200 years. More people are affiliated, even in percentage terms, than ever before in our history. Only one of every ten Americans was a church member in 1776; one out of five in 1860. Today over 60 per cent of the American people belong to a church or synagogue.

Many justified criticisms can be leveled against contemporary American religion. It is overly-centered in institutions and not in men's hearts and lives. It is superficial. Too often, it is thought of as an activity rather than as a permeating, fundamental force in daily life. All too frequently, there is little relationship between the announced position of a religious institution on a public matter and the convictions of many, if not most, of the adherents of the institution. There is a strong tendency to make religion irrelevant and to prefer it that way. "God, says the unwritten glossary of American politics, is a word in the last paragraph of a political speech," wrote the *Christian Century* magazine. Great public obeisance is paid to religious values, religious institutions, religious leaders, but if religionists begin to take faith seriously and to speak out publicly in terms of it, there is a tendency to tell them "to stick to religion."

Nevertheless, American religious groups are determined to make their voices heard as powerful vehicles of public opinion. The church and the synagogue speak frequently on broad moral issues and on specific political, economic, and social matters. In a few areas, religious groups exert virtual vetoes over the legislative process, federal, state, and local (as the Roman Catholic Church on birth control information to foreign countries, the Protestants on an ambassador to the Vatican, Jews on humane slaughter legislation). The attitude of the Roman Catholic Church on, for example, censorship of newsstand literature is not ignored today, nor is the attitude of Protestant groups with respect to religion in public education. And the Jewish group, a tiny minority, yet one of "the three major faiths," plays a disproportionately large and vocal role on such matters as civil rights, immigration, Israel, and church-state separation. Because these religious groups often disagree on public matters, tension inevitably results. And because these are serious issues with profound implications, conflict can be bitter.

One of the paramount facts about today's America that helps to account for the rising temperature of inter-religious tension is: *America is no longer a Protestant country.* Was it ever? It certainly was. In 1776, of every twenty-five Americans, not quite one was Catholic; less than one per 1,000 was Jewish. Richard Niebuhr has said that the United States was the first chance Protestantism had to build a culture. The Protestant imprint was unchallenged on our educational, social, economic, and political life. Though conservative churches like the

Episcopal and Lutheran had great influence and power, the spirit of the radical Protestant churches—first the Unitarian, then the Methodist, the American-born Camp-bellites (Disciples of Christ, Church of Christ), the Pentecostal expressions, the Mormons, and others—these dominated frontier America during all of the nineteenth century.

It is not surprising that, early in that century, European Roman Catholic prelates worked to dissuade their parishioners from moving to America for fear they would be drowned in a Protestant sea. And their fears were not unjustified; hundreds of thousands of Roman Catholics were totally assimilated here and lost to their faith. A primary impulse for Catholic parochial education was the certain knowledge that the public school movement was Protestant-dominated and that Protestant religious practices suffused the schools. Any survey of textbook materials used in nineteenth century American schools tells a startling story of the totally Protestant interpretation of history, philosophy, ethics, even of economics. The very Protestants who worked to erect a "wall of separation" between religion and the state permitted and even insisted on certain violations of the spirit of that principle for their own purposes—from Thanksgiving proclamations to "In God We Trust" on our coins, from government-paid ministers in the armed forces to Protestant-oriented religious observances in the schools. The power in American thought was Protestant, and the churches wielded their power openly.

Some observers have termed the current period the "post-Protestant age." The marked changes, which began to stir at the beginning of this century, have now reached maturity. The waves of immigration between 1850 and 1920 brought millions of Roman Catholics and Jews to these shores. So long as the Catholic tradition was "new, exotic, suspect" (in the words of Professor D. W. Brogan, the British historian), Protestant dominance of the American culture remained sure. Protestantism achieved its largest—and last—civic triumph in the Prohibition Law. But the unpopularity of the law and its ultimate repeal resulted in wide-spread irritation with the Protestant churches. H. L. Mencken and Sinclair Lewis heaped scorn on blue-nosed Protestantism. When the breezes of secularism blew briskly over the land, they hit the Protestant churches with the force of a tornado. Protestant hegemony gradually faded and secularism dominated the American intellectuals. Yet, Roman Catholicism began to rise like a dawning sun.

Only during the past two decades have American Protestants become fully aware of the fact that America is, in effect, no longer a Protestant country. Roman Catholics constitute the largest single denomination in the U.S., with a membership three times as large as the Methodists. Today there are about 62,000,000 Protestants in over 225 denominations, 40,000,000 Roman Catholics, 2,500,000 Eastern Orthodox (Greek, Russian, Armenian, etc.), and 5,250,000 Jews.

Will the United States ever have a Roman Catholic majority? Idle long-range speculation for many, this question appears to haunt some Protestants and some Jews who fear that traditional American liberties might be curtailed by a Catholic majority. This prospect has been called "conquest by fecundity." Current church statistics are shrouded in such confusion and controversy that it is hard enough to fix on present numbers, much less project into a distant future. A prominent Roman Catholic sociologist, Dr. Donald N. Barrett of Notre Dame University, claims that the Catholic population will total more than 86,000,000 by 1990. The sociologist cited a 1957 survey of the Census Bureau which, when figures were added to include Roman Catholics under fourteen years of age, indicated a membership of 43,037,000. He contended that the Catholic population gained by 35.8 per cent in the decade 1950-59 while the general population increased by only 16.6 per cent. "In other words," he said, "41.1 per cent of the total United States growth, 1950-59 was derived from the Catholic sector of the population."

Many other population experts dispute such figures. Arguing that Catholic population growth only slightly exceeds Protestant growth, they contend that the Roman Catholic birth rate will decline as more Roman Catholics move up the socio-economic ladder. Roman Catholics are even more urban centered than Protestants and the urban birth rate is lower than the rural. Roman Catholics have publicly lamented that, despite church teachings, their people now practice birth control to almost the same degree as do non-Catholics. In addition, they point to studies which demonstrate the serious "leakage" from Catholic ranks as a result of mixed (interreligious) marriages. Indeed, a Catholic study found that some 30 per cent of all marriages performed in Roman Catholic churches in 1960 were interfaith ones. Some students feel that nearly half of all Catholics who marry in the United States marry non-Catholic mates. (Mixed marriage is estimated at 8.6 per cent for Protestants and 7.5

per cent for Jews.) In addition, there is controversy about the very methods of counting adherents, and Protestants insist that Catholic groups inflate their statistics by listing every person baptized as a Catholic, irrespective of subsequent membership, affiliation, or disaffiliation. Protestant and Jewish membership figures are also, it should be noted, of questionable accuracy.

PLURALISM

For many years, the "melting pot" theory of American group life was accepted. Into the pot went people from all countries, ethnic and language backgrounds, religious persuasions, and even races. Theoretically, out came *homo Americanus,* presumably in a gray flannel suit. This new species never materialized, and now the very concept has been discarded. America is and will be a pluralistic society in which, ideally, different races, creeds, national, ethnic, and cultural groups try to persuade their adherents to retain their characteristic values generation after generation, even while all Americans try to live together and work together, combining competition and cooperation in a creative and healthy way.

Religious pluralism is not universally beloved in America. Implying as it does a kind of religious co-existence, the very concept is as repulsive to the consciences of some as is co-existence in the international sphere. Roman Catholic Father John Courtney Murray has declared: "Religious pluralism is against the will of God. But it is the human condition; it is written into the script of history. It will not somehow marvelously cease to trouble. . . ." Most Protestants and Jews would be less positive that pluralism offends God's will. But that religious pluralism is a fact of life in the America of the 1960's none but the blind can deny.

Coexistence among faiths within the framework of democratic pluralism has important corollaries. It clearly implies that each faith is obligated to conduct itself with self-restraint according to the rules of freedom and equality, without seeking to impose its will by coercion or by the harnessing of the power of the state to its own sectarian purposes. Under the concept of separation of religion and state, the state is necessarily both secular and neutral as among religions. This does not imply state hostility to religion. It means rather that each religion is equally free to cultivate its own resources without interference or assistance from the agencies of government.

In general, Protestant, Catholic, and Jewish groups have accepted the new concept of a religiously pluralistic America. They are in unblushing competition with one another not so much for the individual souls of Americans, but, in a sense, for the American soul, for the opportunity to shape American culture in the image of the religious ethic of each. Despite their clear inability to cooperate effectively most of the time, they do share enemies—secularism, materialism, apathy, intellectual superficiality, nihilism, and communism. The result: A many-splendored "culture" in a state of kaleidoscopic flux. An inevitable second result: interreligious tensions.

Leo Pfeffer has indicated that America has passed through three main periods of interreligious relations.*

---

* *Creeds in Competition,* Harper & Brothers, New York, 1958.

The first, embracing roughly the Colonial period, was dominated by conflicts over dogma and theology. The second, stretching into the early decades of the twentieth century, was marked by pronounced religious bigotry and prejudice against individuals. The third period is the present, marked by a decline of religious prejudice but a lively "creative competition" among Protestantism, Catholicism, and Judaism on basic public issues, with the beginnings of a more mature, searching conversation among thoughful religionists about universal theological concerns.

The present stage is that of a plural culture-in-becoming. No one religion can dominate the American culture. Each knows this limitation. The growing appreciation of religious pluralism in America was dramatized in November, 1958, when the American Council of Catholic Bishops referred, for the first time, to the various faiths, using the term *faiths* in the plural. Pluralism in America means, inevitably, competitive coexistence among the faith groups and between the faiths and secularism. Competition often spells conflict. Conflict is the price we must pay for competition. It is also prerequisite to progress in any field, as witness the stormy careers of such figures as Moses, Elijah, Jesus, Galileo, Washington, Lincoln, Einstein, and Gandhi.

If Americans learn to take the teachings of religion more seriously, conflict may well increase. If they don't learn to make religious teachings more important, the tensions may die down—but so will religion.

During these years of revolutionary change, each of the major religious groups has been greatly transformed.

The Roman Catholic community in America has

largely lost its prior sense of inferiority, its self-consciousness, its disabling fear of anti-Catholic persecution, and its working-class, immigrant mentality. Just how startling the change is can be symbolized by the fact that, of the 120 well-educated bishops and archbishops in the American Roman Catholic hierarchy in 1961, not a single one was born of a parent with a college education. Today's Catholic laity is increasingly well-educated, articulate, self-confident, aggressive, and politically formidable. They are the products of a great network of educational, social, fraternal, and related institutions within the framework of a vigorous church life.

The coming of age of American Catholicism has been well advertised by the career of John Fitzgerald Kennedy, but he has been merely the symbol of a many-faceted development. Population growth and mobility have made Roman Catholics the major religious group in virtually every large American city. We have demonstrated in this book that Roman Catholics have frequently not hesitated to try to impress their beliefs and concepts not only upon their own followers, but, when they have had the strength, upon the general population as well.

If this volume indicates a swiftly-emerging pluralistic America, and if in principle, at least, successful pluralism requires communication among all the major strands making up the intricate tapestry, the evidence of our chapters raises serious doubts that such communication exists in many areas, and least of all among religionists of the various faiths. The Roman Catholic group, as a matter of religious principle and sociological conditioning, maintains a conscious and strong impulse toward religious separatism in almost every community. Roman Catholic clergymen tend to isolate themselves from the mainstream of American communal life (Catholic clergy have been described as the least accessible group in America), and in certain areas press their laymen to do likewise. The testimony of this volume is eloquent that Catholic withdrawal is manifest in Ministerial Associations in most communities, Health and Welfare Councils here, Community Chests there, interreligious efforts in behalf of civic causes in still other towns. Roman Catholic parochialism goes even further in some communities, to separate organizations for policemen, labor unionists, firemen, and employees of large department stores. In New York City, parallel Protestant and Jewish organizations have sprung up. This calculated divorcement from general community life cannot reduce built-in tensions.

The priest, the rabbi, and the minister may still be linked together in ancient jokes but, in most American communities, they come together in real life only occasionally, usually at rather formal occasions, and they rarely develop a close personal relationship. Exemplifying perhaps an extreme of these distances was a rather poignant letter from a Methodist minister which appeared in the *Pittsburgh Post-Gazette*. "I have preached in Pittsburgh for thirty years," wrote Pastor Hodge M. Eagleson, "and do not know personally a single Catholic priest or Jewish rabbi." The minister proposed an imaginative remedy—a tri-faith fishing trip to Canada—and the publicity attracted a Catholic priest who explained that he had never met a Protestant clergyman. It is presumed that an equally lonely rabbi was flushed out for the occasion. But one wonders about the state of interreligious relations in America if similar stunts must be summoned up as bait in order to get clergymen of various faiths to know one another.

A study of Holyoke, Massachusetts, entitled *Protestant and Catholic*,* found that Catholic and Protestant clergymen not only did not know one another personally but, for the most part, had no desire for closer relationships. Mutual hostility was marked. Said a rabbi about the Catholic priest, ". . . The Catholic proposition [is] 'You serve God in your way and we in *His.*' "

The wide-spread belief of Protestants and Jews that the Roman Catholic Church is a monolithic, united structure is flatly contradicted in the pages of this book. The spectrum of Roman Catholic convictions about our society and its problems can be seen in the irreconcilable differences between the reactionary Brooklyn *Tablet* and the sophisticated and liberal *Commonweal;* or between the late Senator Joseph McCarthy of Wisconsin and enlightened Senator Eugene McCarthy of Minnesota (no kin). Non-Catholics tend to see Roman Catholics in one large, undifferentiated stereotype. But intra-Catholic differences are immense and growing. There are clergy-laymen differences of no small significance. There are personality and ideological clashes among the hierarchy. Ethnic divisions impinge upon many a parish, and rivalry between Irish Catholics and Italian Catholics has increasingly added tang to many a political contest. There are distinctions and even classes among the various religious orders. Regional differences abound. The rigid East

---

* *Protestant and Catholic,* Kenneth Underwood, Beacon Press, Boston, 1957.

Coast churches appear to stand in sharp contrast with the more urbane and relaxed dioceses in the Midwest and Southwest. One has only to recall the anomaly of Cardinal Spellman in New York supporting Franco Spain at the same time that Bishop Sheil in Chicago was condemning it, or to note large Catholic membership in the John Birch Society, a group excoriated by authorized Catholic spokesmen. The Church is proudly authoritarian and lives in Eternity; but in the here and now it is subject to formidable outside pressures which impinge upon it and, equally, to ceaseless internal ferment which bubbles beneath the surface and boils up occasionally to public view. The Church is also universal; but the contrasts between Roman Catholicism in Spain or Colombia with Catholicism in France or Belgium—or, even more, the United States—are so vast that one marvels at the flexibility which embraces all these divergencies within the ample folds of one Mother Church. Yet the stereotype persists among Protestants and Jews.

If non-Catholics have fears about the Roman Catholic Church, Roman Catholics have fears about non-Catholics as well. Catholics discern in both Protestants and Jews a tendency toward thoughtless deification of the gods of liberalism of our age. Catholics worry—out loud and in print—about the loss of religious commitment among both Jews and Protestants. In an ever-more secularized society, Catholics fear, Protestantism and Judaism may blow hither and yon in rootless confusion, bringing America to spiritual sterility. To be sure, the decay of religious commitment and of moral values in the United States has given pause to non-Catholics and Catholics alike, but the latter have appeared to be most vocal.

Said *America,* liberal Catholic weekly, on March 5, 1960: ". . . Unless the current massive pulverization of solid religious and moral convictions is halted, we may yet see our uncommitted State definitely committed to a rampant secularism that is no less hostile to sectarianism than Soviet Russia."

Revealing was a frank editorial which appeared in *America* just prior to the 1960 election. "However John F. Kennedy may fare on Election Day," the magazine declared editorially, "a wide-spread Jewish antipathy to the influence of the Catholic Church in America will persist." Noting that Jews are antagonistic to Catholic positions on church-state separation, censorship, divorce, federal aid, and dealing with the Russians, the magazine continued: " . . . In view of the values which prevail among many educated Jews, we find these attitudes understandable but there is another side to the coin. Many Catholics feel a corresponding distrust of Jewish influence on American life. What the Jewish voter regards as liberal and progressive views often seem to his Catholic counterpart to be inimical to the moral health of the community. Jewish support of extreme liberal positions on such questions as standards for the entertainment industry and the control of pornography—not to mention birth control, divorce, and in some cases even abortion —distresses Catholics."

America continued: "Since Jewish family life is generally exemplary and carefully guarded, these public positions suggest the lack of a sense of responsibility for the moral atmosphere of the community outside the family circle. Devotion to religious liberty is admirable but not when it looks like an alliance with forces seeking the complete secularization of American life. Even flexibility in dealing with the Russians, desirable though it may be, sometimes resembles a willingness to placate them. . . ."

There are deep differences among the faiths in their responses to issues of foreign policy. Among the issues in which interreligious disagreement is sharp is the controversy over U.S. and U.N. policies in the Middle East. Almost all American Jews see the whole region through the prism of the State of Israel, with which they feel a profound, almost mystical, bond. Many Protestants and Roman Catholics, on the other hand, view Israel as the chief source of the tensions which keep the Middle East in a chronic uproar.

Protestant clergymen in particular feel strongly about the lot of the more than 850,000 Arab refugees. Their interest stems not only from Christian charity, but also from the wide-spread missionary and educational activities they traditionally have carried on in the whole area. Protestant denominational universities in the U.S. have been havens for Arab students—and their anti-Israel propaganda. Many Protestant leaders continue to see Israel as a cantankerous foreign element in the simmering pot of the Middle East.

Roman Catholic leaders have centered their harsh response to Israel on its refusal to internationalize Jerusalem. Recently, however, the Vatican appears to have begun to moderate its attitude toward Israel, and it can be anticipated that this change will gradually communicate itself to American Catholic leaders, too.

In general, it must be said that Christian religious leaders display less compassion and friendship toward Israel than does the American population at large, to the extent that Americans have a view and express it. Certainly, the daily general press is more kindly disposed toward Israel than is the Christian religious press.

The equation suggested by *America*—that *secularism is a prelude to Communism*—has penetrated much of the thinking of major religious groups in America. It sometimes leads to the conviction that those who oppose more formal religion in public life are, therefore, the minions of the wicked. Roman Catholic and Protestant spokesmen, increasingly impatient with secular humanism, often tend to set up religion (Christianity) as the flag under which America battles "atheistic Communism." Needless to say, Jews derive little comfort from such formulations, to say nothing of the millions of unaffiliated Americans. Nor is there reason to believe that the uncommitted peoples of the world are disposed to rally to the cause of freedom in the name of Western religion, especially those who know how much of American religious commitment is shallow and divorced from life's real problems.

AMERICAN JEWRY

The Jewish community in the United States has also changed markedly, especially since the end of World War II. In a brief period, American Jewry has been jet-propelled from the periphery of American life, an immigrant, low-income, embattled, defensive group, to a rising middle-class status, a community of highly-educated, mobile, culturally-advanced, predominantly native-born Americans. In an earlier generation, Jewish organizations felt constrained to hover in the background, to avoid entering the lists of public competition or conflict. Anti-

Semitism, it was feared, might get worse. These organizations preferred to find sympathetic non-Jews to fight even the battles for the defense of Jewish rights. After all, many Jews conceded, isn't this a "Christian country"? This fear of anti-Semitism, which reached its peak of anguish during the Nazi period, relegated the Jewish community to a self-imposed status of second-class citizenship.

This sense of inadequacy, of diffidence, of defensive self-abnegation has now declined. In most communities most of the time, Jewish organizations are prepared to assert the values they cherish and to press for them in the public arena. By and large, the current climate of America is hospitable to such Jewish group aspirations. Christians appear to respect Jewish values more than the near-hysteria of that minority of Jews who still think only in terms of, "What will the non-Jew say?" Thus, while American Jewry represents only 3 per cent of the American population, public deference to the balanced representation of "the three major faiths" invests Jewry with respect and opportunities disproportionate to its numbers. Our community studies indicate that Jewish groups are grasping these opportunities with varying degrees of wisdom and success.

In addition, more Jews are in a better position to know the values of their heritage and of our society than ever before. Of the three major religious groups, the Jews are perhaps the best educated and the most strongly impelled in the direction of education and culture. *Fortune** magazine described New York City's 2,250,000 Jews as the *élan* of the city's intellectual

---

* February, 1960.

and cultural life. There are, however, danger signals within American Jewry. While the stubborn liberal streak of the Jews persists, deriving from minority status and history and religious ethic, it is being steadily diluted by pressure toward conformity to the conservative values of suburbia. And the American Jew today is a suburban dweller in unprecedented numbers. His abdication of center-cities has been most dramatically demonstrated in Cleveland ("city without Jews"), but is true everywhere. New maturity, new self-confidence, and new self-acceptance are combining to condition the response of Jews and Jewish groups to the emerging new American society, but the pattern of response is far from unitary or clear.

These studies do indicate that, for the most part, American Jews outside the Deep South are less concerned about anti-Semitism than at any time in the American past. Even the jarring outbreak of swastika-daubings and vandalism against Jewish institutions in 1959-60, and the repercussions of the Eichmann trial in 1961, did not disturb the security of American Jewry for more than a few brief moments. Remaining discriminations against them (country clubs, some posh resorts, certain high-level employment, a few plush neighborhoods) are primarily irritating, not crippling. Jewish leaders are usually not afraid to challenge what they feel to be injustices against them in our society, whether with Jewish ritual implications (Sunday laws which penalize Jewish Sabbath observers, church-state violations) or which affect Jews as involved in the democratic process (the integration fight, changes in immigration laws). Their organizations lead in many community crusades for good causes, particularly in the North. Jews in the South, feeling themselves vulnerable, have not played a prominent role in the struggle for Negro rights.

The Jewish community of the 1960's is primarily native-born (90.7 per cent) and has virtually completed the process of Americanization. Its traditional reverence for education has also been Americanized; American Jews now lavish upon physics, psychology, and medicine the devotion which in earlier centuries was poured into the study of Torah and Talmud. Jews are the least religious, measured by attendance at religious services and statements of belief, of any religious group in America. U.S. Jews appear to be becoming more and more secularized, even while still higher percentages join the synagogues. Their social and political attitudes reflect a lively and liberal humanitarianism which is, at the very least, nicely harmonious with ethical humanism. Yet Jews are very conscious of their Jewish identity which is expressed in terms of a strong feeling for Israel, a sense of connection with other Jews throughout the world, an attachment to some Jewish cultural as well as religious traditions, and a tendency to self-segregation. Jews share exceedingly close communal bonds. Marriage outside the Jewish group is frowned upon, and the intermarriage rate is low. A result is that primary relationships of most Jews are with other Jews. A recent study in Detroit indicated that 77 per cent of the Jews surveyed reported that all or nearly all of their close friends were Jewish.*

Jewish family life, while it boasts a lower divorce rate and is more stable than that of the American family in general, is also undergoing strains and changing relation-

---

* *The Religious Factor,* Gerhard Lenski, Doubleday, New York, 1961.

ships. In many ways, the Jewish group is a remarkably successful minority in America—exhibit A of immigrant group adjustment. But, increasingly, the goals to which American Jews aspire are oriented around American cultural values—happiness, security, popularity, wealth, power, success, and status—more than the historic values of Judaism—piety, love of Torah, prayer, and ethical living under God.

Synagogues and Jewish civic groups battle manfully against these trends and dangers. The gap between them and their constituents is an outstanding fact revealed in these chapters. Still and all, American Jews continue to support their synagogues and national organizations, and these organizations now enjoy strength and status which offer increasing possibilities for deepening Jewish commitments and values on the American scene.

A MINORITY FAITH

American Protestants have suffered a severe historic jolt. This is no longer "their" country. The shock has been most painful in the cities, which now contain the overwhelming majority of the American people, and where Protestants, who dominated rural America, do not hold sway. With over 80 per cent of the Roman Catholic community and 85 per cent of the Jewish community living in twenty-one metropolitan centers of the nation, Protestants have developed a minority response in many of the key cities in America. Revealing was the turmoil which preceded the decision to build the new national headquarters of the huge National Council of Churches of Christ, major institution of American Protestantism, on

Riverside Drive in New York. *Christian Century,* influential independent Protestant weekly, protested against erecting the headquarters in "the Catholic-Jewish canyon that is New York City." The magazine buttressed its stand by citing the experiences of a leading Protestant minister who served a Park Avenue flock for sixteen years. He resigned, discouraged and wearied by leadership of "an embattled minority in New York City."

Our chapters indicate clearly that this new sense of minority consciousness on the part of American Protestants permeates their organizational thinking not only in New York, but in Boston, Philadelphia, Cleveland, Los Angeles, and elsewhere as well. In the face of what they regard as the united and menacing power of the growing Roman Catholic Church, Protestant leaders see themselves as disunited, lacking in authority and strong organization, their power ebbing. Southern Protestantism is defensive, deeply fragmentized over racial, doctrinal, and denominational matters. It has the potential power of numbers, but it gives few indications of a sense of moral responsibility or of religious creativity. Only in Muncie and Nashville, of the cities analyzed here, does Protestantism hold its accustomed sway and its traditional sense of self-assurance.

Protestantism has lost much of its vibrant confidence in its own values. Hard work, self-reliance, sobriety, and thrift are still respected virtues. But the America of the 1960's places a higher premium on consumer consumption, social security, and organizational teamwork. The somber, simple, culturally-parochial, politically-provincial outlook of early Protestantism has been replaced by a complex culture, with radical experimentation in the arts and sciences, in world relationships, and in individual human contacts. Increasing numbers of Protestants have been caught up in the new wave.

The old Protestant ethic has not broken down completely; our textbooks and political speeches are still replete with its remnants. But it is honored in the breach, to the extent that it is honored at all, and it becomes increasingly irrelevant to the demands of the space age.

Seeking to compel sobriety through prohibition proved a dismal failure, and Protestantism paid a heavy price for its dominance in the prohibition movement. Self-reliance is valued—and Americans are being warned increasingly by psychologists and religionists, among others, that the retention of individual identity is a serious need among us—but unemployment compensation and public medical care are more enticing to most people, to say nothing of the security of pension plans and the strength of labor unions.

The responses of Protestantism have been varied. Rev. Billy Graham and others seek to reawaken zeal for the old virtues through fundamentalist evangelism. The Norman Vincent Peales in and out of the pulpit have drained Protestantism of most of its theology and have tried to fill it instead with the sweet wines of pseudo-psychological therapy and the vacuity of positive thinking. Still others, with Reinhold Niebuhr as their prophet, are sponsoring a revival of interest in orthodox theology.

There has been a strong and growing ecumenical movement in American Protestantism. Mergers of traditionally-warring denominations are proceeding apace. One month after the election of John Kennedy, Roman Catholic, as President of the U.S., Dr. Eugene Carson

Blake, leader of American Presbyterians, dramatically proposed a merger of his denomination with the Episcopal, Methodist, and United Church of Christ groups. Such a merger, if consummated, would create a new Protestant denomination with over 18,000,000 adherents. The immediate and enthusiastic seconding of the proposal by Bishop James Pike of the Episcopal Diocese of California added to the drama. As mergers are cemented, the leaders of these larger, stronger, enthusiastic groups may grant their national leadership more authority to fight for ethical causes and may be prepared to compete more vigorously, both nationally and locally, in the inter-religious competitions we see everywhere. On the other hand, these amalgams may be pallid indeed—just to keep the internal peace.

For reasons which these studies do not show, the other rather large religious bodies in America have not yet taken their proper place in communal endeavors. A Greek Orthodox priest was one of four clergymen who invoked at President Kennedy's Inauguration; and Greek Orthodoxy is making a strong bid to become one of "four major faiths." To some extent, the energies of organized Moslem groups are expended in behalf of nationalist groups in North Africa and the Middle East. The various Chinese groups are engrossed in the political struggle of that embattled nation. But it is likely that in not too many decades, new minority religious groups will emerge in America to add their voices and their convictions to the interreligious mixture.

Yet another source of tension has resulted from the so-called religious revival of the post-World War II era. Great pressures are being exerted on all Americans to believe and to affiliate. The right to disbelieve has always been as sacred to America as the right to believe freely. It was this voluntary character of American religion which, in the view of De Tocqueville and other European observers, gave American religion its dynamic quality. The right to disbelieve is in jeopardy in America today. Certainly, the non-believers represent the most important unorganized minority in American life.

Of the first seven U.S. Presidents, only one was a member of a church. Could an American be elected to the presidency today, or to any major public office, if he did not pay weekly public obeisance to some church or synagogue? In the running church-state controversies about religion and public education, described in careful detail in the chapter about Plainview but bursting out in many American towns, the three religious groups virtually negotiate settlements regarding how much and what kind of religion may be reflected in the public schools. But what about atheists, agnostics, non-believers? Who speaks for them? They have become second-class citizens, to some degree. In today's climate, the overwhelming majority of the American people have come to regard atheism as an un-American doctrine, tantamount to and probably connected with Communism. A 1954 study* found that 84 per cent of the people polled would not permit an atheist to teach in a college, and 60 per cent would not permit a book by an atheist in a public library. With the agitation of the Birch Society and the primitives of the extreme right wing, it is not likely that

---

* *Communism, Conformity and Civil Liberties,* Samuel Stouffer, Doubleday, Garden City, N.Y., 1955.

dissent and non-conformity have gained in popularity.

The U.S. Census Bureau, in 1957, made some ambitious studies, finding that 96 per cent of the people identified themselves as Protestants, Catholics, or Jews in response to the question: "What is your religion?" Yet, the combined totals of all church membership figures indicate that some 68,000,000 Americans do not belong to any church or synagogue. Here, indeed, is the great, silent, forgotten minority in American life. If "we are a religious people whose institutions presuppose a Supreme Being," as Justice William O. Douglas has said, where does that leave the 68,000,000? If creeds are in competition, who bespeaks the values of the 68,000,000, and how? Where are their organizations, their lobbyists, and spokesmen? To refuse to give lip service to the emerging American religious faith is becoming a new form of subversion in American life. And as the cold war is falsely posed as atheistic Communism vs. religion, the unchurched and the non-believer may, more and more, find themselves the unwitting victims of the religious revival.

SEPARATION

The most pervasive source of interreligious discord, and perhaps the source of most serious interreligious tensions in America today, is the question of separation of religion and the state. Every chapter of this book echoes with this truth. There is no doubt about the fact that the Jewish community feels most strongly about this matter, takes more absolute positions on almost every specific issue which comes up, is simultaneously most aggressive and defensive in this area. This reaction stems chiefly from the special nature of Jewish history. Jews have had uniformly unhappy experiences with the union of church and state, be the church Protestant, Catholic, or Moslem. Protestants have had no reason to complain about their established churches in England, Scotland, and Scandinavian countries. Roman Catholics have been at ease in South America and in those countries of Europe which are traditionally Catholic.

For the Jewish community, the First Amendment to the U.S. Constitution has been elevated to the status of a virtual Magna Carta, consistently interpreted to mean that a wall of separation should exist between religion and the state.

Of course, the Jewish community's actions are not always consistent with its professions. Jews are militantly, occasionally almost hysterically, sensitive to religious teachings in public schools. On the other hand, the Jewish community did not follow the lead of the Baptist and some Methodist groups in turning down federal funds for sectarian hospitals, under the terms of the Hill-Burton Act. No group has been more zealous about providing chaplains for the armed forces to be paid out of government funds, a practice frowned on as a violation of church-state separation by a few religious groups as well as by some civil libertarians. For the Jewish community, the public school is the crucial church-state battleground, and all compromises are viewed suspiciously by Jews as the "opening wedge." Roman Catholics and most Protestant groups have not the slightest intentions of backing down on their varying positions in this area, and, as a result, a lessening of tensions appears highly unlikely.

Perhaps the most ominous reef in the whole sea of interreligious relations is the question of government aid to sectarian schools. The Roman Catholic community has been increasingly squeezed by grave financial difficulties as costs rise and a higher percentage of its children go to parochial schools. Church leaders have moved from indirect attacks on legislative and judicial bans on any form of public subsidy for parochial education to open demands for such funds. To the Roman Catholic Church, this is not merely a matter of desperately needed economic assistance; it is also, in their view, a serious matter of religious conscience and of civil rights. They consider the current practice an intolerable discrimination against families who prefer religious education to the public school and must, as a result, pay twice for such education.

To Protestantism, this is the key church-state issue. A few denominations are rapidly expanding their parochial school systems. But virtually all major Protestant denominations are taking outspoken national leadership in the fight against subsidies for parochial schools, both on the grounds of protecting the public school system and because they fear Catholic expansionism in general.

Most Jewish community organizations believe that church-state separation requires a continuing flat prohibition against the allocation of public monies for parochial education. A major beneficiary of the public schools, both educationally and in terms of integration into America, most Jews fear for the demise of the unique public education concept if parochial schools become, in effect, a parallel system to public schools. Nevertheless, as Jewish parochial schools have expanded (50,000 pupils in 1961), pressures have begun to develop in traditional Jewish circles for a modification of the Jewish position.

That this issue carries dynamite is obvious. Witness the attack by Francis Cardinal Spellman, on the eve of President Kennedy's Inauguration, on the report of the President's education task force, which did not include public funds for private education in its recommendations. Witness the bitter legislative dispute in New York State in 1961 following Governor Rockefeller's announcement of his plan to give indirect aid to sectarian institutions of higher learning. Witness the bitter and highly-organized clash in 1961 over federal aid to parochial schools which resulted in the gutting of the President's original program. Witness the bitter response to Cardinal Spellman's charge that the President's education program was a "crime" against Catholics and would spell "the end of our parochial schools."

In many ways, the raging struggle over federal aid to parochial schools has an "Alice in Wonderland" aspect. Who could have predicted that a Roman Catholic President would take a position against public aid to parochial schools, which would make him the darling of the most extreme separationists, including the Protestants and Other Americans United for Separation of Church and State (POAU) and the Baptists, while being belabored unceasingly by the Catholic bishops? Who could have anticipated that the first Roman Catholic President would be stoutly defended after his election by some of the very clergymen who had publicly worried about his Catholicism during the campaign? Yet these things have happened.

Cardinal Spellman, spurning the advice of other Roman Catholic leaders, unleashed his attack on Kennedy's education task force on the very eve of the President's Inauguration. Within weeks, the bishops launched the strongest Roman Catholic drive in American history in behalf of tax monies for parochial schools. The President has frequently and ruefully observed that the Church had never made so vigorous a campaign before, that it was only during his administration that a virtual ultimatum (if there is no federal aid to parochial schools, "there will be no alternative but to oppose such discrimination") had been handed down by the bishops. Indeed, *Look* magazine has contended that the hierarchy had deliberately tried to defeat Kennedy in the campaign and, after his election, had set out with calculation to defeat the President's aid to education program. *Look* quoted a Kennedy aide, also a Roman Catholic, as muttering privately, "The bishops put the shiv in us."

President Kennedy may be personalizing the conflict and *Look* may be seeing bishops under the bed. What is more likely is that Roman Catholic leaders chose this particular moment in American history to step up their drive for federal aid for these reasons: (1) The realization that, for the first time, the nation was ready to make a truly massive infusion of public funds to strengthen education in America; (2) The Church's desperate and growing financial squeeze of mounting costs and a shrinking supply of nuns and brothers available to teach without salary; (3) The sobering realization that Catholic intellectual life in America is second-rate and that most Catholic schools seriously lack in excellence; and (4) The belief that standards of public schools would soon be significantly raised by crash programs of public support, thus deepening the gap between Catholic and public education.

No one can predict the long-range outcome of this

struggle. But without doubt this issue may well strain the relationships among American religious groups to a degree no other issue has. The ability of the faiths to cope with these strains will be a major test of America's religious maturity. The outcome eventually will have an incalculably profound effect upon American life.

The failure of the U.S. Congress to adopt an aid-to-education bill in 1961 was undoubtedly due, in large measure, to formidable Roman Catholic opposition. Senator Wayne Morse charged that the Church had stirred up "animosity and misunderstanding" by its all-or-nothing position. For this, Cardinal Spellman branded Morse as "an old friend who has turned against us." Yet there were indications that some Roman Catholic leaders had second thoughts about the unfavorable public relations which the Church undoubtedly elicited in the school fight. Cardinal Cushing of Boston, in October, 1961, appealed to his coreligionists to seek to persuade—and not to coerce—the American public of the Catholic view. He warned against giving the impression that Catholics would kill aid to public education if they didn't get public funds for parochial schools.

Equally significant was an editorial in 1962, in *Commonweal,* Catholic lay magazine. In an obvious thrust at Cardinal Spellman, the editors rebuked Catholic spokesmen who gave vent to "violent pronouncements" on this subject, thus intensifying religious antagonisms.

For reasons we have already indicated, it is usually easier for Protestant and Jewish leaders to come together than for either group to meet with representative Roman Catholics. In addition, Jews share to some extent the widespread, deep-seated Protestant fear of Catholicism. Anti-

Catholicism has been called the anti-Semitism of the intellectual. But it is undoubtedly fed, in addition, by reactions against the methods used by some Roman Catholic groups in asserting their convictions (censorship, boycott, legislative coercion at times) on the social scene.

Writing in the *New Republic,* William Clancy, an articulate Catholic layman, faced the issue squarely: "There can be no doubt that a profound distrust of Catholic intentions toward the free society exists in the United States. And the American non-Catholic community is not entirely to blame for this. The public face of American Catholicism has too often been the face of an ecclesiastical Mrs. Grundy; the voice of American Catholicism has too often been a voice from the past, speaking in the accents of a 'Christian' society that will never return. And the public actions, the group pressures, of American Catholicism, have too often ignored the proper limits of such action within a liberal-pluralist society. The results have been to create that image of Catholicism as a monolithic, antidemocratic power structure which troubles many non-Catholics—and, increasingly, many Catholics, too."

Deep-seated disagreements about specific and fundamental social ideas make clashes between Roman Catholics and non-Catholics an ongoing American reality. The question is not how to remove such conflicts or to prevent them. More important are the questions: are the conflicts healthy, centering about real differences, and are the disagreements carried on in an honest, open manner?

There are indications in our community studies that many interreligious conflicts are healthy and are carried on in an open manner. Some have helped to clarify community issues and to cement individual and group relationships. Sharp conflict has helped to shake the complacency and gelatinous placidity of American communal life, has forced many Americans to face issues more compelling than the treacle spread on the TV screen. It is not at all bad for whole urban or suburban communities to have to learn about religious convictions, ethical principles, and tactical techniques in order to face an issue. This was one of the favorable lessons of the political campaign of 1960.

It is reassuring, as these studies tell us, that recent religious tensions and community conflicts over interreligious differences have led neither to violence nor to lasting enmities in the communities of our land. Scars appear to heal rapidly, friendships frequently spring unexpectedly from battles around a boardroom table or public auditorium, and the next issue descends upon more sensitive, better-informed, wiser leaders and participants. The constructive results of interreligious tensions do not lead us, however, to believe in an unlimited "cold war of religion"; that certainly would be destructive of the essential fabric of American life. But we must face realistically the certainty of openly expressed religious differences and tensions among America's religions.

One of the melancholy aspects of the current interreligious picture is that full use of new maturities and spiritual resources is prevented by the overwhelming ignorance on the part of Americans of religion—their own and, how much the more so, the religions of others. It is not our purpose here to discuss denominational religious education, but the fact cannot be avoided that masses of Americans, less-than-minimally educated in the real purposes and processes of Western religions, tend to think of religion as just another ceremony, an occasional Sunday morning in church or a few times a year in the synagogue, as the agency for giving to life's milestone occasions some intangible extra depth, or as the harbinger of pie in the sky.

This book helps us to see the differential roles which the various faiths play in the contemporary American city. Whereas a generation ago, social class and ethnic differences were among the most important divisions of the American city, today the vital subcommunities of the American city are distinguished by religion and race. This change is seen most clearly within the Roman Catholic community, which has succeeded almost miraculously in creating a single American Catholic community by welding its many ethnic and class elements into a unified whole. Most of the ethnic tensions among Italians, Irish, Poles, Germans, and other Catholics have been submerged in an overarching and flourishing American Catholic Church—a church which Nathan Glazer (*Commentary,* January, 1962) characterized as one of "powerful organization and great fund-raising capacity, puritanism, and sexual prudery (of the Irish as well as the American variety), and a generally narrow and illiberal outlook in politics and social life (though combined with an enlightened attitude on race)."

As has been indicated, the Jewish community has undergone immense changes as well. Like the white Protestant community, it is economically comfortable. Like the white Protestant community, the Jewish community has become on the whole a "status quo" community, quite pleased with things as they are. Continuing irritations and occasional fears on the part of the Jewish community are in no way comparable to the titanic struggle for self-fulfilment in which the Negro community is engaged, or the heavy demands upon society which the Roman Catholic community feels constrained to make in relation to public aid for separate institutions and in relation to the Catholic conception of morality. Thus the Jewish community frequently finds its community relations in the city focusing, in diverse ways, on "Catholic" and "Negro" issues.

The Jewish community in the United States has an exceptional opportunity. For the first time, perhaps in history, a Jewish community has the freedom and the economic resources to devote itself, in good measure, to the general health of society rather than to concentrate its energies exclusively, as was essential in the past, upon fighting for its own security and survival. As of 1962, it is impossible to predict whether the Jewish community can fully exploit this opportunity. A prodigious proportion of Jewish energy is being exhausted in the marvels of fund-raising for Jewish causes. Many Jews have obviously sought comfort behind self-imposed walls of Jewish togetherness. And synagogues and other Jewish institutions, with few exceptions, have not contributed their economic resources and social creativity to such urgent community problems as Negro housing, narcotics, migrant workers, prison reform, and mental health.

It is clear that, despite the buffeting of time and diminishing power, the white Protestant community remains the normative group in American life, is still the symbol of charity and social welfare, and provides the cement which holds together most of the community welfare agencies, community chests, and reforming groups in America. The white Protestant maintains a cherished tradition of communal resonsibility for the victims of social crisis. As Protestants originally founded most of the great reform movements—including those set up to educate immigrants, train ex-slaves, feed the hungry, and rehabilitate the prisoner—so does the Protestant community today, despite the alarming loss of identity it faces in the big cities, stand for community responsibility and social service for all.

INTERFAITH EDUCATION

America's religious groups have been so preoccupied with their individual needs and immediate tasks that there has been only sporadic and largely ineffectual interreligious education. For doctrinal reasons, the Roman Catholic community has been the most resistive to such efforts, but neither of the other great faiths boasts a prideful record in this regard, either.

Far from realizing their full potential for contributing to interfaith understanding, religious groups frequently foster antagonism toward other faiths. A searching three-year study of religious texts has been conducted by Yale University and Dropsie College in cooperation with the American Jewish Committee. The fact of these studies in themselves reflects a growing appreciation of the community relations effects of religious teachings. Preliminary findings indicate that Protestant, Catholic, and Jewish educational materials all leave much to be desired in interpreting their sister faiths to the young student. As Father Trafford P. Maher, Chairman of the Department of Psychology at St. Louis University, pointed out: "Catholic schools tend to pretend there are no other religions. What we really have found is a weakness of omission in

Catholic curricula, rather than contents that were detrimental to other religions." Despite considerable improvement in recent years, many Protestant texts were found to include material felt to be invidious in their treatment of Catholicism and of Judaism and, particularly, the role of the Jews in the crucifixion of Jesus. Jewish materials, generally, were found to lack in imaginative and well-motivated approach to Christian faiths. Textbook revision and the need for more sensitively conceived new curricula are on the agenda of many religious bodies. But bias, hostility, and excessive tribal loyalty are still the bitter fruit of much religious education in America.

There are those in all faith groups who would go further and insist that the fundamental problem in inter-religious relations is doctrinal, and that everything which has been done thus far has been palliative. Until Christianity purges itself of the myth of eternal Jewish guilt for the crucifixion of Jesus, and until Roman Catholicism gives up the "sole true church" concept as a theologically-grounded postulate, true coexistence is not possible, in the view of these leaders.

The religious press also plays a role in shaping the attitudes of Americans toward their own faiths and those of their neighbors. The Roman Catholic press is a stronger journalistic power than that maintained by Protestants and Jews. A strong Catholic press service radiates out of Washington, D. C., serving more than 100 Catholic diocesan newspapers with a combined circulation of 3,500,000. Many Roman Catholic newspapers are official organs of local dioceses. While there is a broad spectrum, ranging from the moderate and enlightened *America* and *Commonweal* among the magazines, and the

Messenger among the newspapers to the hard-shelled St. Paul *Wanderer*, it is fair to say that the Roman Catholic press in the main exerts a conservative and isolationist influence which is often "more anti-Communist than the pope." Waspish criticisms of such groups as the American Civil Liberties Union, the American Jewish Congress, the United Nations, Americans for Democratic Action, and other civil libertarian and international bodies as being "soft" or "left-wing" are much more common in the Roman Catholic press than in either the Protestant or Jewish. The Catholic press is much more open about doctrinal differences as well as social or political outlook. Indeed, much of the Protestant press displays the bland innocuousness which is the bane of contemporary Protestantism. Protestant publications, except some fundamentalist varieties, are generally liberal, humanitarian, shapeless, and inoffensive.

The Anglo-Jewish press is distinguished largely by its striking secularity, its almost universal liberalism, its shoddy journalistic standards, and its limited impact on Jewish public opinion. There are a few well-written, forward-looking Jewish-sponsored magazines which, except for institutionally subsidized ones, have very small circulation.

DIALOGUE

These days a lot of people are talking about interfaith dialogue—but, judging by these chapters, not many are actually dialoguing locally. In most of the communities cited in this volume, ongoing communication among the faith groups simply does not exist. Dialogue has come to mean the process of frank and open communication among the leaders of all faith groups in a community, to discuss the fragile and agitated issues about which there are deep divisions as well as to discuss those matters on which joint action might be taken. A recent study of the conflict in Connecticut over bus transportation for parochial school children reveals the striking fact that at no time in the controversy did leaders of the three faiths in the state meet to try to solve the problem.

There have been some fascinating tentative national ventures into dialogue. In 1958, the Fund for the Republic convened some 150 Protestant, Jewish, and Catholic leaders for several consecutive days of intensive dialogue on a broad gamut of delicate doctrinal and social issues. If it proved that dialogue is necessary and healthy, it also proved that dialogue requires toughness of spirit and thickness of skin. The criticisms by Protestants and Jews of certain Roman Catholic actions were not only frank; they were almost brutal. It was clear that the image projected by the Roman Catholic Church, whether rightly or wrongly, was seen by Jews and Protestants as anti-civil libertarian, authoritarian, arrogant, and inhospitable to religious pluralism. Catholic spokesmen replied, to the surprise of non-Catholic participants, with freely expressed deep divergencies among themselves.

Until now, the process of dialogue has been limited; it has concentrated on issues of public policy on which there is disagreement among the faiths. Yet to come and badly needed is real and continuing dialogue about basic theological differences, deep-seated doctrinal differences, long-standing historic disagreements and conflicts.

But dialogue is not a panacea. The opening of lines

of communication is desirable, but there is no guarantee that what is communicated will clear up misunderstandings and still less that it will lead to practical solutions. (There is not even a guarantee that the words *spoken* are truly *heard*.) Respect for differences—in a sense, co-existence—must be grounded on the realization that some differences may well be irreconcilable. In some matters, the best we can hope for is that we may learn to live together despite deep differences, that we can learn to disagree agreeably.

In an effort to encourage dialogue, many religious thinkers have taken the trouble to set down some basic ground rules for such exchanges. One of the most fair-minded of such statements was formulated by Dr. Robert McAfee Brown, member of the faculty of Union Theological Seminary, who urged that:

1. "Each partner must believe that the other is speaking in good faith."

2. "Each partner must have a clear understanding of his own faith."

3. "Each partner must strive for a clear understanding of the faith of the other."

4. "Each partner must accept responsibility in humility and penitence for what his group has done, and is doing, to foster and perpetuate division."

5. "Each partner must forthrightly face the issues which cause separation, as well as those which create unity."

6. "Each partner must recognize that all that can be done with the dialogue is to offer it up to God."

On the positive side, there are indications in our community studies that American religion is beginning to grow beyond a belief in brotherhood by platitude, beyond that simplistic faith in Brotherhood Week as a form of annual communal salvation. Evidence has accumulated, both in this book and in other studies, that the approach of brotherhood by osmosis simply does not work. We have learned that an annual social contact is no guarantee of lasting positive relationships and that occasional two-faith or even three-faith meetings do not guarantee mutual understanding. The emphasis on shared convictions had a purpose and has achieved it. Now we appear to have grown up enough to be able to face the fact that differences among American religions are real and valid and should not be hushed up or glossed over in the name of a fancied "unity."

1960 saw the beginning of a new break-through in interreligious relations perhaps world-wide in scope. Pope John XXIII's call for an ecumenical conference of all Christians stirred fresh currents in waters which had become fetid during centuries of separation. So did his private meeting with the Archbishop of Canterbury, the first Archbishop of Canterbury to call on a Pope since the Church of England separated from Rome in 1534. Whether these new approaches will bear fruit is speculative, but the approaches themselves are of historic importance. A heightened sensitivity to other religions has been manifest in the Vatican in other ways, too. The Pope pleased many non-Catholics when he revised two church prayers which had long offended Jews. Similarly exemplifying this lessening of distance between Rome and the Jewish people was the Pope's poignant greeting in 1961 to a private audience of American Jewish leaders: "I am Joseph who seeks his brothers."

As another major outgrowth of this process of matura-
tion, there has begun to develop the belief that interreligious effort on behalf of a commonly approved civic
cause is the key to interfaith relations. Interreligious enterprises for better housing, against juvenile delinquency,
for racial integration, for advancing the cause of world
peace (to mention only a few emergent issues), tend
to enrich the causes themselves with religious compul-
sions and at the same time bring members of differing
faiths together in a bond of shared concern. Religious social action is the most promising door our communities
have found to improved interreligious relations. It is to be
hoped that intersectarian organizations like the National
Conference of Christians and Jews will move more vigorously in this direction in order to obtain the increased
respect and support of all faiths. Certainly, no religious
person can be happy about the status of the "brotherhood" movement in the eyes of community leaders or
about the impact of its programs on most of the communities described on these pages.

There are indications that the National Conference of
Christians and Jews is turning a corner in the direction of
a new and more vital program. The 1960 annual report
of the organization was revealing. There is an emphasis
on human equality, civil rights, and "dialogue"—which
has as its purpose not the burial of differences between
religious groups but a proper understanding of them. The
NCCJ has moved into diverse areas in its programming:
labor-management dialogue; education in human relations for policemen, nurses, and others; summer workshops in human relations on university campuses (47 in
1960); a concern for fair election practices (as expressed

in a pamphlet on the religious issue in 1960 campaign, written by Richard Cardinal Cushing, Dr. Edwin Dahlberg, president of the National Council of Churches, and Rabbi Max Davidson, president of the Synagogue Council of America).

With its budget at an all-time high of $2,900,000, and with a substantial grant from the Ford Foundation for a "dialogue" project, the National Conference of Christians and Jews is beginning to exert a realistic influence which may far transcend the indisputable values which resulted, in another generation and another era, from brotherhood for the sake of brotherhood, values no longer obtainable from the traditional techniques. In a typical example of cultural lag, however, most of the communities studied in this volume have not yet felt a strong impact of the new NCCJ programming. In addition, much of Roman Catholic leadership continues to shy away from such interfaith mechanisms. At present, NCCJ increasingly reflects reality; it does not yet create or shape interreligious attitudes in America.

The processes of interreligious communication and cooperation have been kept to a minimum until recently by many factors, a few of which come through clearly in our community analyses. One of them is the tendency for contemporary American theology to be conservative. Theologically liberal groups have been overwhelmed in recent years by the expansion of conservative, fundamentalist groups within Protestantism. Such extremist groups as the Birch Society, the Christian Crusade Against Communism, and similar super-patriotic bodies have found sources of strength in the evangelical, fundamentalist churches. In addition, theological thought and writings have become more somber, neo-orthodox, at times almost nihilistic. Under the impact of European theology, especially the work of Barth, Brunner, and the religious existentialists, American theologians, Protestants especially, with one or two assists from Jews, have moved away from the man-centered, liberal, social-justice-seeking emphasis of the twenties and thirties into brooding over man's helplessness, his inability to lift himself, and his total dependence upon God's inscrutable Grace. Acceptance of this "newer" theology has played a consequential role in interreligious activities. The Unitarian denominational body no longer even tries to become a member of the National Council of Churches. Pulpit exchanges between Protestant denominations are increasingly limited to "safe" speakers, the social gospel speaks cautiously, and the terms of denominational mergers are tending in the direction of more doctrinal orthodoxy rather than less. The price of increased Protestant unity has been increased conservatism.

Fundamentalist Protestantism, both within the denominations in the National Council of Churches and especially those in the frenetic American Council of Churches, the right-wing fundamentalist group, makes no secret of its deep sense of evangelical responsibility toward Jews. Interreligious cooperation is manifestly impossible when a Christian looks upon Judaism as an anachronistic atavism which isn't here to stay, particularly if he, the Christian, does a good enough selling job. Nor can the zealous fundamentalist worry too much about the niceties of interreligious sensitivity. Why should he be concerned if a crucifixion film on TV gives a hostile picture of Jews to millions of viewers? Or if the

Sunday school teachings of his church flash negative images of Jews as Christ-killers upon the sensitive minds of children? Or if a Unitarian parent objects to a trinitarian prayer at a high school baccalaureate service? Dedication to narrow dogma will almost invariably overcome concern for those "unfortunates who have not yet seen the light of revealed truth," or for Catholics whose faith is seen by the fundamentalist Protestant as a medieval hangover filled with superstitious rite and dark secrecy.

There is evidence in our communities, and even more in the national Roman Catholic press, that considerable soul-searching is going on in Catholic circles, and that some decisions have been taken among some Catholic groups to break out of the cocoon which the Roman Catholic Church spun around its adherents in America to protect their "sole true" status and to protect them from non-Catholic depredations. For the Roman Catholic community has paid a heavy price for its self-imposed isolation. There were in 1961 some 5,000,000 children in Catholic parochial schools, 800,000 in high schools, and 350,000 in Catholic universities. Yet, many Roman Catholic leaders are deeply disappointed in the scholarly, intellectual, cultural, and spiritual attainments of American Catholicism. They do not hesitate today to voice this disappointment, and even to indicate that their isolationism has played a role in the relative failure of their communion to create. Similarly, probing self-criticism has been developing within the Roman Catholic community against the negative image the Church projects to millions of non-Catholic Americans. Despite numerical growth, despite conversions of numerous prominent people, Catholicism is not popular with non-Catholics. Sheed and

Ward, a leading Catholic publishing house, recently invited six prominent non-Catholics to set down their unvarnished views of American Catholics and Catholicism. The essays, which added up to an almost embarrassing indictment, were published in full. No effort was made in the book at rebuttal. The publishers explained that the book gave the Catholic a chance at "self-knowledge which comes from seeing himself through the eyes of representative Protestants and Jews of intelligence and good will."*

More and more Catholic leaders are summoning the Roman Catholic community to a greater participation in American civic life. For example, Father Thurston Davis, distinguished Catholic editor, addressing the National Convention of the Holy Name Society in 1959, deplored the failings of "the average American Catholic man or woman who too often just doesn't seem to care about events and trends and procedures on the level of civic life. In most civic, social, and political matters we think, judge, and act too exclusively as Catholics. We tend to stand up and play our full role as citizens only when we as a group are in some way being threatened. We turn out to vote in grand style—as indeed we should—when there is a bigoted bill up to tax our schools, but we don't crowd the polls the way we should as citizens when the issue is a 'neutral urban redevelopment plan or a referendum to put a new wing on the local public library.' "

Accusing American Catholics of "a sort of schizophrenia . . . a lamentable sundering of our political life

---

* *American Catholics: A Protestant-Jewish View,* edited by Philip Sharper, Sheed and Ward, New York, 1960.

from our religious life," Father Davis declared, "We give generously to the foreign missions, but fail even to try to understand the need for 'foreign aid' to underdeveloped nations. We would never think of drawing racial lines at the communion rail (at least I devoutly hope not), but let a Negro or a Puerto Rican threaten to move into our block . . . and some of us see no contradiction in organizing with our neighbors to keep them out."

Similarly, a chorus of Roman Catholic spokesmen has pleaded for greater participation by Catholics in intergroup endeavors, for higher intellectual standards, for less reliance on power plays and pressure campaigns to achieve Catholic ends, for a less hysterical attitude toward Communism, for enlarged understanding of civil liberties and religious freedom, for a clear commitment of church-state separation, for less of the suspicion which instinctively produced cries of "bigot" when Catholic theological or social positions are questioned, and for a less fearful and patronizing attitude toward Protestants and Jews. There is reason to hope that these pleas will not fall on deaf ears as Catholics increasingly achieve that measure of security which obviates the necessity for super-patriotism and isolation. The election of President Kennedy may speed the process of Catholic change.

Although Roman Catholics usually receive more than their share of criticism on the grounds of religious separatism, the truth is that this problem cuts across all faiths and places in jeopardy the American values of cultural diversity. Power struggles in suburbia tend to unfold on a faith basis in public conflicts. Commenting on this in an address to the Plenary Convention of the National Community Relations Advisory Council in 1955, Dr. Dan W. Dodson, director of the Center for Human Relations, New York University, said:

> Increasingly, the individual will have little iden-
> tification unless he operates under one of these
> faith umbrellas. There is good evidence that this
> is so, and that identification under these umbrel-
> las is becoming increasingly more coercive and
> less permissive than ever before. The growth of
> the sectarian fraternities and sororities at col-
> leges and universities, the faith cliques in high
> schools, the decline of the public schools as a
> social center for the youth of the community,
> and the attendant growth of sectarian youth ser-
> vices, all attest to the religious separatism of our
> country and indicate the pressures toward faith
> conformity inherent in our society whereby the
> individual loses identity if he does not join up.

At the same convention, Jewish delegates from all parts of the country agreed that "contacts among Jews and non-Jews in communities were limited in a variety of ways. Exclusiveness was reported to operate almost universally in respect to social contacts. Instances of mingling of Jews and Christians in social intercourse was seen as rare and in many communities non-existent." There was somewhat more contact in business and service clubs.

TRIPLE GHETTO

Indeed there is some ground for fear that America is becoming not a triple melting pot but rather a triple ghetto. Evidence abounds that, while the legal walls of racial and religious segregation are tumbling down in the United States, the walls of self-segregation are springing up. Evidence mounts. Among American Jews, for example, there appears a distinct tendency to seek "Jewish" neighborhoods, to find comfort among Jewish friends, and to belong principally to Jewish organizations. A recent study reported that in one community, where Jews make up 15 per cent of the total population, some respondents to a questionnaire expressed a wish to live in a neighborhood which is 75 per cent Jewish.* Another study† found that 40 per cent of the Jews interviewed had not spent a social evening in the home of non-Jews in the preceding year. The Jewish attitude toward social contact with non-Jews is ambivalent. Jewish parents are eager for their *pre-teen* age children to be in *mixed* groups (Boy and Girl Scouts, school clubs, neighborhood friends), but when their children reach high school age, the parents strongly prefer a minimum of contact with non-Jewish children outside the classroom. In one study,‡ 75 per cent of the parents of even the pre-teen children indicate they would not want their children to have Christian friends of the *opposite sex*. The fear of intermarriage seems to impose a heavy pressure toward separation upon American Jewry. The centripetal attraction of Jewish organizational life is manifest, also. A study in Dade County, Florida, found that, while about three out of four Jewish persons interviewed belong to at least

---

* "Changing Jewish Attitudes," an article in *Journal of Jewish Communal Service,* Vol. No. 4, Summer, 1961.
† *Ibid.*
‡ *Ibid.*

one Jewish organization, only three out of five belonged to a non-sectarian organization.*

Whereas Jewish tendencies toward isolation are largely of a social and communal nature, Roman Catholic separation has a substantial religious motivation. A striking example of religious compulsion was a recent edict issued by Archbishop Joseph E. Ritter of St. Louis, forbidding Roman Catholic students in his diocese from attending non-Catholic colleges or universities without his written permission. In a pastoral letter, the Archbishop said: "Permission will be granted only in individual cases and for just and serious reasons." Efforts to dissuade Roman Catholic children from going on to non-sectarian colleges are applied in various ways in other communities. An article in *College Board Review,* official magazine of the College Entrance Examination Board, reported that some Catholic parochial schools have refused to send either recommendations or transcripts for graduates who apply for admission at non-Catholic colleges. A survey by the *New York Post* confirmed the fact that this practice was carried on by some parochial schools. The *Post* survey also drew attention to another device by which parochial school graduates were prevented from enrolling in non-sectarian universities: the forwarding of transcripts by the parochial school but supplementing them with poor recommendations, frequently inconsistent with the student's grades. Monsignor Raymond P. Rigney, associate superintendent of schools of the New York Archdiocese, told the *Post* that these practices apply only to a "very small segment" of Catholic high schools.

Rabbi Morris Kertzer, a veteran observer of the inter-

---

* Manheim Shapiro, *The Bayville Survey.*

religious scene, has described the "triple ghetto" as it is developing particularly in the suburbs: ". . . we are fast becoming fragmentized into separate entities, with only the most casual communication between us: a nod of greeting when we mow our respective lawns or rush for the commuter's train and bus; a casual contact on a P.T.A. board or at a Rotary meeting, and impersonal business relationships."*

In a shrinking world of color and diversity, millions of Americans—Protestant, Catholic, and Jewish—are living in homogenized white neighborhoods and sending their children to schools where everybody is in the same racial, economic, and—increasingly—religious grouping. Our communities are not preparing Americans for leadership of a changing and plural world.

What is the meaning of all this for the future of America? Predictions are risky but projections of current trends suggest at least reasonable probabilities. In our large metropolitan centers, Roman Catholic influence will continue to grow and white Protestant influence will diminish. Already Roman Catholics make up 38 per cent of the population of our large urban centers over 200,000; white Protestants, 39 per cent; Negro Protestants, 11 per cent; and Jews, 8 per cent. Lensk[†] has suggested that the increasing Roman Catholic influence, associated with the values which characterize the Catholic social heritage, may mean for America in the decades ahead a rising rate of church attendance; a strengthening of family systems; a decline in the importance of intellectual independence;

---

* Paper presented at Biennial Assembly of the Union of American Hebrew Congregations in Washington, D.C., November, 1961.
† *The Religious Question,* by Gerhard Lenski, Doubleday, 1961.

a mounting support for the welfare state; higher birth rates; more restrictions on free speech; enlarged restraints on Sunday business, divorce, and birth control; a lessening restraint on gambling and drinking; and a lowering rate of material and scientific progress.

Lenski may or may not be proved correct. But our own studies do reinforce his deep fear that America may be heading toward a formidable, and conceivably dangerous, "compartmentalization" along faith lines—what we have referred to earlier as the "triple ghetto." If religious pluralism ultimately spells fragmentation—with political, social, and communal life organized along faith lines as in Holland and Lebanon—both religion and the traditions of America will be gravely impaired. The current contest over federal aid to parochial schools—and the disturbing indications that new and highly volatile political groups are mushrooming along essentially religious lines—is one of many portents that religious tensions and conflicts will be an inevitable part of the American landscape in the future. How these conflicts will be handled— with what sagacity, respect for differences, and reliance on democratic processes—will be a crucial challenge to the faith groups and to a plural and free American society.

SUMMARY

What is the over-all message of this book? It has many messages to transmit to Americans, messages both negative and positive. Negatively, our look at ten American communities proclaims that religious leaders and their followers have not yet responded adequately to the urgent social challenges of our day. Negatively, we have learned that some religious differences, both in concept and in expression, are so deep that they should not be expected to yield to the ministrations of good will endeavors. Negatively, we have learned that there are still cancers of interreligious bigotry, isolationism, and hatred in some of our communities. Most important on the negative side, however, we know that indifference to religious values and their social implications is costing us heavily as a nation. And religious leaders must face up to the fact that their teaching and preaching have not yet caught up with the realities of the America of the 1960's—urban, better educated, superficial, nervous.

But our studies have positive messages, too. Some religious leaders in some communities have learned the truth that the interreligious program which is most significant is the one which draws men of differing faiths together to work jointly to bring God's Kingdom just a bit nearer in some area of His world. Some heart-warming successes are recorded here, successes which give hope for the future.

In a way, this book—although it has revealed many flaws in American life—represents a testament to American freedom. Instances of misuse of religious power are adduced in this book, but they do not add up to an insoluble problem confronting the nation. Indeed, a far greater problem than occasional abuse is the failure of religion to make fuller use of its latent power in shaping the ethical conscience of America and impelling public-spirited citizens to righteous action.

This book vindicates anew the workability of the American experiment—and, particularly, the principle of separation of religion and the state on which our religious liberty rests. The proof that our system works shines through these pages. Nowhere in the world is the state less influenced by sectarianism. Nowhere in the world does the church—in the broad sense—flourish as here, where church and state are relatively free from each other. Here, religious groups contend with each other vigorously, but it is a bloodless contention and no group needs to struggle for its right to existence. Here, the habits of mutual respect dull the sharp edges of conflict and encourage accommodation. Freedom of religion is solidly welded in law. In the communities of America, large and small, religious tensions exist. But they exist in a context of a free America which respects individual freedom and exalts equal opportunities for religions no less than for individuals. The tradition of America excludes none by virtue of property or color or religion or creed; and it extends to every religious group the right to follow its deepest commitments. In this all are united. The tradition is sometimes violated—but the tradition remains. And that makes all the difference.

The challenge to American religion is clear and flaming. Religion will fulfil itself not only in saving individual souls. If it is worth adhering to, it will fulfil itself also in saving society—from atomic carnage, from creeping starvation, from indignity and inequality, from every kind of injustice. Mature religious groups have a unique opportunity in today's America to move in that direction. They dare not spurn the opportunity nor fail the challenge of a new age: to keep men human. Unless the moral forces of religion—Roman Catholic, Protestant, and Jewish—are powerfully mobilized in the crises facing our civilization, either that civilization will not survive or, if it does, the survivors will have little use for any religion which failed them in their need.